Human Dignity in Classical Chinese Philosophy

Qianfan Zhang

Human Dignity in Classical Chinese Philosophy

Confucianism, Mohism, and Daoism

palgrave
macmillan

Qianfan Zhang
Peking University
Beijing, China

ISBN 978-1-137-53217-6   ISBN 978-1-349-70920-5   (eBook)
DOI 10.1057/978-1-349-70920-5

Library of Congress Control Number: 2016951225

Cover illustration: © Derek Croucher / Alamy Stock Photo

Printed on acid-free paper

This Palgrave Macmillan imprint is published by Springer Nature
The registered company is Nature America Inc. New York

ACKNOWLEDGMENTS

This book is a collection of cumulative works that have been presented at conferences and published in academic journals over the past 15 years. I am grateful to the journal editors and the organizers of the activities who have helped to bring this work into being. I thank Professors David Archard, Nick Bunin, Sarah Browdie, P.J. Ivanhoe, Chenyang Li, Peimin Ni, Heiner Roetz, David Schiller, Julia Tao, Kam-por Yu, Zhenming Zhai, Dainian Zhang, among others, for valuable academic exchanges and insightful critiques. I particularly appreciate the consistent support of Professor Chung-ying Cheng and Dr. Linyu Gu for a long time.

Chapters in this book are extended versions of my previous publications. Chapter 2 is taken from "The Idea of Human Dignity: A Reconstruction of Confucianism," *Journal of Chinese Philosophy* 27 (2000): 299–330. Chapter 3 is from "Humanity or Benevolence? The Interpretation of Confucian *Ren* and Its Modern Implications," in *Taking Confucian Ethics Seriously: Contemporary Theories and Applications*, ed. Kam-por Yu, Julia Tao, and Philip J. Ivanhoe (Albany, NY: SUNY Press, 2010), 53–72. Chapter 4 appeared as "Propriety, Law and Harmony: A Functional Argument for the Rule of Virtue," in *Governance for Harmony in Asia and Beyond*, ed. Julia Tao et al. (London: Routledge, 2010), 282–314. Chapter 5 is from "Human Dignity in Classical Chinese Philosophy: Reinterpreting Mohism," *Journal of Chinese Philosophy* 34 (2007): 239–256. Chapter 6 is from "Human Dignity in Classical Chinese Philosophy: The Daoist Perspective," *Journal of Chinese Philosophy* 40 (2013): 433–450.

I thank the publishers for granting permission for the use of the published materials in this book. I also thank Rachel Krause of Palgrave

Macmillan for initially contacting me and arranging for the publication of this book.

All translations of the classical texts are my own rendition unless otherwise noted; "trans." means that the translation is taken literally from the work cited, while "see" means my translation is informed by that provided in the cited reference. I am solely responsible for any mistakes.

CONTENTS

CHAPTER 1

Introduction

More than five decades ago, in the wake of great atrocities committed during World War II (WWII), the United Nations appealed to the "recognition of the inherent dignity and of equal and inalienable rights of all members of human family" as "the foundation of freedom, justice and peace in the world."[1] In the following year, the Basic Law of the Federal Republic of Germany (*Grundgesetz*, 1949) honored human dignity in its very first article as the controlling norm. Since then there has been a consensus among the nation states that human dignity is an important moral and legal concept that should be taken seriously at both national and international political order.[2]

The salience of the dignity concept is not diminished in the new millennium, when economic expansion and technological advancements quickly bring together the peoples of diverse cultures hitherto separated by the geographical barriers. While the closing of distances creates opportunities for mutual understanding and cooperation, it also creates occasions for conflicts and distrust, which sometimes lead to violent confrontations. The tragic incidence of September 11, 2001, was but a climax reached by decades of ethnic and cultural conflicts, and foreboded the escalation of violence in a world of diminishing physical distance and engulfing cultural disparity. The cultural and political conflicts in the contemporary world have much to do with the clash of the senses of dignity in different cultures. When the Jihad suicides attacked the western civilians, they might have acted out of the belief that this was *the* way to vindicate their

© The Author(s) 2016
Q. Zhang, *Human Dignity in Classical Chinese Philosophy*,
DOI 10.1057/978-1-349-70920-5_1

own dignity, while their attacks obviously devastated the dignity and basic rights of the victims.

It seems paramount that, in order to guarantee the world peace, justice, and prosperity, the governance of a harmonious "global village" requires a global constitutional order based on the moral discourse of human dignity. Such discourse may not produce a universally agreed understanding of human dignity, but it will help to improve consensus and reduce tensions among nations of different cultures. This book is but a modest contribution from the classical Chinese perspective, which developed a rich conception of human dignity before and during the Warring States (*Chunqiu Zhanguo*, 770–221 B.C.) period.

THE QUEST FOR DIGNITY

Important as it is, the dignity concept has not been intellectually explored and politically utilized among nations of the world today. While many developing nations were beset by economic hardships and political repression, developed liberal democratic nations were caught by the explosion of various political, economic, and social rights. The USA, for example, was preoccupied with the Civil Rights Movement in the 1960s and with the welfare rights in the 1970s. Despite the conservative turn, the world continued to be inundated with the "rights-talks" in the 1980s. Individual rights in different realms of human life—rights to free speech and free exercise of religion, rights against legal and political discriminations based on race and sex, right to procedural fairness in welfare hearings, right to physical freedom of woman versus potential rights of an unborn life, and so on—seemed to be the only ground that people in liberal democracies were willing to accept as the basis for good life. Yet, rights are not self-justifying, and "rights-talks" would remain groundless without some unifying conception of human beings. Although the postwar rights movements did contribute to improving the social, economic, and political status of the disadvantaged sections of the population, they shifted the focus of political, legal, and philosophical debates away from the central question about the meaning of human dignity and, without even attempting to answer this question, many invented rights remained unjustified.[3]

Recently, however, there seems to be a renewed interest in the idea of human dignity among philosophers and legal scholars. Within the western liberal tradition itself, some philosophers come to treat dignity as the philosophical foundation for the existence of rights.[4] A US Supreme Court

Justice even made effort to found the new constitutional rights on the basis of human dignity.[5] The concept of dignity is also used, implicitly, as a device to reconcile Confucianism, primarily a duty-oriented ethics, with the rights-based modern liberalism.[6]

Unfortunately, the recent rise in references to human dignity has hardly contributed to its conceptual clarity. The concept, which Dworkin notes rightly as broad and vague,[7] has caused much confusion in literature. It has been used by authors of different convictions to stand for different meanings and with different implicit assumptions, often never made explicit and articulated. It has been employed variously to mean, among other things, the Kantian imperative of treating human being always as the end and never as means only,[8] the "intrinsic humanity divested of all socially imposed roles and norms,"[9] the inherent worth belonging equally to all human beings,[10] the actually developed and mutually recognized moral status of a person,[11] the act and the capacity of claiming one's rights or the self-controlled expression of rights,[12] the right to secure inviolable moral status against degradation and disgrace in the context of the Due Process and the Equal Protection clauses of the Fourteenth Amendment in the US Constitution,[13] self-respect implying respect for others as opposed to purely self-centered esteem,[14] the quality or state of being worthy and esteemed which requires respect for one's physical or psychological integrity,[15] full realization of human power and rational existence,[16] the existentialist "authentic dignity of man" as found in man's thrownness into the truth of Being,[17] the universally shared human reality as given by God or the unique value of human being created in the image of God,[18] and the all-embracing Confucian ideal of humanity (*Ren*) composed of "concentric circles" of the self, the family, the state, human society, and the cosmos.[19] While some of the connotations are vague and unclear in themselves (e.g. what is meant by the *end* as opposed to mere means? What is full realization of human power?), others conflict with one another (e.g. human dignity as intrinsic quality universal to all vs extrinsic characters present only in some achieved human beings). It is perhaps not far-fetched to say that the current discussions of human dignity are mired in the stage of conceptual chaos. A recent comprehensive survey of this subject across major civilizations of the world indicates that there are many unanswered questions about the concept of dignity.[20]

Before we begin systematic discussion of the classical Chinese perspective, I present below a brief account of the western understanding of human dignity.

THE CONCEPT OF HUMAN DIGNITY IN THE WEST: AN OVERVIEW

Like the notion of individual rights, human dignity is a western concept. But in the prevalent rights-oriented ethical discussions today,[21] "human dignity" is not among the terms that are often talked about. And in those academic works that do mention the phrase (even in their titles), it is often left undefined and is used to express moral convictions the authors take for granted to be self-evident.[22] In reality, of course, the concept of dignity is anything but self-evident. Having comprehensively surveyed the conceptual development in the history of western philosophy, Spiegelberg finds it compelling to conclude that the meaning of "human dignity" remains vague and inconsistent, and the clarification of the concept still poses a "genuine challenge" to contemporary philosophers.[23] To facilitate comparison with the Confucian idea of human dignity discussed below, I provide here a brief account of the conceptual development in the West.[24]

Since the Greek philosophers, the concept of human dignity has evolved in the entwined development of two traditions in the West: secular and religious. From the beginning human dignity was implicitly associated with freedom and reason. In the Platonic anatomy of the soul, reason is the best and the highest part; it is the divine substance, the partaking of which elevates the soul and makes it immortal. For Aristotle, men are dignified in virtue of reason because it brings order to their individual and social lives.[25]

When it came to the Christian scale of value, however, human reason was relegated to a minor place. For Augustine, human beings *are* reasoning creatures, yet reason is not the end in itself, but only the means to a higher end.[26] Fundamentally, faith is the precondition to right reasoning, and the faith in God, the perfect and highest good, is to be chosen freely by human will.[27] Free will, then, seems to be the ultimate locus of human dignity.[28] In the same vein, Descartes elaborates further that mankind can be said to partake a part of its Creator, not in its limited capacity for reason, but in the unlimited free will.[29] In a sense, human being has dignity because he is created in the image of God, and carries within him a portion of divine substance.[30] Under the influence of the humanist movement since the Renaissance, the Christian view of human nature took further positive development. Indeed, one of the earliest clear expressions for the "dignity of man" came from a young medieval priest.[31] Yet the Christian notion of *human* dignity seems to be necessarily limited in certain aspects.

After all, it is precisely the free will that makes men consciously abandon their belief in God and deviate from his commands, thus falling into sin and evil.[32] Consistent with the Christian theological belief, it seems, human dignity could not possibly originate *within* human being, but must come from some external source.[33]

With the Enlightenment, "the dignity of man" became a general ideal independent of particular religious doctrines and acquired its modern meaning. Most prominently, Kant combines freedom and reason in one to derive a unique notion of human dignity. For Kant, one's dignity (*wurde*) comes exclusively from the inner, unconditional worth of moral law and the capacity for autonomous law-making.[34] Everyone is in essence a free and rational being, capable of making for himself the moral laws that applies universally.[35] In virtue of the self-legislating capacity, human beings are able to live in the "kingdom of ends," where they treat each other as the beings of intrinsic, irreplaceable worth (as opposed to goods tradable and replaceable at certain prices).[36] The universal, categorical imperative would command everyone to treat others as well as himself as ends in themselves and never merely as means to other ends.[37] Yet, as several authors have contended, the Kantian notion of dignity is difficult to conceive because it is associated with moral freedom, which exists not in the observable phenomenal world (which Kant, under the influence of the Newtonian and Laplacian view of the cosmos prevailing at his time, believed to be mechanically determined), but only in the non-observable and incomprehensible noumenal world ("the thing in itself").[38]

Despite its problem, the Kantian conception of human being as a morally autonomous and self-legislating creature, who must be treated as the end in itself and not merely as means, remains unsurpassed as the basis for the western concept of human dignity. Indeed it became all the more appealing in light of the traumatic human experience in the twentieth century, especially during and after the two World Wars, in which the dignity and basic rights of millions of men and women were systematically trampled by totalitarian dictatorships. To permanently prevent the resurrection of monstrosities committed by the Nazi regime, the Federal Republic of Germany absorbed the elements of Kantian moral philosophy in its postwar constitutional practice. Most notably, the German Basic Law declares in its unalterable opening article that "The dignity of man shall be inviolable. To respect and protect it shall be the duty of all state authority."[39] The clause of human dignity has led to an admirable body of jurisprudence developed by the German Constitutional Court and is treated as the controlling norm by which all individual rights are interpreted.[40] The philosophical cornerstone of the German constitutional jurisprudence remains the Kantian tradition, infused with the Christian natural law and social democratic thoughts.[41]

On the other hand, moral idealism in Kant's philosophy took a radical subjective turn in the existentialist development during the war period.[42] In searching for a secure place for human freedom and dignity in a hostile human environment, the existentialists turned to the inner world of human consciousness, and identified the dignity of man with the freedom of choosing and making oneself. Radical and unfettered freedom now becomes the sole foundation of all values. In a representative work,[43] for example, Sartre underscores the famous existentialist theme: "Man is nothing else but that which he makes of himself"; "Man makes himself; he is not found ready-made; he makes himself by the choice of his morality, and he cannot but choose a morality."[44] Through free choice a person becomes responsible for his actions. Indeed, Sartre goes beyond Kant's universality of moral laws when he declares that human being not only legislates for himself, but is also "a legislator deciding for the whole of mankind," and thus become "responsible for myself and for all men."[45] But, although Sartre seems to agree with Kant that certain form of morality is universal, he rejects any notion of a *priori* moral laws, and insists that "One can choose anything,"[46] as long as the choice is made freely. He further rejects the Kantian version of humanism, which takes man as the end in itself and as the ultimate value. To the contrary, the existentialists would "never take man as the end, since man is still to be determined."[47] Of course, at the same time, the existentialists reject the Christian theology as the proper account of human morality. There is neither a God who created mankind with fixed human nature nor the Ten Amendments which inexorably order human beings to refrain from doing certain things; every man is completely free and responsible for every action he takes, even though it is taken without any rational justification. As existentialism treats individual choices as fundamentally groundless, irrational, and absurd, it has often been attacked for advancing moral nihilism. For our purpose, the radically subjective orientation of existentialism seems to have undermined its chance of success in searching for human dignity.[48] After all, it is difficult to make sense of human responsibility without any guiding principle, or to see the dignity in human beings as moral agents whose value choices are entirely without rational ground. A solid basis for human dignity and freedom is yet to be established.

In seeking to provide the philosophical foundation for the respect and protection of individual rights, several attempts have been made recently to reinvestigate the meaning of human dignity. While authors in the Judeo-Christian tradition continue to maintain that human dignity is to be ultimately based upon the theological premise that God created human beings in his own image,[49] there are encouraging developments within the secular tradition. The concept is explicitly discussed in a recent volume edited by Meyer and Parent,[50] which explores the essential relationship between human dignity, constitutional rights, and American liberal values. Perhaps the most systematic and consistent treatment is provided by Alan Gewirth,[51] who seeks to use his "dialectically necessary method" to derive the existence of human dignity. For Gewirth, the concept of human dignity contains both empirical and inherent aspects.[52] While the contingent features of acquired desirable characters (such as gravity, composure, confidence, and self-respect) belong only to certain human beings and to different degrees, the intrinsic worth is shared by all human beings to an equal degree. Questions still exist, however, as to the relationship between the intrinsic and extrinsic aspects of dignity and its moral implications. In what sense is inherent dignity shared by all human beings, making a criminal on par with a saint?[53] Should individual differences in extrinsic dignity make any difference to one's political and social rights? Should the notion of inherent dignity impose any duty on the person to acquire extrinsic dignity, besides giving him the right to demand respect from others, an aspect on which almost all relevant discourses so far have focused?[54]

Since these questions have not been satisfactorily answered in the existing literature primarily interested in finding justifications for individual rights, I will now turn to the classical Chinese teachings for additional insight.

THE THEME AND STRUCTURE OF THE BOOK

In this monograph, I argue that the classical Chinese philosophy, namely Confucianism, Mohism, and Daoism, can contribute something unique to the conceptual understanding of human dignity. The book is divided into seven chapters. The second chapter defines the concept of human dignity primarily from the Confucian perspective. The entire moral and political philosophy of Kongzi is centered on the notion of human dignity, that is, something held to be inherently noble and respectable in every human being. The aim of his lifelong activities was to (re-)establish a social order in which the unique human virtues (*De*, sometimes translated as potential or capacity) can be effectively cultivated, respected, and protected. Among them the primary virtues are *Ren* (humanity) and *Yi* (righteousness). While *Ren* is a moral character possessed by an altruistic personality, *Yi* essentially stands for reciprocity expressed in the Golden Rule: "Do not impose on the others what you do not wish others to impose on you."[55] Kongzi believes that every human being is able to acquire these virtues through learning and practicing, thereby becoming a gentleman (*Junzi*),[56] a morally noble person. A state will become noble if it has many gentlemen and is ruled by them. Order and harmony will be secured in such a state since everyone in it is demanded to respect the virtues in others, and disrespect would simply diminish one's *Yi* and thus his own dignity. Thus, a person shall never act in a way that will either directly degrade others or deprive them of the opportunity to realize their virtues.

The third chapter concerns the Confucian concepts of *Ren* and *Renzheng*, for the way the Chinese government treats its people is rooted deeply in the Confucian tradition, and unless this cultural tradition is changed, the nature of its political and administrative processes will remain the same. Despite recent shifts in law and policy to the more favorable side of the disadvantaged population, it is unlikely that problems of this kind will be eradicated overnight. Laws can force conformity of overt behavior, but they cannot change the minds from which such views are formulated. At the bottom, we need some moral inspiration that will allow us to change our views by searching more deeply in our minds for principles that will lead to us treating other people, especially disadvantaged groups, with dignity and kindness. This chapter claims that we do not have to look far for such inspiration, for Confucianism has much to say about the ways to resolve our social problem today. Although China has physically changed beyond recognition from its remote past, its social makeup and the problems of its governance remain by and large the same. The political culture that shapes the Chinese government today is still under the influence of the Confucian tradition, a tradition that consistently identifies a good government as one that serves the best interests of the people.[57] Yet, this apparently benign starting point may end up in paternalistic despotism if care is not taken to distinguish the Confucian moral concept of *Ren* from its political applications, *Renzheng*.

The fourth chapter examines particular aspects of the moral debates from a social and historical perspective. Specifically, it focuses on the Confucian-Legalist lines of arguments about the relevance of basic moral norms to social order and harmony. By reviewing the dilemmas of narrowly rational society—primarily the Prisoner's Dilemma and the related collective action problem, I seek to provide a partial defense for the crucial functions of traditional social rules and norms as embodied in the Confucian system of *Li* (propriety). Following Mengzi and Xunzi, I argue that a harmonious society presupposes a set of basic and widely subscribed rules and norms governing the behavior of its members, which I broadly designate here as the "constitution of society," written or unwritten, and that *Li was* such a constitution that had held the traditional Chinese society together. The history of traditional China has refuted the Legalist belief that a narrowly rational state can be sustained solely by laws and punishments tailored to human interests. The social dilemmas revealed by the modern rational choice theory further discredit Legalism as a feasible political program. Aiming to resolve the pervasive social dilemmas, I argue that the cultivation of personal virtues through common moral practice seems to be necessary for holding a society together and bringing about social harmony and cooperative actions. Indeed, Confucian *Li* had become such a vital part of the Chinese culture that, by seeking to abolish the entire body of *Li*, the radical modernization efforts which culminated in the May-Fourth Movement necessarily undermined and eventually destroyed the binding force of the constitution of the traditional Chinese society, and created decades of war and turmoil. The chapter is concluded with a discussion on the relevance of *Li* as a living constitution to our global society today.

The fifth chapter shows how the Mohist teaching can be construed to correct some of the practical imperfections in Confucianism and defend it against several objections raised against modern utilitarianism for potential violations of human rights. Requiring only the general sentiment of universal love for all human beings, Mohism has built in certain checks against the majoritarian abuses. Indeed, one author has gone so far as to compare the Mohist principle with the Kantian categorical imperative that demands the treatment of everyone as an end in itself.[58] Of course, Mohism does have its own problems. Although it tends to equalize social relationships by subjecting everyone equally to the universal principle, Mozi ultimately fails to provide a moral basis for autonomous human actions owning to the lack of metaphysical foundation for human virtue and dignity. Thus, Mohism cannot substitute Confucianism for the purpose of developing a coherent conception of human dignity, but it does illustrate that utilitarianism is not necessarily against the notion of dignity, but can make a unique contribution to its conceptual development by supplying certain parts missing in Confucianism and, in doing so, helps to formulate a more complete picture of human dignity.

The final chapter discusses the Daoist contribution to the idea of human dignity in the classical Chinese philosophy, particularly in aspects that had been ignored by the Confucians and the Mohists. By criticizing the traditional morality and reviving the faith in a primitive, self-sufficient life, Laozi and Zhuangzi add an important dimension to the classical understanding of human dignity: individual freedom, particularly the freedom of living under the minimum burden, direction, and oppression of the state. The article is divided into two main parts. First, it explores the Daoist moral philosophy centered on the Way and human freedom. Distinguishing itself from other schools of Chinese philosophy, the Daoist takes the self as the ultimate end of human pursuit, thereby recovering human dignity from excessive burdens of social or familial obligations that tend to crush individual personality. Second, it discusses the Daoist political program as a way to realize its moral ideals and examines the extent to which the early Daoists have succeeded in building a consistent theory to effectively pursue a free personal life. I argue that, although the Daoists express the romantic longing for personal freedom, their unnecessarily radical hostility against reason and institutional building has prevented them from formulating an effective mechanism to gain, protect, and maintain such freedom. The chapter ends with a brief comparison of the Daoist conception of human dignity with those of the Confucians and Mohists, and concludes that all three classical schools, if reasonably construed, should support the view that the establishment of a liberal constitutional scheme is necessary to preserve dignity for every human being who lives in a modern society.

A constitutional theory based on dignity has many implications for practical life. One advantage it has over a theory based purely on individual rights is that it has the inherent capacity of resolving the conceptual tensions arising from the "conflict of rights" among persons or groups (including nations). This is so because the notion of dignity itself implies mutual respect, which tends to prevent excessive competition at the complete disregard of the rights and interests of other individuals or groups. Consistent with the principle of reciprocity (*Yi*), the full recognition of one's own dignity naturally entails the respect for the dignity of others: if one desires to make others respect his person, he must respect others first, regardless of differences in race, sex, age, or political beliefs. The same holds true for the nations in the world today. For instance, if a developed nation desires its economic interest be respected and effectively protected in a developing nation, then it should respect the latter's needs of eradicating poverty and improving the basic conditions necessary for the full development of human potentiality. Only with the universal respect for the dignity of human life can different peoples establish mutual trust and cooperation, which are pre-requisites for securing global peace and harmony in a new era.

NOTES

1. Universal Declaration of Human Rights, Preamble.
2. See Matthias Mahlmann, "Human Dignity and Autonomy in Modern Constitutional Orders," in *The Oxford Handbook of Comparative Constitutional Law*, ed. Michel Rosenfeld and András Sajó (Oxford, UK: Oxford University Press, 2012), 371.
3. The Universal Declaration itself contains several "economic, social, and cultural rights." For example, "Everyone, as a member of society, has the right to social security and is entitled to realization …of economic, social and cultural rights indispensable for his dignity and the free development of his personality." (Art. 22) "Everyone who works has the right to just and favorable remuneration ensuring for himself and his family an existence worthy of human dignity, and supplemented, if necessary, by other means of social protection" (Art. 23, sec. 3). Similar statements are also contained in the Preamble of International Covenant on Economic, Social and Cultural Rights, adopted by the United Nations in 1966. See the collection of documents in Ian Brownlie ed., *Basic Documents on Human Rights* (2nd Ed., Oxford: Clarendon Press, 1981). In all occasions the phrase "human dignity" is left undefined.
4. See, for example, Alan Gewirth, "Human Dignity as the Basis of Rights," in *The Constitution of Rights: Human Dignity and American Values*, ed. Michael J. Meyer and William A. Parent (Ithaca: Cornell University Press, 1992), 10–28.
5. J. William Brennan, "The Constitution of the United States: Contemporary Ratification," *University of California at Davis Law Review*, 19 (1985), 8; see also Jordan Paust, "Human Dignity as Constitutional Right: A Jurisprudentially Based Inquiry into Criteria and Content," *Howard Law Journal*, 27 (1984), 150–158.
6. See contributions in Wm. Theodore de Bary and Tu Weiming ed., *Confucianism and Human Rights* (New York: Columbia University Press, 1998).

7. Ronald Dworkin, *Taking Rights Seriously* (Cambridge: Harvard University Press, 1978), 198.
8. *Ibid.*
9. Peter L. Berger, Brigitte Berger, & Hansfriend Kellner, *The Homeless Mind: Modernization and Consciousness* (New York: Random House, 1973), 89.

10. Gewirth, "Human Dignity as the Basis of Rights," 12.
11. A.I. Melden, "Dignity, Worth, and Rights," in *The Constitution of Rights*, ed. Meyer and Parent, 29–46.
12. See, respectively, Joel Feinberg, "The Nature and Value of Rights," *Journal of Value Inquiry* 4 (1970): 257, and Michael J. Meyer, "Dignity, Rights, and Self-control," *Ethics* 99 (1989): 527.
13. Meyer and Parent, *The Constitution of Rights*, 47–72.
14. Charles Murray, *In Pursuit of Happiness and Good Government* (New York: Simon and Schuster, 1988), 112–129.
15. Louis Henkin, "Human Dignity and Constitutional Rights," in *The Constitution of Rights*, ed. Meyer and Parent, 210.
16. Myres S. McDougal's notion in W. Michael Reisman and Burns H. Weston ed., *Toward World Order and Human Dignity* (New York: Free Press, 1976), 48–51.
17. Heidegger's reply to Sartre, see H. Spiegelberg, "Human Dignity: A Challenge to Contemporary Philosophy," in *Human Dignity: This Century and the Next*, ed. Rubin Gotesky & Ervin Laszlo (New York: Gordon & Breach Science Publishers, 1970), 53.
18. See, respectively, Jurgen Moltmann, *On Human Dignity: Political Theology and Ethics* (Philadelphia: Fortress Press, 1984), x; Brad Stetson, *Human Dignity and Contemporary Liberalism* (Westport, CT: Praeger, 1998), 15–17.
19. Tu Weiming, "Epilogue: Human Rights as a Confucian Moral Discourse," in ed. Wm. Theodore de Bary and Tu Weiming, *Confucianism and Human Rights* (New York: Columbia University Press, 1998), 302. In the same collection of works, see also Irene Bloom, "Fundamental Intuition and Consensus Statement: Mengzian Confucianism and Human Dignity," 96, and compare with Cheng Chung-ying, "Transforming Confucian Virtues into Human Rights: A Study of Human Agency and Potency," 146.
20. Marcus Düwell et al. ed., *The Cambridge Handbook of Human Dignity: Interdisciplinary Perspectives* (Cambridge: Cambridge University, 2014), 42.

21. For how the center of natural law doctrine in the West shifted from duty to rights around the resurgence of natural law theories in the sixteenth and seventeenth centuries, see John Finnis, *Natural Law and Natural Rights* (Oxford: Clarendon Press, 1980), 205–210.

22. For example, Herschel Baker, *The Dignity of Man: Studies of the Persistence of An Idea* (Cambridge, MA: Harvard University Press, 1947), which bears "dignity" in the title, but refers to it only sparingly in the entire book; the same is true with Ernest Bloch's *Natural Law and Human Dignity*, trans. Dennis J. Schmidt (Cambridge: The MIT Press, 1986), which does not even have the word in the index. The French book by Thomas de Koninck, *De la dignite humaine* (Paris: Presses Universitares de France, 1995), has a general title, but is in fact limited only to child treatment (see Hugo Meynell's book review, "Politics of Human Dignity," *The Literary Review of Canada*, February 1996, 6–7). The most relevant treatment of the concept can be found in two edited works: Gotesky and Laszlo's *Human Dignity: This Century and the Next* (1970) is more philosophically oriented (see especially Spiegelberg's analytical essay), while Meyer and Parent's *Constitution of Rights: Human Dignity and American Values* (1992) is by and large tied to issues arising from American constitutionalism (but see Gewirth's contribution therein).

23. Spiegelberg, "Human Dignity: A Challenge to Contemporary Philosophy," in *Human Dignity*, ed. Gotesky and Laszlo, 39–62.

24. For a more detailed review, see J. Prescott Johnson, "Human Dignity and Nature of Society," in *Human Dignity*, ed. Goteskyand Laszlo, 317–349.

25. See Baker, *The Dignity of Man*, 100–105.

26. Vernon J. Bourke ed., *The Essential Augustine* (2nd Ed., Indianapolis: Hackett, 1974), 19–32.

27. St. Augustine, *City of God*, trans. Henry Bettenson (London: Penguin Books, 1984), 190–196.

28. Johnson, "Human Dignity and Nature of Society," 330–338.

29. *Discourse of Methods*, Book IV.

30. Augustine, *ibid.*, pp. 458–463.

31. Giovanni Pico della Mirandola, *Oration on the Dignity of Man*, trans. A. Robert Caponigri (Washington, DC: Regnery Gateway, 1956).

32. Augustine, *City of God*, 195.

33. See Yu Ying-Shih, *The Modern Interpretation of Traditional Chinese Thought* (Nanjing: Jiangsu People's Press, 1989), 24–48. For an

argument that human dignity is saved by redemption through Jesus Christ, see John Warwick Montgomery, *Human Rights and Human Dignity* (Dallas, TX: Zondervan, 1986), 208.

34. Immanuel Kant, *Grounding for the Metaphysics of Morals*, trans. J.W. Ellington (3rd Ed., Indianapolis/Cambridge: Hackett Publishing, 1993), sec. 411. See also Thomas E. Hill, *Dignity and Practical Reason in Kant's Moral Theory* (Ithaca/London: Cornell University Press, 1992), 76–96, and Leslie Arthur Mulholland, *Kant's System of Rights* (New York: Columbia University Press, 1990), 102–139.

35. Kant, *Grounding for the Metaphysics of Morals*, sec. 421–423, 452–453. As Kant himself acknowledges, he is indebted to Rousseau on at least two key points: that everyone, however low in social rank, has intrinsic worth and that freedom means self-legislation (which is, for Rousseau, to make the general will one's own will).

36. See H.J. Paton, *The Categorical Imperative: A Study in Kant's Moral Philosophy* (Chicago: University of Chicago Press, 1948), 185–198.

37. Kant, *Grounding for the Metaphysics of Morals*, sec. 428–429. For Kant's connection between human dignity and treating man as the end, see Yang Zu-han, *Confucianism and Kantian Moral Philosophy* (Taipei: Wenjing Press, 1987), 40–41. This notion of human being is widely accepted among Continental philosophers after Kant. Hegel states, for example, that "Man is only an end in himself (or final end) through what is divine in him—by what has from the beginning been called reason and ...freedom." Carl J. Friedrich ed., *The Philosophy of Hegel* (New York: Random House, 1954), 19.

38. See, for example, Meyer and Parent, *The Constitution of Rights*, 53.

39. *Grundgesetz*, Art. I.

40. See Donald P. Kommers, *The Constitutional Jurisprudence of the Federal Republic of Germany* (Durham: Duke University Press, 1989), 308–309.

41. Kommers, *Constitutional Jurisprudence*, 312–314.

42. The subjective tendency is already present in Kant, who seems to have established only that human beings can *think* of themselves as being free.

43. Sartre never devoted systematic attention to the question of human dignity. His relevant concern is mostly reflected in his *Existentialism and Humanism*, on which my discussion here is focused. For a book by an existentialist author bearing the title of human dignity, see Gabriel Marcel, *The Existential Background of Human Dignity* (Cambridge: Harvard University Press, 1963), 128–135, 158. The

discussion on human dignity there is only sporadic, however, and does little to clarify the meaning of the concept.

44. Jean-Paul Sartre, "Existentialism and Humanism," in *Existentialism: From Dostoevsky to Sartre*, ed. Walter Kaufmann (Cleveland/New York: World Publishing Co., 1956), 291, 306.

45. Sartre, "Existentialism and Humanism," 292.

46. Sartre, "Existentialism and Humanism," 308–309.

47. Sartre, "Existentialism and Humanism," 310. For a thorough discussion on the existentialist view of human existence and freedom, which leads to a peculiar notion of responsibility, see Sartre's *Being and Nothingness: A Phenomenological Essay on Ontology*, trans. Hazel E. Barnes (New York: Washington Square Press, 1956), 76, 565, 598, 603, 797.

48. Spiegelberg, "Human Dignity: A Challenge to Contemporary Philosophy," 51–53. For a critique of Heidegger and Sartre in comparison with Confucianism, see Yu Ying-shih, *The Modern Interpretation of Traditional Chinese Thought*, 24–48; about a comparison between western and Chinese philosophy on moral personality, see Xu Fu-guan, *The Basic Characters of Confucian Spirit, Its Limitations and Rebirth* (Hong Kong: Democracy Review Press, 1951), 1–10.

49. Moltmann, *On Human Dignity*, 15–31; Montgomery, *Human Rights and Human Dignity*, 208–217.

50. Meyer and Parent, *The Constitution of Rights: Human Dignity and American Values*.

51. Gewirth, "Human Dignity as the Basis of Rights," 10–28.

52. For a similar distinction between "intrinsic" and "extrinsic" dignity made in the Christian context, see Brad Stetson, *Human Dignity and Contemporary Liberalism* (Westport, CT: Praeger, 1998), 15–17.

53. Gewirth, "Human Dignity as the Basis of Rights," 10; compare with Melden, "Dignity, Worth, and Rights," 31.

54. The only exceptions are those made in the Christian context, see, for example, Moltmann, *On Human Dignity*, 10; Montgomery, *Human Rights and Human Dignity*, 192.

55. *Analects*, 12: 2; 15: 24.

56. "Gentleman" here is gender neutral. Unless specified or made clear by the context, none of the masculine words in this book suggest any gender bias.

57. The "three-represents" doctrine, originally proposed by the former General Secretary of the Communist Party, Jiang Zemin, and recently

enshrined in the preface of the 1982 Constitution, is a good example. One of the "represents" is "to represent the most basic interests of the majority of the people."

58. See Benjamin I. Schwartz, *The World of Thought in Ancient China* (Cambridge, MA: Harvard University Press, 1985), 146.

CHAPTER 2

Human Dignity: A Reconstruction of Confucianism

In this chapter, I seek to clarify the concept of human dignity by introducing the contribution of classical Chinese philosophy to this subject. As I indicate in the title, however, it is a reformulation of the Confucian view, for the word "dignity" was neither explicitly mentioned in classical Confucian text nor systematically explained by traditional interpretations. I nevertheless argue that it is the most adequate concept for understanding and interpreting Confucianism, which discovered the dignity of man in the innate virtues (*De*) unique to mankind by which every man and woman is enabled to live a morally decent and materially self-sufficient life. The chapter is divided roughly into two parts. After a brief review of the conceptual development in the West, I explain, primarily in the words of Kongzi and Mengzi, the meaning of human dignity as exemplified by a Confucian gentleman. Next, I discuss the connection between the Confucian concept of dignity and the western concepts of rights and duties. Conceding that Confucianism failed to espouse the modern ideas of democracy and liberty, as some might contend,[1] I argue that the idea of human dignity, which *is* firmly rooted in Confucianism, does contain the potential of receiving new interpretations that can bring about basic compatibility between the Chinese cultural tradition and the prevailing western notion of liberal democracy. While human dignity implies a universal demand for its protection and respect, and thus is primarily a duty-oriented concept, the universal duty imposed on the state and society does

© The Author(s) 2016
Q. Zhang, *Human Dignity in Classical Chinese Philosophy*,
DOI 10.1057/978-1-349-70920-5_2

confer definable rights to the individual. I argue, indeed, that compared to the Hobbesian theory of natural right, on which the western liberal tradition is founded, the Confucian concept of human dignity can accommodate a more balanced and consistent view of rights and duties.

The Confucian Concept of Human Dignity

Although human dignity is explicitly a western concept, it has a close Chinese correlate. Its literal translation today is *Zunyan* (尊严), a word often used in conjunction with a familiar Confucian term, *Renge* (人格), which is sometimes translated as "moral personality." The latter word had a rather tortuous history. It was first used in Japanese to express "persona," a psychology term. When it was introduced to China, however, it became associated with the ideal Confucian personality and acquired moral connotations.[2] In expressing the idea of human dignity, it is perhaps better that the two Chinese words be used jointly,[3] so that *Renge* expresses, in Hare's terms,[4] the descriptive element, and *Zunyan* the prescriptive element, of the normative concept. Although neither word appears systematically in the classical Confucian texts, this concept (denoted as human dignity from now on) best captures the moral teachings of Kongzi (孔子 551–479 B.C.) and Mengzi (孟子 372–289 B.C.).

In Confucianism, human dignity is a composite normative concept and, as such, implies conceptual elements on three related but distinct dimensions: descriptive, prescriptive, and emotive. The first two dimensions define the normative meaning of a value concept. On the descriptive or cognitive dimension, the concept contains the belief in the basic facts or, more precisely, the possibilities of human life, based on empirical observations of social interactions among human beings. This is the relatively objective realm of "is" or "can."

The prescriptive or evaluative dimension, on the other hand, presupposes the subjective valuation of these facts or possibilities, from which the prescriptive notion of "ought" is derived. On this dimension, the concept implies evaluative determination of what types of human life, actions, or dispositions to act are to be regarded as "good," noble, or praiseworthy, and positively prescribes a duty to develop, maintain, and preserve—at least refrain from harming—the conceived good.

Finally, the emotive dimension entails the behavioral manifestations that naturally ensue from believing in and subscribing to the norm. It can include, for example, the exhibited psychological satisfaction and confidence derived from continuous moral practice prescribed by the norm, or the natural sentiments it arouses in the common people, such as approbation for what they perceive as conforming (thus desirable) behaviors and antipathy to what they view as deviant practices. In this way, the emotive dimension furnishes a partial empirical "proof" for the universal presence of the norm within normally developed human beings. I shall explain below the term "human dignity" along these three dimensions.

The Meaning of Dignity as Exemplified in Confucian Gentleman

Descriptively, human dignity stands for a set of beliefs about human life or the kind of life that human beings are capable of living. Here, the concept contains two aspects about human nature: the potential and the actual, which roughly corresponds to Gewirth's notion of "inherent" and "empirical" dignity, or Stetson's notion of "intrinsic" and "extrinsic" dignity.[5] The vision of unique human potentials sets the end for a good life, and requires active pursuit to actualize these potentials. The Confucian idea of human dignity is thus closely related to its central concepts of innate virtues, the personality of gentleman (君子 *Junzi*), and the Principle of the Mean (中庸 *zhongyong*). It should be noted that, unlike virtues in the Greek sense which stand for acquired moral habits, "virtues" used here to translate the Chinese word *De* (德) means potentials in a human being, and is sometimes translated equivalently as potency, power, or capacities. In other words, the Chinese "virtues" are not primary faculties ready to carry out certain types of actions (e.g. the quality of justice as propensity to act justly), but only secondary faculties that enable a person to acquire the primary faculties (e.g. the ability to become a just person through some effort).[6]

The Confucians believe that human beings are endowed by Heaven (天 *Tian*, equivalent in meaning to Nature) with a set of innate virtues. In one occasion, Kongzi makes a remark about himself that "Heaven produced virtue in me."[7] Mengzi further develops this assumption of human nature into an ontological doctrine. Everyone is endowed from Heaven, he says, with four beginnings (四端 *siduan*) of "heart-mind" (心 *Xin*); they are the seats for four cardinal virtues: humanity (仁 *Ren*), righteousness (义 *Yi*), propriety (礼 *Li*), and wisdom (智 *Zhi*).[8] While the heart-mind for shame and distaste (for one's own bad behavior) is the seat of feeling for justice, the heart-mind for compassion is the origin of humanity. Humanity and righteousness are the inborn moral qualities, which defines the essential character of a human being and without which a man would be reduced to a mere animal. With adequate education, learning and self-cultivation, these innate capacities will be actualized in a person, making him a mature gentleman. It is to be noted that, since very early time in Confucianism, gentleman became a respectful title for anyone who acquired high moral status. As Liang Qichao (梁启超), a prominent intellectual in the late Qing (清) dynasty and the early Republic era, points out, "*Junzi* is not a word denoting one's social status; it is a word that denotes one's moral status. In other words, *Junzi* represents a person who has perfected his *Renge*."[9]

To Kongzi, one becomes a gentleman when he has succeeded in culti-vating balanced virtues based on the central Principle of the Mean. Kongzi makes it unambiguous that a gentleman is one who consciously follows the Principle of Mean, by which he unites himself with Heaven. The abil-ity to act according to the Mean becomes the definitive criterion for distin-guishing a gentleman from a mean-spirited "petty man" (小人 *xiaoren*), a "small person" with low moral status.[10] Thus, "a gentleman acts according to the Mean; a petty man acts contrary to the Mean. Because a gentleman maintains the Mean, he always acts to a perfect degree."[11] As a result, in a gentleman, we find several primary virtues in a harmonious proportion: "Benevolent, he is free from worries; wise, he is free from perplexities; courageous, he is free from fear."[12] The best example is Kongzi himself, who is praised for being "gentle but serious, awe-inspiring but not harsh, respectful but calm."[13] Continuous self-cultivation is the road to becom-ing a sage (圣 *sheng*), who has acquired perfectly balanced virtues:

> *Only the perfect sage in the world has quickness of apprehension, intelligence, insight and wisdom, which enable him to govern the world; magnanimity, gen-erosity, benignity and tenderness, which enable him to embrace all men; vigor, strength, firmness and resolution, which enable him to maintain firm hold; orderliness, seriousness, adherence to the Mean and righteousness, which enable him to be reverent; reasoned articulation and refined penetration, which enables him to exercise proper discrimination.*[14]

Now, one may contend that the Principle of the Mean is too general to guide concrete human conduct, and the specific virtues are either too vague (e.g. what is the meaning of humanity, *Ren*?) or, once they received a fixed interpretation, quickly become dogmatic and anachronistic (e.g. to be *Ren* is to respect one's parents and, thus, when one of them dies, to mourn for three years). Further, even the Confucians might not agree among themselves as to which virtues (e.g. *Ren* or *Li*?) should be placed

at the highest hierarchy and govern others, or how they should be interpreted. While these contentions do carry some force, they by no means
undermine the basic Confucian idea that every human being is endowed
with a set of unique potentials that characterize him as a human; and
such traditional virtues as humanity, justice, wisdom, courage, and propriety of conduct, still receive wide approbation today, even though their
interpretations may be disputed and modified over time. In other words,
while the descriptive content of what constitutes human dignity may vary,
there is nevertheless a consensus that a meaningful content is there. We
should reject the dogmatic tendency in Confucianism and admit, with
MacIntyre,[15] that our conception of human nature is not static, but a dialectic progress that changes with time, circumstances, and the improvement of human understanding. Yet, this does not preclude society from
accepting, at any given time, a prevailing view about human nature upon
which its moral judgment is based.

One essential virtue, whose social acceptance does have withstood the
test of time, is righteousness (Yi). A Confucian gentleman is above all a
righteous person, who always directs his action according to justice as
required by the Principle of the Mean. Thus, "a gentleman stands in the
middle, without inclining to either side."[16] He ties himself fast to that
principle, without being swayed by such external influences as profits,
power, or financial difficulties.[17] "A gentleman does not give up his righteousness when he is poor; nor does he deviate from the Way when he is
prosperous....If poor, he cultivates his virtue in solitude; if prosperous, he
strives to bring virtue to the whole world."[18] Nor is the norm of his behavior affected by his socio-political status: "In a high position, he refrains
from treating his inferiors with contempt; in a low position, he refuses to
court the favor of his superiors. He rectifies himself, and seeks for nothing from the others."[19] Nor should the state of politics distract him from
following the path of justice: "When good principles prevail in his government, he tenaciously pursues his goal.... When bad principles prevail in
the country, he maintains his course to death without changing."[20]

Firm commitment to righteousness confers physical and moral independence upon a gentleman. By claiming more than one deserves (e.g.
undue prestige or salaries), the acts of injustice indicate a state of dependence on the others—the signature of a morally inferior mind. On the
contrary, a gentleman relies not on the changeable wills of other persons,
but on his own effort through which he can bring about the actualization of his innate qualities endowed from Heaven, thereby achieving true

autonomy.[21] Having identified himself with the Way of Heaven, a gentleman will act on his own initiative, independent from any pressure, power or opinion of others. He is to act justly under all circumstances, with or without the awareness or presence of the others. For even if nobody on earth knows his virtues and vices, the omniscient Heaven and he himself would know; and an unjust action merely degrades his personal dignity, making him feel the shame in his mind. For this reason, a gentleman must take care of his virtue even when he is in solitude.[22]

Meanwhile, once a gentleman has sincerely examined himself according to the principle of justice and left his mind free from any sense of moral shame or guilt, he becomes the most courageous of all, and cannot be compelled by any external force, least by the fear for other men's power. Thus, from his disciple we learn the great courage of Kongzi: "on self-examination, if I find that I fail to be righteous, I would not threaten a single man, be he in an inferior status; but, on self-examination, if I find that I *am* righteous, I will go forward even against a crowd of a million men."[23]

To summarize, a Confucian gentleman is a person who has actualized in a balanced fashion the innate virtues endowed from Heaven as a human being. He exemplifies the Confucian ideal moral character that any person can attain through continuous moral learning and practice. In the words of Mengzi, a gentleman is

> to dwell in the magnificent house of humanity, to stand in the right place of propriety, and to walk on the great path of justice; when he succeeds in obtaining an office, to practice his principles together with his people; when his effort is frustrated, to persist in the practice of these principles alone. Wealth and honor cannot corrupt him; poverty and low status cannot move him (away from justice); and power and force cannot subjugate him.[24]

The Prescriptions of Dignity: Individual Cultivation and Universal Respect

The Confucian concept of human dignity not only implies the factual recognition of the unique human possibility of becoming a gentleman, but also bestows value on the realization of such possibility. And, like every value, it depends on the evaluative effort of the subject himself.[25] An uncultivated person has the equal potential to become a sage or a villain; it encumbers on human beings themselves to value the former and condemn

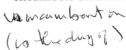

the latter. The great Confucian authority, Xunzi (荀子 313–238 B.C.), once says that "Water and fire have essences (气 Qi), but not life; herbs and trees have life, but no knowledge; birds and beasts have knowledge, but no sense of justice (Yi). Humans have essence, life, knowledge and, in addition, a sense of justice; thus he is the noblest on earth."[26]

But even if we are convinced that human beings indeed possess the innate sense of justice, it does not necessarily follow that it is the *noblest*; to thus value mankind above everything else, which gives rise to the unique pride for being a human, is itself a value judgment. It is an anthropocentric view of *Homo sapiens*, individually and as a whole, since it means that we simply value human lives above all other things. This (and, to a Confucian, only this) life is worth living, precisely because it is believed to be a process of continuous actualization of the unique potential worth present in every human life. The "radical world optimism"[27] is the very essence of Confucianism and, more generally, the Chinese humanist tradition.

The belief in human dignity presupposes an irreducible worth attached to every person insofar as she/he is a human being. This is best illustrated in the Mengzian theory of human nature,[28] which enables Mengzi to develop a positive doctrine of human value. Mengzi assumes that everyone is born with a noble body together with the capacity to develop it. Man is set apart from other animals perhaps by only a slight difference, yet it is precisely this small difference that makes man unique. The unique value of man lies not in his material body—because that he shares with all other animals, but exclusively in his moral faculties as embodied in his heart-mind (*xin*). Responsible for moral and rational thinking, the heart-mind is the noblest organ endowed by human being and, unlike the material body whose advantages are unequally inherited by different individuals, the moral heart-mind is endowed equally in all men and women. As a result, "everyone possesses in himself the noble value."[29] The individual moral differences lie not in the natural endowment, but in the posterior development of the innate potentials. Mengzi distinguishes the "noble" or "great" body (the heart-mind where humanity resides) from the "ignoble" or "small" body (sensuous organs giving rise to passion and desire). "While a gentleman follows his great body, a petty man is driven by his small body."[30] Unlike a petty man who is preoccupied with his selfish material desires, a gentleman takes care to cultivate his sublime moral character by pursuing humanity and justice, which enables him to lead a life that is worthy of his noble nature. Humanity and righteousness are true nobility endowed from Heaven, and cannot be substituted by human nobility (such as high social status and comfortable material life). While the human nobility is contingent on individual fortune and limited necessarily to a few, the inherent nobility of Heaven is absolute and universal to all human beings.

Now, it may be contended that the Confucians valued not so much the potentials inherent in man as the actually developed qualities exhibited in a gentleman. Munroe observes, for example, that traditional Chinese society had consistently rejected the ideas of democracy and mass political participation precisely because of the Confucian emphasis that only those who had actually developed virtues had the right to participate in politics.[31] Merits in arguments of this type aside, however, they cannot support the assertion that the Confucians did not value the pure potentials in *every* human life. There are plenty of passages in the classical Confucian texts that point to the contrary. For Kongzi, human beings *in general* worth more than anything on the earth, and cannot be arbitrarily harmed or destroyed even by the highest ruler of the state. He strongly condemned, for example, the custom of using figurines in the kings' burial because the figurines were made to look too similar to real people[32] (instead of only those with gentlemanly outlook). When a horse stable caught on fire, he asked, without mentioning horse, whether *anyone* (rather than only men of elevated moral status) had been hurt.[33] Likewise, Mengzi clearly sees the same worth in a human baby in his famous example where he attempts to illustrate the existence of humanity by the spontaneous feeling of compassion.[34] Suppose we witness a baby approaching a water well, he argues, we would be prompted by our natural compassion to go forward and save her from the danger.[35] Had Mengzi not valued the potentials innate in a human being, we would seem to have no reason to save the baby, for she is yet to develop any of her unique human potentials. In this case, an undeveloped human child should not worth more than other animals, and we should not feel more compelled to save her than to save, say, a cat about to fall into a well. But Mengzi would argue, I believe, to the contrary: whenever a human life, whose multifarious potentials are yet to be actualized, faces such danger, the matter is of an entirely different order. Thus, although Mengzi intended to use this example to illustrate the presence of humanity in every human being as a potential virtue, it can be plausibly extended to show the general Confucian concern and respect for the innate human potentials. Whether a person has actually developed these potentials (as he ought to), they are regarded to have value by themselves and deserve respect from others. In the Confucian view, then, the potential virtues innate in every human being are an inseparable part of human dignity.

On the other hand, as a value concept, human dignity also carries a prescriptive component. It places high premium on certain potentials innate in every human person and treats them as the irreplaceable good, which positively requires the individuals to cultivate these unique potentials by learning and practice in order to become fully developed men *and*, at the same time, to respect the same potentials in every other man and woman. Further, the concept can be plausibly so construed as to demand that the state and society should respect, protect, and help cultivate the virtues in every individual, thus providing everyone with certain basic rights, both in the negative (liberty) and positive (claims) senses. The prescriptions entailed by human dignity, then, contain three distinct aspects: the self, the other, and the collective.

First, a Confucian gentleman is a person who values his inborn virtues and takes care to preserve and develop what he believes to be noble in him, and he is said to have developed dignity precisely because he act in accordance with his innate nobility. Significantly, the Confucians did not stop here, but further required the conscious cultivation and actualization of these inborn capacities. To see this we need only mention the classic *Great Learning* (大学 *Daxue*), which prescribes a systematic program for self-cultivation (*xiushen*). Having cultivated the virtues, a Confucian gentleman practices and displays them overtly in his daily actions, giving rise to an appearance that commands respect from others. Thus, the Confucian dignity combines both the internal and external aspects of a human being; it presupposes the potential unique to mankind and, taking its value for granted, requires every man and woman to make a good effort to develop it in daily life. When the dignity is fully developed, it would spontaneously display itself in one's appearance and behavior, as a part of acquired habits.

Second, the gentleman's sense of justice presupposes his conscious recognition of the same basic worth in all other persons that command his respect. The respect for others is the natural extension of his self-respect, since a just man must obey the basic rule of reciprocity, which Kongzi takes to be *the* Way for every gentleman: "whatever you do not wish others impose upon you, nor do you impose on others."[36] Thus, when his student asks about the practice of virtue, he says: "When you leave home [to govern a people], behave [cautiously] as if you were receiving a great guest; to employ the people as if you were assisting a great ceremony.

Do not impose on the others what you do not wish the other to impose on you."[37] If a gentleman wants himself to be respected, then, he must first respect others and treat them as human beings who, like him, are endowed with moral and intellectual faculties capable of being fully developed. To imitate the absolute justice of Heaven, a gentleman must refrain from doing anything that might prevent anyone from actualizing his/her potential and achieving full dignity. Thus, his respect is due not only to cultivated gentlemen with comparable moral achievements, but also to every ordinary person, whose innate capacities make human improvements always possible.

But even that is not enough. For a gentleman is concerned not only with interpersonal moral conduct, but also with the ideal state and society in which he prefers to live. While he respects every human being in the universe, it would be quite rational for him to require others to pay reciprocal respect for himself. Further, he should also like to be able to require that we all (not only he himself) respect the basic dignity of any other person. Human dignity requires universal respect, from which no one ought to be excluded. For this purpose, recognizing the weaknesses and limitations in individual human beings, a gentleman should concern himself with setting up proper laws and social institutions to secure such an end, that is, to prevent everyone from taking actions that would diminish anyone else's (and his) dignity. These laws and institutions establish what are in nature private rights, because they protect the dignity of every citizen against private encroachment from others. Last and most important, he should be concerned, above all, with establishing fundamental rules that can prevent these institutions themselves, especially the state, from exercising powers in such a way as to defeat the very aim for which they are erected. We thus need a constitution that can limit the powers of the state and social organizations, and provides basic rights to every individual against public encroachment. Although, historically, the Confucians were not always conscious of the need for the institutional balance of powers, it seems to be reasonable to derive these basic institutional requirements from the Confucian concept of dignity.

The Sense of Dignity in a "Shame Culture"

Is there any ground for holding this fundamentally optimistic self-evaluation and for believing that the distinctive virtues in a human being make him nobler than other animals? It is true that, even if we can prove that we are in fact endowed with the Confucian virtues (e.g. the innate abilities to acquire, among other things, humanity and justice), we are by no means logically compelled to confer highest value on them or even regard them as "good" at all.[38] Without endorsing existentialism as a whole, we may nevertheless agree that human beings are free to value or devalue everything existing. Nor is it feasible to empirically demonstrate the universal existence of these virtues in every person. Yet, at least a partial vindication can be made to support the self-consistency of holding such a belief. That is, for those who *have* succeeded in developing their virtues, they do feel the existence of the inner worth, as shown in the psychological satisfaction and self-confidence; on the other hand, if they undertake actions contrary to the opinion they hold about their moral nobility, they will have a distinctive experience of feeling degraded. Further, even ordinary men and women have a sense of dignity within themselves which, though perhaps not consciously articulated, shows itself when their self-esteem is harmed by degrading treatments. Thus, it does seem plausible that some sense of dignity is universally felt in every human being.[39] This leads us to inquire the third and the last dimension of human dignity: the emotive dimension, which contains both positive and negative aspects.

First, as stated earlier, the quality of righteousness in a Confucian gentleman gives him the sense of moral independence, and allows him to correspond with the Way of Heaven without having to blindly follow others.[40] This presupposes a considerable degree of confidence in his own moral righteousness, which is to be exhibited in easy but dignified outlook that naturally commands respect from others. In the words of Kongzi, one becomes a gentleman "when he maintains a dignified ease without being arrogant; when he is majestic without being fierce."[41] As he explains further, "whether [the gentleman] has to do with many people or few, or with things great or small, he does not dare to indicate any disrespect—is not this to maintain a dignified ease without any arrogance? He adjusts his clothes and cap, and throws a dignity into his looks, so that, thus dignified, he is looked at with awe—is not this to be majestic without being fierce?"[42] The "dignified ease" (泰 *tai*) here stands for an appearance of magnificent composure that comes from the gentleman's confidence in his own worth.

Second, and negatively, a gentleman refrains from injustice because he feels the shame in doing unjust things to others—things that are not worth his effort and the commission of which would make him feel degraded. "Hence a gentleman feels no shame upon self-examination, and brings no embarrassment to his own will."[43] And freedom from any sense of moral shame gives him both the confidence and courage that are found lacking in a petty man. The conscious feeling of self-respect within oneself, as reflected in the sense of shame, distinguishes a gentleman from a petty man. While a petty man can do anything, however low, without feeling degraded, a gentleman is fully conscious of the worth inherent in him and will do only those things that are consistent with or can help to actualize his worth.[44] For this reason he regards himself highly.[45] If a gentleman committed a certain action that was not worthy of his nobility, then he merely degraded himself to a level lower than his intrinsic moral quality—a degradation for which he would feel shameful. Thus, Kongzi insists that a gentleman should "maintain the sense of shame in his own conduct"[46]; those who would do anything without feeling shame lack the very moral quality to do the right thing. As Mengzi puts it aptly: "A man must first know what he ought *not* to do, before he can do what he ought to do."[47] And both Kongzi and Mengzi have furnished examples for the kind of things that will make a gentleman feel shameful. A gentleman, for example, "thinks it shameful if his words exceed his deeds,"[48] because he would then make false claim on something which he did not do. And "a gentleman feels shameful if the prestige he receives exceeds his virtue."[49] Likewise, "it is shameful if, serving as an official in the court, he cannot practice the principle of good government" because he would then receive many benefits for doing nothing[50]; for Kongzi, "a good minister should serve his king through the Way and, finding it impossible, retire."[51]

It may be objected that the sentiments for dignity is not universal, but present only in those cultivated gentlemen who have succeeded in developing their innate virtues. Even for those who do not believe in human virtues or fail to make any conscious efforts to cultivate them, however, they nevertheless feel offended when they are treated less than what they deserve, implying that they do attribute some worth to themselves—though perhaps unconsciously and inconsistently. This is particularly obvious when they are mistreated by others. Even a beggar would feel degraded if someone throws food on the floor for him to pick up, as if the latter were feeding an animal.[52] As long as one has not lost the minimal sense of self-esteem, he would feel offended if his employer treats him merely as a machine for producing profit or government agents push him around rudely, as if they were taming a wild beast. In these situations, one would feel humiliated because he thinks that he deserves better treatment than what a mere animal or machine receives. Although he may purport to ignore or even consciously reject the worth inherent in him, thereby degrading himself and inviting despises from others, his aversion against the maltreatment implies that he still thinks himself to have some value. Thus, it can at least be argued that the sense of dignity is not limited to those cultivated persons; rather, it is universally found in every human being, even though the degree of such sentiment may vary. The general presence of such a feeling in every human being may not establish conclusively the existence of innate human virtues, but does suggest the reasonableness of the Confucian belief in the basic worth of human person.

What is human dignity, then? What does it amount to say that human being is a dignified creature? According to Confucianism, human being is dignified because he is born with a set of innate virtues unique to human race and the capacity of fully realizing these virtues that make him a mature person, and because he respects himself (and other men and women) by attributing high values to these unique virtues, which lead him to consciously develop them. As a result, human dignity is a composite idea that consists in the innate potentials believed to be uniquely endowed by every human being and held at the highest irreducible value, plus the extent to which these potentials is practically realized through conscious self-cultivation. An action is dignity-enhancing if it cultivates, practices or exhibits one's virtues; it is dignity-reducing (thus degrading) if it fails to exercise virtues or prevents anyone from cultivating or exercising virtues. Those who adopt this positive view of mankind, seeing the same worth and virtues in themselves, take lifelong efforts to cultivate them for the betterment of themselves, striving to achieve the highest dignity possible for a human being. Having cultivated these virtues, they take pride in them and display an overt confidence in their daily behavior; on the other hand, if they happen to have done things that tend to diminish or prevent the realization of virtues, they would feel degraded and shameful. They assume that everyone ought to see these virtues in himself and in others as something noble and worthy, and thus make a conscious effort to respect and to cultivate them in order to make himself a better human being; failure to do so would justly invoke moral disapproval from other members of society. Finally, they further require the state and society to not only respect, protect and refrain from degrading the dignity in every man and woman, but also provide the basic social conditions that make it possible for everyone to attain a dignified way of living.

THE DOUBLE IMPLICATIONS OF HUMAN DIGNITY: BALANCING RIGHTS AND DUTIES

It is commonly asserted, however, that the Chinese tradition in general and Confucianism in particular lacked any clear conception of rights. While this appears to be obviously true from even a cursory scan of classical Confucian works, it would be a mistake to infer that Confucianism is inherently opposed to individual rights, including basic political rights. I argue below that the Confucian concept of human dignity can easily accommodate the notion of rights as a device for cultivating individual virtues. To hold this view may require us to modify the traditional conception of personhood and to reject the dogmatic strain within Confucianism which took the legitimacy of tradition for granted. But doing so does not undermine the basic argument that, leaving the descriptive content of human dignity open to future modifications, as mankind acquire more experience and better judgment, Confucianism can adapt itself to changing circumstances and conceptions of human nature. In fact, with the overall optimistic assumptions of human nature, Confucianism can derive a balanced view of duty and rights, and provide a more consistent foundation for the commonly held belief in human worth and dignity than modern liberalism in the West. This section is divided into two parts. First, I briefly review the western liberal theory of individual rights as represented by Hobbes and point out its deficiencies. Second, I discuss the possibility and the necessity of deriving individual rights from the universal duty of respecting human dignity in modified Confucianism that is so reformulated as to be consistent with the basic social facts.

The Primacy of Rights over Duty in Western Liberalism

Belief in human dignity is often implicitly assumed in modern liberalism, a dominant ideology in the western liberal democracies. On June 27, 1998, for example, former President Bill Clinton made the following remarks in the historic city, Xi'an, the first stop in his recent trip to China:

> *Respect for the worth, the dignity, the potential and the freedom of every citizen is a vital source of America's strength and success.... In this global information age ....a commitment to providing all human beings the opportunity to develop their full potential is vital to the strength and success of the new China as well.*[53]

Yet, paradoxical enough, modern liberalism seems to be incapable of providing a solid philosophical foundation for the widely held belief in human dignity. It is simply difficult to find any worth or dignity in human beings from its basically negative view of human nature. And, without dignity and worth, many basic and now widely accepted rights would lose their legitimate ground.

It is well known that the western idea of individual rights is originally derived from the social contract theory of Thomas Hobbes.[54] In his *Leviathan*, Hobbes postulates a state of nature, in which egoistical individuals, with limited resources (including material goods and honor) and without mutual trust and a common government, find themselves trapped in "a war of all against all." To escape such a miserable condition, every person rationally enters a compact with every other person to put themselves under a sovereign. From such an original promise, enforced by the common power, is derived a set of natural laws which command each individual to keep peace and observe the terms of compact. The duties thus prescribed, however, are strictly conditioned upon the original purpose for which the compact was made at the first place: the preservation of individual life. This is indeed the "inalienable" natural right that Hobbes finds in every rational human being. Every human government must work toward the preservation and security of life; failure to do so constitutes a fundamental breach by the sovereign, which brings back the state of nature, where every individual is absolved of all duties toward others and regains natural liberty. The primacy of natural right over duty is obvious, as there is no equivalent "natural duty," but only duties *derived* from rights. The notion of natural right is further extended by John Locke to include the right to liberty and property. Although, in Locke's theory, the natural laws maintain their binding force in the state of nature, the fundamental asymmetry between rights and duty would remain *if* the biblical authority of God is left out.

Despite its wide acceptance today, the social contract theory of rights contains several difficulties.[55] First, without presupposing the a priori validity of transcendent divine command, the existence of human duty would depend entirely upon the prudential calculations of one's self-interest, and is thus made secondary to rights. Among other things, the Hobbesian theory can support only a weak notion of duty; that is, a person observes his duty not for its own sake, but only because it furthers his self-interest, and his duty stops as soon as the cost of obeying it apparently outweighs the benefits. Prudential considerations, however, depend on the actors' foresight and circumstances in which they are situated, and the ensuing uncertainty necessarily undermines the binding force of certain basic duties (e.g. "Don't steal" or "Act justly under all circumstances"). Second, without the sanction of an external divine authority, which requires belief in a particular religious doctrine,[56] the primacy of natural right of self-preservation in the Hobbesian theory makes it difficult to even accommodate other widely held rights, such as personal liberty and property. If human beings are by nature selfish, unjust, vile, and rapacious, it seems doubtful whether they are worthy of any rights other than bare preservation.

Finally, and most significant for our purpose, it seems to be very difficult to consistently derive from this theory the widely held "recognition of the inherent dignity" in the Preamble of the Universal Declaration of Human Rights, or respect for "the worth, the dignity, the potential and the freedom of every citizen," to which Mr. Clinton alluded in his China trip. If everyone is, as Hobbes depicts, an egoistical animal preoccupied with his self-interest, and his apparent observance of law and duties arises only from the fear for the punishments of the sovereign power, then it is difficult to find any worth and dignity in human beings. If we act by nature like thieves and robbers, then the mere appearance of law-abidingness does not change who we really are, and few would find that theft and robbery are worthy or dignified way of life.

The basic problem with the modern liberal theory of rights is, then, its low estimation of human being contrary to the widely held practical beliefs.[57] Such an initial assumption makes it too difficult to derive the notion of innate dignity or worth, and makes basic duties too easily overwhelmed by the prudential concerns of self-interests. For this reason, modern liberalism is criticized, perhaps with some justice, for adopting an unnecessarily dim view of human nature and for ignoring the inherent moral potential in a human being. By undermining social duty and legal constraints on personal gratification of desires, it is charged,[58] the radical individualistic tendency in modern liberalism dehumanizes human beings. I argue below that Confucianism, while fundamentally a duty ethics and despite its own problems, provides a salutary correction to such a tendency and, if properly construed, is capable of accommodating a well-balanced theory of rights.

From Universal Duty to Universal Rights: A Confucian Transformation?

We have already seen that, as a consistent implication of the Confucian belief, the universal respect for human dignity carries the demand that the state and society must protect and help to cultivate the innate virtues in every individual human being, and this task is probably best achieved by providing a constitutional system of basic rights. It is nevertheless true that such a system of rights has been conspicuously lacking throughout the Chinese history. It appears as if that, by emphasizing social duty, the traditional China were diametrically opposed to the modern West. The reason for such difference lies partly in the different conception of equality. As Munroe points out,[59] the classical Chinese philosophers recognized only *natural* equality in the sense that everyone is born with innate virtues as unique human potentials, but denied *actual* equality that all human beings could in fact develop their nature to such an equal extent as to entitle them to equal respect.

In Confucianism, such a distinction had justified the hierarchical structure of society and the denial of popular participation in government. By focusing on the capacities that the people have *in fact* developed through learning and education, the Confucians had limited the participation in government to a small group of elites, and ignored the notion of innate moral rights developed in the West, which entitles every adult to some form of participation. As a result, Confucianism had never developed an explicit notion of "rights"—not modern political right to participation, not the Lockean right to property in virtue of one's labor, not even the Hobbesian natural right to self-preservation. Similar to the classical and Medieval counterparts in the West, Confucianism was decidedly duty-orientated. In what the Chinese view as a just society, one's "right" (i.e. social, economic, and political privileges) was to be made strictly proportional to the degree of actually developed worth and ability. The state and society must be run by the most virtuous and worthy, who almost always remain a small minority, and it seemed to them patently absurd to allow the ignorant, selfish, myopic, and morally immature mass to choose their own leaders. To the contrary, Kongzi and his followers were simply concerned with how to make men virtuous and, at the same time, make the virtuous men rule.

In a sense, the Confucians were quite right. If one is truly incompetent in a certain vocation (e.g. political participation), then both justice and common prudence require that he should refrain from engaging in it, but leave it instead to those who are capable. And mere rights, freedom, and participation are not the only things about which the people ought to care; indeed, these alone are insufficient to sustain a sound social and political institution.[60] Rather, they presuppose something else as their foundation, that is, the development of the people's virtues and the primary means by which the virtues are acquired: proper education and upbringing. After all, hardly anyone wants to live in a society full of "rights" and "freedom," but bereft of basic order, norms, values, and a sense of duty—a society in which everyone feels free to do whatever he wants, without any moral constraint. Such a society would be necessarily one of "petty men," among whom numerous conflicts, strifes, infringements, and oppressions are bound to occur. On the other hand, a democracy worthy of its name presupposes a society of gentlemen who, having developed their virtues and become mature citizens, are capable of exercising their "rights" intelligently. Thus, for good reasons, self-cultivation has occupied the central position of Confucianism; it is the very path toward the making of virtuous and dignified citizens.

To be consistent with the Confucian assumption of natural equality, however, even *xiaoren* ("petty man") is, after all, a person (*ren*) and must be treated as a human being with the inborn potential virtues. For those who choose to accept the Confucian view of human nature must believe that *every* man and woman is equally endowed with the innate virtues and think highly of them.[61] Even a petty man deserves some respect for his innate nobility in virtue of being a human—better, nobler, and worthier than other animals. Thus, to a Confucian gentleman, it is morally inadequate to treat anyone—a petty man, even a criminal—like a mere animal. The failure to cultivate one's virtues should never lead a gentleman to merely despise one's person, but should rather urge him to help the petty man by all means to cultivate the virtues and become a gentleman. The belief in human dignity may further inspire a gentleman to devise a better system of education, among other things, in order that everyone can have a reasonable opportunity to actualize his virtues and to maximize, as it were, his dignity.[62] At least, social and political schemes should never be designed to merely put down a petty man and make him docile simply for the sake of societal peace and order. As everyone is endowed by Heaven with the innate virtues, which afford him some basic dignity, everyone is an end in himself, more than a tool for any other end, however grandiose.

Thus, it can be plausibly argued within the Confucian framework that an ordinary person should have some right in discussing and deciding public issues that will ultimately touch upon his life, and many such issues might be plain enough to be understood by a common mind with reasonable education. Further, to become a gentleman presupposes a set of favorable social and political conditions, which had been denied to most ordinary men and women in traditional China. A person need be given the basic education and some opportunity for practice before he can intelligently participate in government. Without these opportunities, he will most likely remain an uneducated and underdeveloped "petty man"— not because he wishes to remain politically ignorant and incompetent, but because he lacks the fortune (at least an adequately provided family, among other things) that is beyond his control but is nevertheless necessary for his moral development. Since the mass of people were deprived of the opportunity to become morally developed gentlemen, the apparently "just" traditional system of merit was based ultimately on injustice. In this sense, a social and political system that guarantees a minimum set of rights—to participate in government or otherwise—seems to provide more fairness because it can afford relatively equal opportunity for personal development of innate virtues.

Still, the notion of "rights" does not so easily fit with the dignity of a Confucian gentleman. The problem of rights lies deeper in the Chinese practice, for even a gentleman seemed to have only duties, but no reciprocal rights, before his parents, rulers, and society in general. Somehow it appears inadequate—even distasteful—to a gentleman to fight for his own rights and interests, especially in the form of factions and parties, for "a gentleman is dignified, but does not wrangle."[63] It is true that the Confucian duties are never unilateral, but always reciprocal.[64] Thus, the king and his officials, the husband and his wife, and the father and his sons have their own duties to perform toward each other. And, if a duty (e.g. benevolence of a king) is insisted and recognized by every member of society, then it is in effect transformed into a kind of right toward the recipient of its performance. But, in practice, such condition is hardly ever met. Generally, in a relationship between two unequal parties, the moral persuasion of duty alone is seldom sufficient to prevent the powerful party from abusing its power. As a result, contrary to equilibrium and harmony as prescribed by the Principle of the Mean, the imbalance of power frequently led to egregious abuses in the Chinese political history. During those periods, no matter how dignified a gentleman was in private life, his dignity would disappear before the state, against which he had no protection.[65] Even private complaints must be made with caution, as Kongzi himself taught: "When good government prevails in a state, one should speak and act boldly. When bad government prevails, act righteously, but speak with reserve"[66]; otherwise, one would merely put his life, together with the security and welfare of his family, in jeopardy.

Before the state, then, even a gentleman could not maintain his dignity because he was compelled to restrain his action and speech out of fear for an omnipotent power. This is incompatible with the earlier image that, as a mature, just and courageous person, he should be without any fear for actions (including public speeches) he thinks to be just and proper. As a rational being, it seems, he would desire to live in a better institutional arrangement in which his moral autonomy can be effectively preserved. Indeed, a central theme that continues to preoccupy the contemporary neo-Confucianism has been to extend from "sageliness inward" (內聖 neisheng) to "kingliness outward" (外王 waiwang)—a political system that is conducive to the realization of endowed virtues and, thus, the enhancement of human dignity.[67]

Therefore, to consistently follow the Principle of the Mean, it seems necessary for a Confucian gentleman to adopt some institutional mechanism to guarantee his basic right in order to minimize the possibility that his dignity is degraded. Nor should a gentleman feel shame in exercising and defending his rights in democratic politics, as the partisan competitions can now be carried out through entirely peaceful and dignified constitutional procedures, without having to "wrangle." Quite the contrary, in the spirit of the Mean, the secure independence of a gentleman requires a certain balance of power between an individual and the state, in order that nobody is so overwhelmed by the omnipotent power of the sovereign as to become the mere object of political control. When this independence is endangered by the natural disparity of power between the state and individuals, the Principle of Mean demands the implementation of a system of rights, so that the power of the stronger can be checked peacefully, and the balance restored, secured and enforced by an effective legal artifice. Such a balance can be guaranteed by a rationally designed Constitution based upon a set of fundamental values, which are shared by a people who have commonly agreed to respect the dignity of every member in society.

It may be contended, at last, that such a universalistic notion of respect could not be consistently derived from Confucianism, an ethics primarily concerned with particularistic duties. The Confucian concept of general love (*Ai* or *Fan Ai*), for example, is not to be confused with the Mohist notion of undifferentiated, universal love. Rather, the Confucian love was graded according to the proximity of natural human relationships, enforced by a hierarchical system of propriety (*Li*), which prescribed different rules for treating one's family members, superiors, inferiors, friends, and members of society. And the Confucian notion of "intimate love" (*qin*) is further restricted, by definition, to be within one's family. I argue, however, that the clear distinction between particularistic love and general respect constitute the strength rather than weakness of Confucianism. This is best seen in the context of the central concept of humanity (*Ren*), which the Confucians define as a radiating process beginning naturally from within one's family and extending to more remote social relationships.[68] According to Mengzi, humanity and intimate love are applied to things of different orders: while a gentleman is humane to whole mankind, he owes special filial duty only to his family members.[69] Humanity for ordinary people (*Ren min*) lies between the intimate love for one's kin (*qin qin*) and the general care for things (*ai wu*): although humanity is above ordinary care for things, it does not carry with it the unique emotional feeling for one's kin. For Mengzi, indeed, the Mohist universalization of social relationship is to ignore one's parents (无父*wufu*), a fault no less grave than that committed by its egocentric opposite, the Yangist denial of all social duties, which leads to the neglect of one's king (无君*wujun*).[70] To the Confucians generally, it would be against human nature to prescribe such universal Christian command as "You should love your neighbor as yourself."[71] Among other things, love as an intense emotional feeling and obligatory commitment is necessarily limited only to a few, to whom one owes his special debt (parents) or who otherwise occupy prominent places in one's family life (husband, wife, children, and other close relatives). Yet, if intimate love is to be restricted to one's family and cannot be universalized, general respect as a personal attitude is *not* constrained by such physical limit, and *can* be reasonably required to extend over all members of society.

SUMMARY

To sum up, the Confucian view of human dignity presupposes the potential virtues equally endowed by every human being and their irreplaceable value. Under this view, everyone has the basic dignity due to these innate virtues and deserves some respect. A Confucian gentleman, to be sure, is a person who consciously cultivates, practices, and displays his virtues, and his dignified appearance invites general respect. He not only always seeks to perfect his own virtues, but also helps others, within his ability, to improve theirs. Although the respect to a particular individual can be made proportional to the extent to which he has actually acquired human virtues, the innate human potentials that constitute the irreducible core of human dignity entitle everyone to at least a minimum respect. In this sense, even an infant has as much innate dignity as any adult, and should receive only those treatments that will help her to develop the inborn potentials as she grows up. A criminal also has the same innate dignity, even though it is manifestly contradicted by his grievous behavior; but even he should be treated in such a manner as to help him to recover his innate virtues and to see the worth in himself, so that he becomes capable of developing them on his own initiative. The legitimate actions of a state, society, or private persons are limited to those that do not inhibit anyone from attaining one's full dignity.[72] A legitimate public institution must fulfill the duty to provide favorable social conditions and a compatible legal framework so that everyone has the basic opportunity to develop the inner worth and become a dignified member of community. To this end, society is obliged to establish an equitable constitutional system of basic rights. Construed in this way, the Confucian idea of human dignity can provide a sound philosophical basis for the modern notions of human rights and freedom, together with a balanced theory of reciprocal duties. Such a reconstruction of Confucianism can help us understand, I hope, the connection between two types of universal ideals to which the United Nations appealed over half a century ago, that is, "the dignity and worth of the human person" and "the equal rights of men and women."[73]

NOTES

1. See, for example, Li Chenyang, "Confucian Value and Democratic Value," *Journal of Value Inquiry*, 31 (1997): 183–192.
2. See Zhu Yilu, *Confucian Ideal Personality and Chinese Culture* (Shenyang: Liaoning Education Press, 1991), 1–18. The earliest source I can find that explicitly attempts to connect the western concept of human dignity with Chinese *Renge* is Zhang Dongsun, *Rationality and Democracy* (Hong Kong: Longman Books, 1946), 47–82.
3. See Zhang Dainian, "The Concept of Human Dignity in the Classical Chinese Philosophy," *International Confucianism Study* 2 (1997), 18.
4. R.M. Hare, *Freedom and Reason* (London: Oxford University Press, 1963), 10–27.
5. See, respectively, Alan Gewirth, "Human Dignity as the Basis of Rights," in *The Constitution of Rights: Human Dignity and American Values*, ed. Michael J. Meyer and William A. Parent (Ithaca: Cornell

University Press, 1992), 12–14; Brad Stetson, *Human Dignity and Contemporary Liberalism* (Westport, CT: Praeger, 1998), 15–17.

6. For confining the notion of virtues to socially beneficial human abilities and propensities, see Cheng Chung-ying, "Transforming Confucian Virtues into Human Rights: A Study of Human Agency and Potency," in ed. Wm. Theodore de Bary and Tu Weiming, *Confucianism and Human Rights* (New York: Columbia University Press, 1998), 145–146.

7. *Analects*, 7: 22; see Wing-tsit Chan, Source Book in Chinese Philosophy (Princeton: Princeton University Press, 1963), 32.

8. *Mengzi*, 6A6.

9. Liang Qichao, *History of Political Thought in the Pre-Qin Period* (Taipei: Zhonghua Books, 1972), 381.

10. As to the Confucian distinction between *xiaoren* and *Junzi*, see Yu Ying-shih, *The Modern Interpretation of Traditional Chinese Thought* (Nanjing: Jiangsu People's Press, 1989), 160–177.

11. *Principle of the Mean*, sec. 3; also see sec. 4, 5, 9. In addition, "a gentleman follows the path of Mean, and feels no regret even though his virtue is unknown and neglected by the world." *Principle of the Mean*, sec. 11, trans. James Legge, *The Four Books* (Hong Kong: Wei Tung Book Co., 1971), 7.

12. *Analects:* 9: 29; see Legge, *The Four Books*, 126.

13. *Analects*, 7: 38.

14. *Principle of the Mean*, Ch. 31; see Chan, *Source Book in Chinese Philosophy*, 112

15. Alasdair MacIntyre, *After Virtue* (2nd Ed., Notre Dame: University of Notre Dame Press, 1984), 222–223.

16. *Principle of the Mean*, sec. 10; see Legge, *The Four Books*, 7.

17. Thus, "a gentleman seeks the Way rather than material support.... What worries him is not poverty, but that he fails to attain the Way." *Analects*, 15: 32.

18. *Mengzi*, 7A: 9; see Legge, *The Four Books*, 305.

19. *Principle of the Mean*, sec. 14; see Legge, *The Four Books*, 11.

20. *Principle of the Mean*, sec. 10; trans. Legge, *The Four Books*, 7.

21. "A gentleman seeks in himself, while a petty man seeks in the others." In *Analects*, 15: 21; see Legge, *The Four Books*, 137. "A gentleman must first acquire the virtues before he may require them in the others; he must rid himself of the vices before he can prohibit them in the others." *Great Learning*, sec. 10; see Legge, *The Four Books*, 12.

22. 慎独 *shendu*; see *Great Learning*, sec. 6.
23. *Mengzi*, 2A2; see Legge, *The Four Books*, 63.
24. *Mengzi*, 3B2.
25. J.L. Mackie, *Ethics: Inventing Right and Wrong* (London: Penguin Books, 1977), 15–49.
26. *Xunzi*, "Kingly Government," Ch. 9; see Homer H. Dubs, *The Works of Hsuntze* (Taipei: Cheng-wen Publishing Co., 1966), 136.
27. That is, the lack of belief in the original human sin and the resulting guilt, see Max Weber, *The Religion of China*, trans. Hans H. Gerth (New York: Free Press, 1951), 235.
28. See Irene Bloom, "Fundamental Intuition and Consensus Statement: Mencian Confucianism and Human Dignity," in *Confucianism and Human Rights*, ed. Wm. Theodore de Bary and Tu Weiming (New York: Columbia University Press, 1998), 104–108.
29. *Mengzi*, 6A17.
30. *Mengzi*, 6A4.
31. Donald J. Munro, *The Concept of Man in Early China* (Stanford: Stanford University Press, 1969), 49–83.
32. See *Mengzi*, 1A4.
33. *Analects*, 10: 17. I owe this example to Professor Ni Peimin in response to a question raised by Professor Li Chenyang at the panel discussion at the Twentieth World Congress of Philosophy.
34. See Peter L. Berger, Brigitte Berger, and Hansfriend Kellner, *The Homeless Mind: Modernization and Consciousness* (New York: Random House, 1973), 89–95, for an argument of similar conceptual understanding in the West and for an illuminating discussion of how the process of modernity and the disintegration of traditional social institutions led to the transition from the particularistic concept of "honor" to the universalistic concept of "human dignity."
35. *Mengzi*, 2A6.
36. *Analects*, 15: 24.
37. *Analects*, 12: 2.
38. For a general argument that "good" is an indefinable, non-natural quality, see G.E. Moore, *Principia Ethica* (Amherst, New York: Prometheus Books, 1902 [1988]), 2–21, and further discussion in Mackie, *Ethics: Inventing Right and Wrong*, 50–63.
39. This is recognized even by the utilitarianist J.S. Mill, who argues that the "sense of dignity, which all human beings possess in one form or other" is identified with one's "unwillingness...to sink into what he

feels to be a lower grade of existence." *Utilitarianism*, Ch. 2; quoted from Spiegelberg, "Human Dignity: A Challenge to Contemporary Philosophy," 64, n. ii.

40. "A gentleman is friendly, but do not follow blindly." *Principle of the Mean*, sec. 10; see Legge, *The Four Books*, 7.

41. *Analects*, 20: 2; see Legge, *The Four Books*, 183.

42. *Ibid.*

43. *Principle of the Mean*, sec. 33.

44. "A gentleman can stay with his poverty; but a poor petty man will do anything [to improve his lot]." *Analects*, 15: 2.

45. For a Greek but similar description of the "great man," see Aristotle, *The Nicomachean Ethics*, trans. David Ross (Oxford: Oxford University Press, 1980), 89–95. Compare Max Weber, *The Religion of China*, trans. Hans H. Gerth (New York: Free Press, 1951), 228–229 for the contrast between "shame culture" and "guilt culture" in the west, which presupposes the original sin in human nature.

46. *Analects*, 13: 20; see Legge, *The Four Books*, 113.

47. *Mengzi*, 4B8.

48. *Analects*, 14: 27.

49. *Mengzi*, 4B18.

50. See *Mengzi*, 5B4.

51. *Analects*, 11: 24; see Legge, *The Four Books*, 89.

52. *Mengzi*, 6A10. The distaste for the lack of respect is clearly expressed by Mengzi: "To feed a man without love, is to treat him as a pig; to love him without respect, is to keep him as a domestic animal." *Mengzi*, 7A37.

53. Bill Clinton, "Remarks at the Arrival Ceremony in Xi'an, China," 25 June 1998, http://www.doc88.com/p-9788189619188.html, last visit on May 4, 2000.

54. See, for example, Leo Strauss, *Natural Right and History* (Chicago: The University of Chicago Press, 1953), 80–85.

55. The "difficulties" here are referred to substantive ones. The logical difficulties, such as the "naturalistic fallacy" that Moore charges the naturalists for committing, seem to be rather minor. G.E. Moore, *Principia Ethica* (Amherst, New York: Prometheus Books, 1988), 37–58. If Hobbes can establish that self-preservation is universally desired by every rational animal, then the opposition against defining such desire as a "good" (i.e. the natural right) carries little force. The transition from "is" to "ought" does have a logical problem of

violating the "Hume's Law." Yet, the problem is not so serious if one omits the prescriptive element inherent in the "ought," so that ethics can be identified with factual inquiry.

56. For example, the Christian God in Locke's *Two Treatises of Government*.

57. But partial corrections can be found in, among other works, Butler's *Five Sermons*, Hume's *Enquiry Concerning the Principles of Morals*, and *The Theory of Moral Sentiments* by Adam Smith.

58. Brad Stetson, *Human Dignity and Contemporary Liberalism* (Westport, CT: Praeger, 1998), 4–8, 165–166.

59. Munroe, *The Concept of Man in Early China*, 49–83.

60. On defending Confucianism against morally nihilistic freedom without basic values and norms, see Xu Fu-guan, *Confucian Political Thought and Democracy, Liberty and Human Rights* (Taipei: The Eighties Press, 1979), 284–293.

61. For the common assumption of all classical Chinese philosophers about the natural equality innate in every man, see Munroe, *The Concept of Man in Early China*, 1–14, 49–50.

62. Thus, "the Way of great learning lies in the brightening of virtue, in renovating the people, and in the end of the perfect good." *Great Learning*, Ch. 1.

63. *Analects*, 15: 22; trans. Legge, *The Four Books*, 137.

64. "As a ruler, he abided in humanity. As a minister, he abided in reverence. As a son, he abided in filial piety. As a father, he abided in deep love. And in dealing with the people of the country, he abided in faithfulness." *Great Learning*, sec. 3; trans. Wing-tsit Chan, Source Book in Chinese Philosophy (Princeton: Princeton University Press, 1963), 88.

65. The same can be said to have occurred—much more frequently but perhaps at a reduced scale—in the traditional family, which is supposed to be both the foundation and a miniature of the state. Similar opposing arguments made below apply, though with some difficulties owing to the secular nature of Chinese metaphysics of life, which I will not get into here.

66. *Analects*, 14: 3.

67. See Fung Yu-lan, *A Short History of Chinese Philosophy* (Derk Bodde ed., New York: The Free Press, 1948), 8. For an argument for the possible compatibility of Confucianism with the notion of human rights, see Xia Yong, *The Origins of the Human Rights Concept* (Beijing: China Politics and Law University Press, 1992), 177–192.

For the neo-Confucian effort to derive a compatible political mechanism from the Confucian ethics, see Xu Fu-guan, *Confucian Political
Thought and Democracy, Liberty and Human Rights*, Ch. 4. For a
critique on the alleged failure of such effort, see Jiang Qing, "From
Heart-Nature Confucianism to Political Confucianism," in Liu Shu-
xian et al., *Collection of Papers on Contemporary Neo-Confucianism*
(Taipei: Wenjing Press, 1991), 153–178.

68. *Principle of the Mean*, sec. 20.
69. *Mengzi*, 7A 45.
70. *Mengzi*, 3B9.
71. *Matthew*, 22: 39.
72. This says nothing against setting up penal institutions for those crimi-
nals, whose dignity has fallen below the minimum that can be toler-
ated by the community. But these institutions cannot be created *merely*
for the sake of punishment or the maintenance of public order; they
must treat these people as human beings, aim to help them to find
their own worth, and make them capable of becoming a gentleman
upon their own efforts. This is very much in line with the Confucian
thinking of the reformative function of law and punishment.
73. Universal Declaration of Human Rights, Preamble.

CHAPTER 3

Humanity or Benevolence?
The Interpretation of Confucian *Ren* and Its Modern Implications

INTRODUCTION

If we had the fortune of inviting a sage of the Warring States period, say, Mengzi, to visit China today, he would find the landscape transformed beyond recognition. Yet, to his surprise, he would also find many problems familiar to his distant age. Despite rapid economic development over the past three decades, China, like many developing nations in the world today, is still a peasant-dominant society plagued by poverty. In 2014, peasants still constitute over half of the massive 1.4 billion population.[1] Even in cities where the living conditions are comparatively better, relative poverty and pressure of life is on the rise owing to a variety of factors—high housing cost in metropolitans, expensive education, the lack of effective medical care, social insurance programs, and so on. And poverty is not nearly as serious a problem as the moral, institutional, and environmental crisis. One need not deliberately search the Internet to find dramatic headline stories.[2] The recurring episodes of air, water, soil, and food pollution are attributed as much to the morally irresponsible economic actions as to the relentless official drive for economic development as the primary source of its authoritarian legitimacy at the expense of the nation's environment. Official corruptions have been so characteristic of every level and branch of government that the public began to display "fatigue" to the exposure of official scandals. City demolition in the name of "renovation"

© The Author(s) 2016
Q. Zhang, *Human Dignity in Classical Chinese Philosophy*,
DOI 10.1057/978-1-349-70920-5_3

and rural land being taken under the pretext of "urbanization" have created much grievances to the dislocated and occasionally wars between the government and the civilians who are about to lose the most vital part of livelihood. So much so that, in the end of 2009, a woman named Tang Fuzhen poured petroleum over and set fire to herself when she failed to keep from her house the demolition team sent by the township government in Sichuan province.[3] She died in hospital after a few days, and the tragic news agitated much public anger across the nation.

I suppose sages like Kongzi and Mengzi faced just this kind of society when they tenaciously put forward their theories in order to save the declining moral and political order from a total collapse. Of course, the specific situations are necessarily different: back then they (especially the rulers) worried that the population pool was too small to undertake major projects or aggressions, now we are trying everything to contain if not cut down the too enormous population; they had a static and uneducated peasant, we have a migrating peasant handicapped by the state sponsored discriminations and restrictions; they suffered from bloody wars actively initiated by ambitious kings and dukes, we suffer from modern industrial accidents, air and water pollutions, and food poisoning of various sorts, which cost equally large life tolls as a result of insufficient care taken by the "parent-like officials" (父母官 fumuguan) who are motivated less by public necessity than by prospects for their personal promotions; they had court plots and regicides, we have patricides, infanticides, wrongful deaths of innocent people, and so on.[4] But the nature of the problems is nevertheless the same. Were Mengzi asked to comment on the Tang Fuzhen case, he would unhesitatingly point to the root cause of the tragedy, that humanity (仁 Ren) and benevolent government (仁政 Renzheng) have been missing! China today and China two millennia ago confront precisely the same moral and political predicaments.

The purpose of this chapter is to identify the original meaning of Ren,[5] a concept that has occupied a central position in Confucianism. The word was of relatively late origin, and found its popular use only after the Analects (论语 Lunyu), where its meaning was articulated for the first time by Kongzi. But so many meanings have been attributed to Ren, sometime inconsistently by the same philosopher, that to translate it as "humanity" would already be to assume the conclusion of analysis. The word could also be translated, for example, as "care," "love," or "benevolence."[6] However, none of these translations, taken in their ordinary senses, can properly capture the true meaning of Ren as the highest moral ideal for every Confucian. This chapter seeks to discover a consistent development of the idea among the works of Kongzi and Mengzi and to establish the conceptual linkage between *Ren* and humanity in the Kantian sense, that is, to treat a human being "always at the same time as an end and never merely as a means."[7] References to Kant are made in this essay primarily because both the Kantian and Confucian ethics are humanistic ethics centered on the respect for human dignity. Although there are important differences between the Confucian approach and Kant's rationalistic approach, they do seem to corroborate each other and eventually agree upon major moral premises.[8]

In the next part of the chapter I argue that, as a moral concept, Confucian *Ren* goes beyond the limit of the materialistic concept of benevolence and agrees with a formulation of the Kantian categorical imperative. The original idea of humanity, as illustrated in the *Analects*, implied the requirement that one ought to respect others as ends in themselves and adopt actions that are acceptable to other human beings. More than a century later, Mengzi went further and developed an ontological theory for humanity based on the assumption that human beings are good by nature, thereby confirming the ultimate source of value inherent in human beings. Together with the notion of the "gentleman" (*Junzi*), the concept of *Ren* forms the core of Chinese humanism, which takes for granted that everyone is endowed by Heaven with the moral capacity for humanity and justice. To be consistent with the moral requirement of *Ren*, everyone must be treated as a moral being as such and is not to be reduced to a mere animal solely concerned with welfare needs and benefits.

Yet the Confucian concept of *Ren* has not always been consistently applied. While, in the matter of personal ethics, *Ren* as the highest moral ideal must be understood to mean "humanity," it was reduced to the limited significance of "benevolence" in the sphere of governance. This is true for the political philosophy of all Confucian schools, which had inherited the early Zhou (1046–771 B.C.) idea of the rule of virtue (德治 *dezhi*). Limited by the historical conditions of the time, they all took for granted the legitimacy of the existing social order and the monarchical form of government, and for that reason laid great emphasis on loyalty and obedience to the kings. Under that presupposition, however, they insisted that the kingly government must work for the welfare of the common people; hence the notion of "benevolent government" (仁政 *Renzheng*). The two apparently conflicting positions were united by the underlying assumption that the common people, though endowed with moral and intellectual faculties, were nevertheless incapable of sufficiently developing themselves to take care of their own welfare, much less to resist the tyranny of their rulers. The purpose of government, then, was mainly to provide protection and nourishment for the people's physical lives and, if possible, some moral education to help them rise above the animal status.

In the third and fourth parts of this chapter, I discuss the purpose of government as understood by the two leading schools of Confucianism, represented by Mengzi and Xunzi. Although the two schools are diametrically opposed with respect to their assumptions about human nature, they share the same problem in under-estimating the people's moral potential and taking for granted the legitimacy of their political regimes. As a result, the people are not taken as moral ends in themselves, but by and large as subjects of their own needs and desires, the satisfaction of which would reply upon the benevolence of government. I argue that such an understanding of *Ren* (as in *Renzheng*) is inconsistent with the ideal of humanity originally conceived by Kongzi and Mengzi and is ultimately based on negative assumptions about people's moral and intellectual capacities, which had been taken for granted since the early Zhou dynasty. Having misconceived the basic mission of government, neither Mengzi nor Xunzi was able to present morally persuasive arguments to their rulers. Unable to count on the people, they were compelled to rely upon the goodwill of rulers, and appeal to their self-interest in a benevolent government—an approach with little moral force and very limited practical success in the Chinese history.

Finally, I explore certain passages in the works of Mengzi and Xunzi that require the government to transcend mere benevolence, and offer the possibility of building a new political philosophy consistent with the original moral conception of *Ren*.

REN AS HUMANITY

The idea of *Ren* expresses one of the central assumptions of Confucian humanistic philosophy, that is, every individual is endowed with the inner moral faculty from Heaven and is capable of self-perfection without the further aid of a transcendent divine power. As Kongzi says of himself: "Heaven produced virtue in me."[9] Mengzi goes even further to state: "All things are already complete in me. There can be no greater delight than to feel sincerity upon self-examination."[10] Although Kongzi himself rarely talked about human nature,[11] he did indicate that *Ren*—the moral faculty that distinguishes a person from mere animals—is the very definition of a human being. Thus, "Humanity is [the distinguishing character of] the human being (人ren)."[12] The Confucian mainstream represented by Mengzi generally assumed that the moral nature, derived directly from Heaven, is innate in every human being. Through constant learning and self-cultivation, everyone can develop his true nature and choose a way of life that conforms to the Way of Heaven. Thus, since the early days of Chinese intellectual history, humans have been regarded as moral beings, who are able to use reason to control their needs and sensuous inclinations for pleasure and to understand the higher purpose for which they were created.

The Original Meaning of Ren in Kongzi's Writings

In the *Analects*, the central meaning of *Ren* is general love for mankind,[13] as manifested by the proper manner in which one deals with his family, friends, and the state.[14] As defined by Kongzi and Mengzi, *Ren* is a radiating process of love, which starts naturally from within one's family, and extends to more remote social relationships to include friends and members of society in general. Thus, "those who are humane, beginning with what they [naturally] love, proceed to what they do not [naturally] love."[15]

The notion of "general love" (*fan ai*), however, means more than the mere provision of benefits. Indeed, *Ren* and ordinary love are applied to things of different orders: while a gentleman loves all creatures, he is humane only to the people.[16] Thus, *Ren*, or general love, signifies a higher feeling due to human beings. Most important, the proper manifestation of humanity presupposes two moral criteria: one mental and the other behavioral.

First, the notion of *Ren* presupposes a goodwill in a person that leads to his apparently benevolent actions. Unlike the "propriety" (礼*Li*) shown by one's overt behavior, *Ren* refers to the inner quality of a person's mind. To Kongzi, the appearance of propriety would amount to nothing, had it not come from a genuine good heart.[17] In fact, *Ren* has also been identified with two characteristics of mind: faithfulness (忠*zhong*) and reciprocity (恕*shu*), which formed a "unifying thread" that runs through Kongzi's own philosophy of life.[18] The inner quality of *Ren* can be cultivated by the practice of the five virtues: "gravity (恭*gong*), liberality (宽*kuan*), truthfulness (信*xin*), diligence (敏*min*), and benevolence (惠*hui*),"[19] among which material benevolence and generosity is only one of the constituting elements.

Second, the good quality of mind ought to be reflected in one's respectful manner of treating others, suggesting that everyone possesses something that is worthy of respect. A person of *Ren* is to be "sedately grave when staying at home; reverently attentive in the management of business, and sincerely loyal in dealing with others."[20] Had Kongzi viewed human beings as mere receivers of benefits, who would seem to deserve little respect, the prescription of respectful manner would have been entirely superfluous. Thus, the concept of *Ren* implies a great deal more than a benevolent outcome; in order to be *Ren*, one must achieve such a result through a respectful form of behavior and, more important, with a good heart.[21]

Various expressions of *Ren* can be subsumed under a general rule that is similar to Kant's categorical imperative[22] and the perfect duty of refraining from doing harm to the others: "Do not do to others what you do not want them to do to you."[23] Although Kongzi had not elevated this rule of conduct to the height of universal law as Kant did, the idea is nevertheless similar. It plainly suggests that, to satisfy the moral requirement of *Ren*, I should not impose upon others what I think would be harmful to me (and usually also to others); to the contrary, I ought to make sure that every action I take must not only suit my own purpose, but also be acceptable to all others. Indeed, Kongzi would hold further that *Ren* positively requires one to help the others:[24]

> A person of *Ren*, wishing to establish himself, seeks also to establish others; wishing to be prominent, seeks also to make others prominent. The art of achieving *Ren* is to think of others by what is nigh in ourselves.[25]
>
> c near, close

This passage further implies the idea of treating every person as an end, not merely as a means, and suggests strongly against the interpretation that identifies Confucian *Ren* with mere benevolence. If, following Kongzi and Mengzi, I think of myself as a moral being, and treat myself as an end rather than a means to any other end, then "to think of others by what is nigh in ourselves," I should treat the others as moral beings and ends in themselves as well. I should not reduce myself to a mere receiver of benefits provided by others, nor should I treat others merely as such receivers of benefits. The morality of my actions (which may well be benevolent), then, cannot be derived solely from the incentive to benefit others by satisfying their needs,[26] but must come from my respect for their true nature as moral beings. This implication, simple as it may sound, was not fully realized when the later Confucians turn to construct "benevolent politics."

Now it is commonly conceded that the Golden Rule does not always produce morally acceptable results, but do so only when certain conditions are satisfied.[27] In a footnote in his *Grounding of Metaphysics of Morals*,[28] Kant himself treats the Golden Rule as an imperfect deduction from his universal maxim, being both underinclusive in the sense that it may fail to include certain moral duties (e.g. duty to aid the needy, for someone may be callus enough to insist that everyone should live on his own means and this is true even when he himself turns out to be in the needy position) and overinclusive in that it may include certain non-moral or immoral elements (e.g. a criminal may ask the judge to put himself in his shoes and exculpate him). For Kant, the Golden Rule is necessarily subject to exceptions and limitations since it depends on the contingent feeling and interest of the subject.

Kant is largely right about the limitations of the Golden Rule, which essentially serves as a reflexive device to use our self-interest to check against our excessive selfish inclinations. It forces us to be conscientious about the consequences of our attitudes and actions toward others, but it does not always work well. Here we explore two related problems that might pose as challenges to the Confucian Golden Rule, but these challenges are successfully met by Confucianism.[29]

First, that the application of the Golden Rule depends on the interest and feelings of the subject means that it would always work for "good" people but not necessarily so for "bad" people. In some circumstances, if the subject is reckless enough about his own interest, he may delightedly choose to deny his moral duty toward others without expecting reciprocal duty to him. This is particularly true for the positive form of the Golden Rule. A bad judge, for example, may choose to set a criminal free when he expects himself to commit crimes and get away from punishment, despite the fact that in doing so he would do damage to criminal justice and social order, and eventually endanger his own security. This challenge does not seem to apply to Kongzi, however, because he wisely limits at least the positive form of the Golden Rule to the right subject—the person of humanity, who will help others to establish themselves according to their particular characters, abilities and weaknesses. Kongzi seems to expect that the Golden Rule should not be applied universally to all, but only to those who have cultivated proper moral motivations, and to those uncultivated people (i.e. the petty men) only in circumstances where such application will not produce undesirable moral implications.

Second, in this connection it is possible to limit the Golden Rule expressed in the *Analects* to "horizontal" relationships.[30] In other words, when Kongzi preaches to do to others what you like others to do to you, or refrain from doing to others what you dislike others to do to you, it is possible to interpret the "others" here to mean persons of equivalent status rather than everyone in the world; outside your class, this type of reciprocity may cease to have any effect. There is no textual basis to hold such a limited interpretation, however, since Kongzi himself never stated such limitation. Confucianism is, to be sure, a particularistic ethic with ubiquitous unequal vertical relationships: a king is not supposed to receive the same etiquette from his ministers as the ministers from the king; a child is supposed to pay respect to his parents, and from them obtain care in return. Yet the lack of exact parity does not prevent the Golden Rule from operating. The rule would only ask the king to think about the way he would like to be treated by his king were he a minister, and that is the way he should treat the ministers; and so do parents and children. In fact, Mengzi has already contemplated a roughly reciprocal relationship between the king and the ministers:

> *If the king regards his ministers as his hands and feet, the ministers will regard him as their heart and mind; if the king regards his ministers as dogs and horses, then his ministers will regard him as any other man; if the king regards his ministers as mud and grass, the ministers will regard him as a bandit and an enemy.*[31]

The takes and gives are not exactly equivalent (nor do the Confucians think they ought to be), but a pattern of parity is here, and there is no reason to insist that this pattern applies only to the court relationships. In specific applications, of course, the Confucians are mindful of individual weaknesses, and would not simply render whatever one would like putting oneself in the other's shoes. For example, how should a gentleman (*Junzi*) treat a petty man (*xiaoren*)—should he think of what he might need were he a petty man, just as a criminal asks the judge to think pretending to be a criminal? That would have been absurd for the Confucians, so the Confucian Golden Rule must be interpreted to mean the switch of situations without switching moral characters; otherwise, it would be quite impossible for the person of humanity to help establish others since he would not have known what is good and how to become good at the first place. When Yan Yuan, Zhong Gong, SimaNiu, and Fan Chi asked about how to practice *Ren*, Kongzi gave each a different answer tailored to their abilities;[32] when Zi Gong, Duke Jing of Qi, Minister Ji Kang, Zi Zhang, Zi Lu, Zhong Gong, and Zi Xia asked about how to govern a state, Kongzi again gave each a different advice, this time according to what they would need in view of their deficiencies.[33] The positive formulation of the Golden Rule means only that, when a person of humanity meets someone with inferior capacity (in the Confucian moral view), he is to provide that person with whatever means necessary for moral cultivation. So the answer given by a Confucian magistrate to that astute criminal would be: "I am not like you at all, so I cannot apply your logic; but had I become as depraved as you, I would do such and such in order to get back to the right course of moral life." The fact that the Confucians would find it objectionable to punish for its own sake does not mean that they are compelled by the Golden Rule to exonerate crimes.[34]

Humanity and Human Nature: The Moral Construction of Mengzi

Although Kongzi introduced the central concept of *Ren* to Chinese moral philosophy, he did not elaborate upon its metaphysical foundation. A more systematic theory of humanity had to await Mengzi, whose doctrine later came to dominate Confucian thought. Like Kongzi, Mengzi firmly believes in the human moral capacity for self-perfection. The ultimate source of morality is the human heart-mind, which is good by nature. A human being possesses an innate knowledge of *Ren* and has the inborn capacity to be humane: "*Ren* is [the unique character of] the human being. When embodied in human conduct, it is the Way."[35] Human evil arises not from human nature, but from human failure to resist the pernicious influences of the outer world. Thus, the proper end of mankind lies in the conscious effort of learning and self-cultivation, through which one recovers his easily lost good nature.

Mengzi asserts outright that *Ren* is rooted in the "heart-mind" (心 *xin*) of every person.[36] Everyone is endowed by Heaven, he says, with four sprouts of the "heart-mind"; they are the sources for humanity (*Ren*), righteousness, propriety and intelligence:

The feeling of commiseration is found in all men; the feeling of shame and dislike is found in all men; the feeling of reverence and respect is found in all men;

> *the feeling of right and wrong is found in all men. The feeling of commisera-*
> *tion is humanity; the feeling of shame and dislike is righteousness; the feeling*
> *of respect and reverence is propriety; the feeling for right and wrong is wisdom.*
> *Humanity, righteousness, propriety, and wisdom are not drilled into us from*
> *outside. We originally have them with us. Only we do not think [to find them].*
> *Therefore it is said, "seek and you will find it, neglect and you will lose it.*[37]

While the heart-mind for shame and distaste (for one's own bad behavior) is the origin of the feeling of righteousness, the heart-mind for compassion is the origin of humanity. Thus, *Ren* is a moral quality with which everyone is born, which defines the essential character of a human being, and without which a person would be reduced to a mere animal. The feeling of compassion plays a key role in establishing Mengzian theory of humanity:

> *All men have something that they cannot bear. Extend that feeling to what they*
> *can bear, and humanity will be the result. All men have something that they*
> *will not do. Extend that feeling to something that they will do, and righteous-*
> *ness will be the result. If a man can give full development to his feeling of not*
> *wanting to injure others, his humanity will be more than what he can ever put*
> *in practice.*[38]

The Mengzian theory appeared to plainly contradict many people's common experiences in his time, when the previous political and social order established by the Zhou dynasty was dissolving, and feudal kings and warlords preyed upon one another. In fact, it is quite possible that the lack of humanity in the actual world at that time is what prompted early Chinese sages to appeal to this very ideal. Despite the apparently cruel human reality, however, Mengzi insisted that the heart-mind of *Ren* is still innate in every ordinary human being, and on proper occasions it even compels one to act according to the moral ideal of *Ren*.[39] Mengzi attempts to illustrate the general existence of *Ren* using the human urge for actions that are based upon the natural feeling of compassion, free from all contaminations of material motives.

> *Now, when humans suddenly see a child about to fall into a well, they all have*
> *a feeling of alarm and distress, not to gain friendship with the child's parents,*
> *nor to seek the praise of their neighbors and friends, nor because they dislike the*
> *reputation [of lack of humanity if they did not rescue the child]. From such a*
> *case, we see that a man without the feeling of commiseration is not a human.*[40]

Thus, *Ren* as the defining character of the human being seems to be present in every person. We all would be urged by our natural compassion to go forward and save the child from the danger without any exterior motives; presumably even a criminal would feel the same urge within.[41] This is precisely what Mengzi means by "Yao and Shun (尧舜) were the same as other men."[42] We all share the innate "moral sprouts" that will generate compassionate feelings when prompted by certain instances and, when cultivated properly, will grow into a full moral character.[43]

Of course, the example given here cannot "prove" the existence of humanity. As Kant points out, humanity as a transcendental ideal cannot truly be proved by mere experience of feelings, which always find exceptions. For however compelling this example might be to an ordinary person, some people may never feel compelled to save the baby. Nor is compassion as a natural feeling necessarily limited to human beings; many animals may act in the same way. Thus the imaginary urge to take benevolent actions out of compassion cannot establish that *Ren* is the unique moral character common to every human being. Kant may also be interpreted as objecting to the use of compassion—a natural feeling—for supporting a moral argument. To be moral, one must act not only in conformity with the moral law, but also for the sake of the moral law. In other words, the ultimate motive for a moral action must be the duty itself, not merely some kind of feeling.

Although Mengzi does differ from Kant by presupposing a transcendent heart-mind as the seat of *Ren*, the objections made above are not fatal to his arguments. After all, compassion is a feeling associated with our imperfect duty—the duty to help others whenever we can. And we need not take the example to mean that compassion is the only motive that induces a moral action; rather, we can interpret it to signify the power of the inner moral faculty, just as the feeling of respect signifies the presence of the Kantian moral law. More important, compassion illustrates our consciousness of the worth inherent in the lives of others. This is probably as far as anyone can go in demonstrating the common moral presence in human nature, and we would be on the verge of obstinacy to beg for an absolute proof.

Therefore, despite their profound differences, it seems possible to reconcile Mengzi's theory of human nature with Kantian ethics. Kant is particularly valuable for our purpose because he developed a systematic theory on humanity and human dignity—concepts that occupy a central position of Confucian ethics. Obviously, his approach differs from the

Confucians' empirical or intuitionist approaches since he is exclusively concerned with a secure *a priori* foundation for moral principles, which he thinks are not to be derived from empirical observations or perceptions that are both predetermined and susceptible to exceptions. For Kant, moral laws, unlike the laws of nature, are laws of freedom to be grasped by reason,[44] and "freedom (independence from being constrained by another's choice), insofar as it can coexist with the freedom of every other in accordance with a universal law, is the only original right belonging to every man by virtue of his humanity."[45] Yet, Kant's rationalistic approach is not without its own problems, and his exclusive grounding in reason and absolute rejection of a legitimate place for moral feelings seem to originate from the outdated cosmological assumptions that are no longer tenable today. With a more plausible assumption, it is at least possible to find the two approaches corroborating and complementing each other, and the rationalistic framework will be enriched by incorporating moral feelings into it. From this perspective, it seems that Mengzi is quite justified to appeal to feelings of compassion in order to demonstrate the moral "sprouts" of humanity (which Kant would think belong to the unknowable noumenal world) at work.

If we can take for granted that the natural feeling of compassion is present (albeit to different degrees) in most of us, it seems to suggest two things. First, although it does not establish the metaphysical existence of morality, it is consistent with the idea that we can act morally, beyond all selfish, reward-seeking motives. Second, it implies that the beneficiary of my moral action represents a good in itself, whose suffering of a misfortune somehow compels my moral conscience. For I certainly lack the same degree of compassionate feeling for the suffering of all animals.[46] It will not be surprising if I do not feel the same urge when it is a cat approaching the well; but it is entirely different if a human being is about to suffer from the same fate. And I have the urge to do everything within my capacity to save the child, not out of any concern for myself, not even for my natural love for a cute creature, but solely for the simple reason that the child, as a human being, is a good that, being absolute and universal, manifests unique worth to the entire world. Construed in this way, compassion, taken by Mengzi to be the manifestation of *Ren*, does seem to imply the intrinsic value of human life.

Toward a Notion of Dignity

Based on his theory of human nature, Mengzi developed a positive doctrine of human value. A human being may differ from other animals only slightly, yet it is precisely such a difference that makes the person unique. His unique value lies not in the material body—because that is something he shares with all other animals, but exclusively in the moral and intellectual faculty as embodied in his heart-mind. The heart-mind, responsible for moral and rational thinking, is the noblest organ endowed to human beings, and enables him to lead a meaningful moral life. Thus, Mengzi distinguishes the "noble" or "great" body (the heart-mind where humanity resides) from the "ignoble" or "small" body (the sensuous organs, which give rise to passion and desire). "While a gentleman (*Junzi*) follows his great body, a petty man (*xiaoren*) is driven by his small body."[47] A petty man knows only to satisfy his base desires and ignores the moral aspects of his nature and, as a result, leads a life not so distinct from that of a mere animal. By contrast, a gentleman takes care to cultivate his sublime moral character by pursuing *Ren*, which enables him to lead a life that is worthy of his noble nature. Mengzi assumes that everyone is born with the noble body together with the capacity to develop it. Thus, "everyone possesses in himself the noble value."[48] True nobility lies in humanity and righteousness, which is endowed by Heaven and cannot be substituted by human nobility (such as high social status and a comfortable material life). While human nobility is contingent on human fortune and limited to a few, the nobility of Heaven is absolute and universal to all human beings. Mengzi recognized, behind the veil of extreme social inequality at the time, a basic human equality grounded in moral capacity. He went so far as to assert that, "a sage belongs to the same type as the common people"[49]; one becomes a sage not because he was born with more *Ren* than others, but because he is able to consciously cultivate *Ren* throughout his life.

Thus, the difference between a gentleman and a petty man lies not in what one can do, but in what one will do. Human beings always have the capacity to become *Ren*, and will reach the kingdom of *Ren* as long as they want to—as long as they can keep their selfish desires and passions in check.[50] Like Kant, both Kongzi and Mengzi believed that human beings have the freedom of will to choose how they will live their lives. Thus, "whether to be *Ren* depends on oneself," not on others.[51] Those who give up the effort to be *Ren*, thus abandoning what is noble in their nature, are merely degrading themselves and inviting disgrace from others.[52] Endowed with reason and the freedom to choose, a person is fully responsible for his own moral development and thus is seen as a morally autonomous being.

Only by virtue of being a morally autonomous being is a human being regarded as an end in himself. A person is endowed by Heaven with the innate moral capacity for justice and humanity, an inestimable worth that distinguishes him from other animals. While animals are seen as instrumentally useful to mankind, a human being is an end to himself and is to be respected as such. The distaste for the lack of respect is clearly expressed by Mengzi: "To feed a person without love, is to treat him as a pig; to love him without respect, is to keep him as a domestic animal."[53] To treat someone with *Ren*, it is not enough to merely satisfy his material needs or even to love him; he must be respected as an ultimate end.

There is little justification, then, to reduce Confucian humanity to mere benevolence. In other words, humanity is not benevolence in its ordinary sense; rather, it is absolute benevolence, a principle by which Heaven made a person complete in his physical, intellectual, and moral faculties. To follow the principle of humanity, one must treat oneself and others truly as autonomous ends who, endowed with these innate capacities, were created for a higher purpose than to serve as mere subjects of their sensuous needs and desires. This is an important point to which we will return in applying *Ren* to the political realm, a point that, from the Confucian experience, can easily be forgotten. Without reference to intrinsic worth, all that is left in *Ren* is pity, which would fetch us right into benevolent politics as it did for the classical and later Confucians.[54]

THE ESSENCE OF "BENEVOLENT GOVERNMENT" AND ITS LIMITATIONS

Mengzi was the first in the Chinese history to extend the notion of humanity (*Ren*) and invent the term of "benevolent government" (*Renzheng*). He wanted to replace the "way of the despot" (霸道 *badao*) or the way of force with the "kingly way"(王道 *wangdao*)—the way of moral power,[55] and he expounded on this ideas systematically throughout his work. His new ideal was based on the traditional theory of the "rule of virtue," which initially provided political justification for the establishment of a new dynasty, the Zhou. Like Kongzi, Mengzi accepted the traditional legends about virtuous kings, who served as paragons for all rulers in his theory of government. It was these ancient kings, he asserted, that had brought to the people physical security, material prosperity,[56] education, and decent morals, without which the people would have led merely animal-like lives.[57]

Let me begin by acknowledging that the notion of benevolent government is not just a Confucian ideal, but one that is very much alive in the

Western world. Indeed, this ideal is gaining even more support today than it did two millennia ago, as different parts of the world are entering the welfare society. Since scientific and technological advances have made it possible to dramatically improve the social and economic conditions of mankind, there is every reason for a humanistic state to eradicate misery and poverty that have hitherto denied the opportunity for the full development of human potentials to the vast majority of the human population, and Mengzi was only prescient when he proposed the *Renzheng* ideal in such an economically backward society. Having said this, though, I am still convinced that *Renzheng* and *Ren* are two fundamentally different notions. As I shall argue below, although they share the same word (仁), *Renzheng* as a political ideal does not quite reach the high moral elevation of *Ren*, and one cannot successfully reconstitute the basic tenets of *Ren* by reading passages about *Renzheng*. Just as Western welfare society is not necessarily what Margalit calls a "decent society," a Confucian benevolent government pursuing *Renzheng* may well fail to be truly *Ren*.

A Welfare Society

Simply put, a benevolent government represents the ideal of a welfare society, where the old, the isolated, the helpless, and the common people in general are taken care of by the government. A benevolent government must meet two requirements. Negatively, it must refrain from hurting and exploiting its people, primarily in the form of taxation and mandatory draft of public labor. Positively a benevolent government must promote social welfare and protect the common people "as if it were protecting infants," so that "the neighboring people revere it as they revered their parents."[58] For this purpose, a benevolent government must begin with salubrious economic policies, especially the reasonable distribution of land.[59]

Even though no one today is obligated to accept his design of "well-shaped land" (井田 *jingtian*) system, in which the public land is to be surrounded and nourished by the private land blocks, one cannot fail to be struck by the prescience of Mengzi's concern over clear definition of land property rights. China today is beset precisely by the same problem, caused by the monopoly of the ill-defined "public" ownership of land, which has provided ample occasions for official corruptions and, at the same time, contributed to depriving the common people of their basic shelter—both of which would be strongly condemned by Mengzi. Even though China eventually enacted the Property Law in 2007, it is still grappling with such slippery legal jargons as "public interest" and "reasonable compensation." Had the Communist regime paid slightest heed to the Mengzian teaching over two millennia ago, how many conflicts and tragedies would have been prevented today!

Of course, the Mengzian welfare society is more than physical security and comfort of life; otherwise, in his own view, human beings would not be different from well supplied animals. In an ideal state, the people must also be provided with, in addition to food and clothing, adequate education that teach them proper social relations and rules of conduct.[60] It is therefore necessary to devise a reasonably complex education system, so that the people will be taught with different levels of knowledge about human relations. And good education not only places the common people in a harmonious social relationship, but also predisposes them to peaceful governance: "Good politics is less helpful than good education in winning the heart of the people (得民 *demin*). Good politics keeps the people in awe, but good education makes people love it."[61]

Condemnation of Tyranny

If a ruler cannot bring much welfare to its people, at the very least he must not purposefully undertake to hurt them, especially by engaging in wars aimed to augment his own territory and property. Mengzi strongly condemned those rulers who maintained luxuries of their court lives by taking away the basic goods necessary for the people's sustenance, driving them to starvation and destitution in the wild. He equated these exploitative activities to be "leading beasts to devour men" and "killing with policies," no less than killing with knives.[62]

Even today very much the same words can be said about the rulers who failed to perform the duties they owed to the people. If the government failed to implement the minimum standards for safety or health and caused great harms to human lives, then the leaders cannot simply say that it is the mines or floods or the private food processors to be blamed, but the rulers themselves are to be blamed for failing to take the people's lives seriously enough and avert their dangers. This is why China nowadays has implemented the "official responsibility system," which holds the chief administrators responsible for local disasters of natural or human origins.[63]

Mengzi did not stop laying down general criteria that the "parent-like officials" must meet, but targeted against specific rulers who had failed to practice benevolent politics. For example, he reproached King Hui of

Liang for lack of humanity, as "a person of humanity reaches what it does not love from what he loves, a person of inhumanity reaches what it loves from what he does not love."[64] What King Hui did was more than failing his duty; he positively drove his people to fight for his territory and suffered from great defeat, and to secure victory, he further drove his beloved brothers to the deadly cause. For Mengzi, this is many times worse than the use of figurines in the burial—a practice strongly condemned by Kongzi.

To be consistent, Mengzi also condemned those abettors of the tyrant, who could not have fulfilled his multitudinous ambitions without their assistance: "Today those who serve the king always say: 'I can extend territory and fill depository for you.' Today's so-called good ministers were called in ancient times the thieves to the people."[65] These abettors, abandoning the right course of government, are to be rejected by the Confucians: "When a ruler failed to practice benevolent government, all those ministers who enriched him were rejected by Kongzi. How much more would have he rejected those who are vehement to fight for him?"[66] The right way is that, if the king commits a major error, the ministers should advise him; if he refuses to follow after repeated advices, then ministers in his family should "replace him with someone else," and ministers outside the royal family should simply leave.[67]

If the king ultimately fails to abide by the principles of humanity and righteousness, then he will lose the qualification to maintain power, and virtually become a lone usurper (一夫 yifu). So when asked about the King Tang's exile of the despot Jie (桀) and King Wu of Zhou's (周武王) expedition against the last emperor Zhou of the Shang dynasty (商纣王), Mengzi answers: "He who injures humanity is a bandit. He who injures righteousness is a destructive person. Such a person is a lone man. I have heard of killing a lone man Zhou, but have not heard of murdering of a king."[68] Such a revolutionary doctrine laid the foundation for the legitimacy of rebellion against tyrannical rulers, long before Locke invented the similar notion in his social contract theory.[69]

Persuading Rulers

To establish benevolent government, Mengzi endeavored to persuade the rulers of his time with their own interests, and put forward the story that "the benevolent [ruler] is invincible," an idea which he borrowed from the primitive natural law doctrine of the rule of virtue. Briefly, a benevolent government is in the best interest of the rulers, he asserted, because benevolence would enable them to maintain the people's support and thus to enjoy a stable rule, without having to face major challenges arising from popular discontent.[70] Here, Mengzi is essentially making a liberal argument with a paternalist turn: The rulers should adopt liberal policies that put minimal burden on the subjects, not necessarily because the subjects deserve them, but because these policies are ultimately beneficial to the rulers.[71]

On the contrary, a government without benevolence would be hated by the people and, having lost their support, would be brought quickly to ruin. The fate of rulers ultimately depends on the "hearts of people" (民心 *minxin*):

> *Kings Jie and Zhou lost their empire because they lost the people and they lost the people because they lost the hearts of the people. There is a way to win the empire. Win the people and you win the empire. There is a way to win the people, win the hearts of the people and you win the people. And there is a way to win their hearts. It is to collect for them what they like and do not do to them what they dislike.*[72]

Ultimately, only benevolent government would enable a king to enjoy his power; the interest of a true king is perfectly consistent with that of his people. The ruler is supposed to share his happiness with his people; in fact, only then can he hope to partake of true happiness.[73] Without appealing to the unknown entity of Heaven, Mengzi was able to interpret the dynastic vicissitudes of history solely in terms of the natural causality of human actions. In fact, among "opportunities provided by Heaven," "advantages afforded by the Earth," and "the harmony of men," the human factor is regarded as the most important.[74] In order to gain "the people's heart," a ruler needs only to "collect for them what they like, and not to impose on them what they dislike."[75]

Back to Human Nature: The Foundation of Benevolent Government

Mengzi is quite consistent in applying his theory on human nature to his moral persuasions. We all have compassion for others, and the rulers are no exceptions since humanity is also in their nature. "All men have the mind that cannot bear [to see the suffering of] others. The ancient kings had this mind and therefore they had a government that could not bear to see the suffering of the people."[76] Indeed, this is where Mengzi begins to introduce his famous well example to illustrate that the feeling of compassion is present is everyone, and one is to recall that even such a mediocre ruler as King Xuan of Qi would be compassionate enough to spare an ox when he happened to see its dreadful appearance before slaughtering.[77]

Thus, just as the feeling of compassion is instrumental for illustrating the presence of humanity in everyone, it is equally important in initiating a benevolent government. It is because the benevolent sage cannot bear to see the sufferings of mankind that he brought us benevolent government. "If the sage exercises his effort, and continue with the government of compassion (不忍人之政 burenrenzhizheng), then humanity (Ren) will cover the whole world."[78] And according to the Confucian doctrine long established since the Zhou dynasty, the ruler's benevolence is what legitimates the enjoyment of their special power and privileges:

> The three dynasties won the title to rule the world with humanity, and lost the title with inhumanity. And this is the cause by which the state prospers or declines. An inhumane emperor cannot maintain the world, and an inhumane lord cannot maintain his kingdom.[79]

Although the Mengzian theory on benevolent government and welfare society is "politically correct" even today, the account of its philosophical underpinning differs fundamentally from what he uses to account for individual human nature. There he did use the same well and ox examples to show that the feeling of compassion is the manifestation of humanity in every human heart, but he also made it abundantly clear that humanity, together with other beginnings of "heart-mind," is the noble part that all human beings share with the sage-kings Yao and Shun, and that everyone is able to develop these moral beginnings with studious efforts of self-cultivation, by which he would eventually become like Yao and Shun. Here, however, all that is left is simply the feeling of compassion for the suffering of the poor multitude, and a philosophy about human dignity is quickly reduced to a strain of pity ethics.

The cause seems to lie at least partly in Mengzi's examples themselves. When he uses the well or ox example, his purpose is to illustrate that we as observers who imagine ourselves watching some helpless creatures (a crawling baby unaware of imminent danger or an ox being led to the slaughterhouse) about to suffer serious harm will experience a feeling of compassion. When he presents the story to the rulers to persuade them to adopt benevolent government, however, he simply has the common people take the position of these inept creatures and appeals to the rulers (who are now in the position of an observer with ability to offer some help) for compassion. From this perspective, it is easy to understand why Mengzi has been so consistent in identifying rulers with parents and people with children—indeed, sometimes domesticated animals. When he reproached an official who complained about the loss of people due to a bad harvest, he said:

> *In bad years thousands of the old and weak among your people wandered in ditches, and the stronger dispersed to other places. Now if someone accepts others' cattle and sheep for grazing, he must manage to develop adequate land and sources for grass. If he cannot get these, should he return the cattle and sheep to the owner, or should he instead wait and see them all die?*[80]

To be sure, Mengzi does not mean that the people are just "cattle and sheep" (though he did seem to imply that they belong to some "owner"), but it is clear that not much respect is given to them here. These examples are inherently problematic when extended to the political context because the common people are put in the naturally inferior position. Of course, Mengzi could have argued that we experience our compassion for the baby not purely for the sake of pity, but also for the respect due to her innate good (indeed, it may be argued that even an ox has some innate good), so likewise the ruler should show compassion for the people out of respect and not simply pity. But in any case, Mengzi never pushed his arguments in that direction since he never explicitly argued that the ruler should practice benevolence out of respect for the people's potential virtues, and his writings leave with a pervasive sense that the people are merely the subject for compassion even in an ideal benevolent government.[81]

Thus, while Mengzi preserves the source of nobility and potential worth for every human being, this aspect seems to be lost in his theory of benevolent government. At least, he appears to use different kinds of arguments in different situations: one can imagine that, when he confronts an individual person, he would exhort him to take more care of his "noble body" than his "petty body" and become a morally cultivated gentleman who is worthy of respect; when he confronts a king, however, he would appeal to his compassionate feeling for the poor masses, and the arguments about innate nobleness would simply disappear. Benevolent government is created purely out of pity for the common people.[82]

Now Mengzi is not necessarily inconsistent between his moral theory on the one hand and political theory on the other. After all, he merely argues that we all have the right "beginnings" for moral development; most of us may eventually fail to develop these beginnings, and he seems to have acknowledged that such is the case at least in his time, when he argues that the Ox Mount is barren not because it was this way, but because it is reduced to barrenness by external forces (yet is now barren nevertheless).[83] If we are not brought up in the right environment or we fail to cultivate ourselves due to the lack of resolve, then we may well wound up with the same situation as Mengzi faces in his time, when apparently the vast majority sought after profits and took no interest in humanity and righteousness.[84] In such a situation, moral ideal and reality are separated apart, and it might be quite appropriate for Mengzi to appeal to the human potentials for moral development on the one hand, and return to prudent concern for reality in his political advices on the other. If most people are uncultivated and inept creatures who must be both constrained and nourished by a benevolent government, then little difference would their potential innate dignity make since the noble body would have been covered by thick layers of vulgar inclinations by the time they reach the age of maturity, just as the Ox Mount was reduced to barrenness.

And Mengzi does distinguish the natural capacities from what is actually acquired. "It is the nature of things to be unequal," he says, "Some are twice, some five times, some ten times, some a hundred times, and some one thousand or ten thousand times as valuable as others. If you equalize them all, you will throw the world into confusion. If large shoes and small shoes were of the same price, who would make them?... How can these doctrines be employed to govern a state?"[85] Although everyone is born equal with the heart-mind of humanity and righteousness, individual differences grow apace in the cultivation processes; in the end the vast majority remained uncultivated, only the few went through proper training and fully developed their moral potentials. So the few gentlemen who accomplished moral cultivation differs from the multitude, as if by their second natures, and it is only proportionate to the nature of things that they should be treated differently. "The difference between humans and animals is slight. The common people lose it, but the gentlemen keep it."[86] While the gentlemen can tolerate poverty and observe principles of humanity and righteousness in adversary conditions, the common people cannot and must be provided with basic means of livelihood.[87]

Whether the distinction between the natural and actual capacities is legitimate or not, it appears to be convincing that the Confucian notion of *Ren* does take on different meanings when it is applied to different subjects. While the moral theory of *Ren* is founded explicitly on innate dignity and the potential of self-perfection in every human being, the word loses this meaning when it is applied to politics, with the result that the *Ren* in *Renzheng* means only "benevolence" on the part of government.

Weaknesses in Mengzi's Argument

This part will provide a critique of the Mengzian theory of "benevolent government" and argue that *Renzheng* is an inadequate extension of *Ren* as a moral concept into the political sphere. Let me begin by acknowledging, however, that we moderns (or postmoderns) all support benevolent government, and Mengzi proves to be extremely prescient since the Chinese today face precisely the same kind of predicaments as he did more than two millennia ago: many patients in rural areas die at home for the lack of medical care; many young laborers wander into the cities just to earn a living and have put up with an array of invidious discriminations; the people are exposed to polluted air, unclean water, insecure food, and dangerous environment that are harmful and detrimental to their lives. Are these not "driving people to the ditches" or "killing with policies?" Benevolent government is precisely what China lacks and needs today, even though I would support it more as a result of sound institutional arrangement aimed to respect human dignity than an ideal motivated by compassion for human sufferings. It is pointless to blame Mengzi or Xunzi today for not having invented a political theory that would appear more favorable in the modern judgment; any serious thinker, however imaginative or even utopian, will necessarily ground his presuppositions in the political and social reality of his time, and the monolithic political framework since the Zhou dynasty had framed the political imagination of all classical Chinese thinkers, among whom the Confucians were not alone. Nor do I deny that the notion of benevolent government, imperfect as it may be, did induce some rulers in the long Chinese history to exercise moderation during their terms—for example, to reduce taxes, announce amnesties, and repeal cruel corporal punishments.[88] But I do suggest that the Confucian argument can be made more persuasive and more consistent with its moral propositions if it draws more inspiration from the moral *Ren*, without which the pursuit for benevolent government would ultimately fail.

It is entirely understandable, of course, that Mengzi appeals to the rulers' self-interest in his political persuasions. If we put ourselves in Mengzi's shoes, it is not difficult to feel the convenience (even the necessity) of the way he presents his arguments to King Hui of Liang and the like. Like all intellectuals of the classical age, Mengzi faces a dilemma set by the longstanding political institution of China: He wants to convince a ruler of mediocre moral quality to do the right thing—to stop waging wars and exploiting his people, to lower taxes to prepare for bad years, and so on. Now, for sage rulers like King Wen (文王) and Lord Zhou (周公), it is obviously unnecessary to persuade them to do such and such, but for mediocre rulers like King Hui, who is essentially a petty man preoccupied with personal profits (利 *li*) in maintaining his state, what kind of arguments can possibly move these self-interested rulers to practice humanity and righteousness, which would immediately benefit only their people? Naturally, Mengzi would have to appeal to their self-interest; otherwise, they would simply remain unconvinced: Why be just? Why be humane? What do these moral constraints mean to *my* concerns—more population and territory, more power and more security in enjoying my power? These are precisely the questions that King Hui put to our intellect at the very opening of *Mengzi*, and unsurprisingly Mengzi is almost obligated to answer in the affirmative: you need to follow the path of humanity and righteousness in order to keep and perhaps even enlarge your profits! If you want to maintain your state, then stop worrying about profits since that will simply be counterproductive: if your ministers and subordinate officials also begin to seek profits as you do, then your kingdom would be in danger; so at least from a long-term perspective, extol moral virtues and practice benevolent government, since that will bring security to your kingdom.[89] If the king followed the principle of justice and benevolence, he would be able to secure his interest as some sort of "byproduct." This is the crux of Mengzi's arguments in all the passages involving court persuasions, and they are probably the best arguments to be made in the political settings of his time.

Just note, however, how much the style of argument can differ in a different political framework: if the rulers were popularly elected, Mengzi will hardly need to go through all the troubles to persuade them that to practice benevolent government is good not only for the state, but also for themselves: unless they are idiots, they surely know that they would lose everything in the next election if they do not. If Mengzi is still interested in traveling to the court from afar, his role would be changed to that of a policy adviser: his job is no longer to convince the rulers *why* they must practice benevolent politics, but simply to tell them *how* to do it. Imagine how much stronger the Mengzian position would now be in such a political framework, where the rulers' interests are structured in such ways that it is rational in itself for them to follow the moral and political principles.

But such an institutional strength was unavailable—in fact, unknown—to the classical Chinese intellectuals of Mengzi's time. When they appear before the court, they are already assigned a weak position, from which they cannot appeal to moral principles straightforwardly since the rulers' interests are not institutionally structured and constrained to be in accordance with these principles. This weakness is not one of their own, but a feature of the multitude to be ruled, and it merely passes on to them when they take the role of the multitude's spokesmen before the unaccountable ruler. This is why Mengzi takes pains to convince King Hui that he should share enjoyment with his people (与民同乐 *yumintongle*), as that would actually increase his own enjoyment. And when he meets King Xuan of Qi, he warns against the risk of the ruler's "enjoying" his lot without his people since that usually means that the ruler would not care enough about their needs, and that their discontent would eventually put an end to his enjoyment.[90]

Although these arguments are well made, the weakness of the Mengzian position dictates that they cannot entirely be effective.[91] It was quite fortunate that King Hui agreed with Mengzi that he would enjoy more with people than enjoying alone (so that their conversation could continue), but one cannot help ask what if he turned out to be a completely depraved person, who simply did not care about enjoyment with others? Anyway, if enjoyment with the people turned out to be a plus at all for the ruler's own enjoyment, it was likely to be a minor plus to a mediocre ruler, and thus insufficient to push him toward the right course against his other desires. And if the people thought that King Wen's garden was too small (because he shared with the people) and King Xuan's was too large (because it was turned into a trap for the people who will be severely punished if they dared to enter), so what as long as there was not an open rebellion?[92] Of course, the fact that King Xuan asked this question showed his concern about the people's attitude to him, but we cannot be sure at all that such a concern would be deep enough to make him change his way of governance.

There are inherent limits in the type of causal arguments that Mengzi makes. After all, humanity and righteousness are to be pursued for their own sake, and their pursuit may well be neither necessary nor sufficient for bringing about worldly successes. As Kant points out, only the moral law contains necessity and universality; the rule of prudence is always met by an indefinite number of exceptions in the empirical world we live in. Without a necessary connection between moral worthiness (benevolence) and material rewards (status and power), there is a serious risk that the notion of benevolent government can be reduced to a mere fiction, hardly producing any incentive for or deterrence to bad rulers. In the course of Chinese history, many evil rulers simply enjoyed their reigns unpunished, at least in "this life," and good rulers might never get due rewards.[93] An oppressive regime could last long, provided that it could maintain forceful control over the helpless people, and a benevolent government might be quite short-lived. So, the Legalists could jeer at the Confucians in the example of King Yan of Xu, who lost his kingdom while practicing benevolent government.[94] When a ruler looks at mixed results and realizes the lack of a definite connection between virtue and rewards, he may simply take the Mengzian story about the "invincible humane person" (仁者无敌 renzhewudi) as a "noble lie" conjured up to coax him into sparing alms. Even though Mengzi might be quite correct about the overall correlation between benevolence and the stability of the empire, and even though he could perfectly predict that such violent regimes as the Qin (秦) dynasty would quickly come to ruin, a willful and capricious ruler might still ignore this prudent advice, jeopardize his own long-term interest, and take stupendous measures that would catastrophe to his people.

Mengzi is unequivocal about his standpoint, of course, when he puts forward the order of importance in which the people is to be the highest and the kings the lowest.[95] When he appeals to the ruler's interest, he is really inducing the ruler to act for the interest of the ruled, which he regards to be the *true* interest of the ruler. Yet, although in the Confucian normative framework the ruler's interest ought to be identified with that of the ruled, in reality they do differ and at times even conflict with one another. The problem is how to bring these essentially different interests together. Ultimately this problem is not to be resolved by moral persuasions; it is to be resolved only by making a better institutional arrangement. In this sense, perhaps we should limit our expectation on what Mengzi can achieve through moral argumentation. But I do not think we should be despair about the practical efficacy of moral persuasion. Nor do I think that Mengzi did all he could in presenting the most persuasive arguments he could have made, drawing more fully from the rich theory he himself developed about human nature. In particular, when advocating for benevolent government, he seemed to have ignored the potentials of humanity in every common person, and appealed exclusively to the rulers' compassion and (perhaps *true*) self-interest. While the exclusive reliance on the rulers' self-interest tends to equivocate the moral force of his arguments, the lack of sufficient emphasis on the moral potentials of ordinary people risks to treat people as mere receivers of imperial largess, thus further deprives the people's legitimate claim of moral strength.

The Mengzian arguments are predestined in a sense because they are based on his evaluation of the moral and political realities of his time. If the people are inept as a matter of fact and must rely on a benevolent government for sustaining basic livelihood, then Mengzi would have no alternative but to appeal for the goodwill of the rulers. On the subject of *Renzheng*, the *Mengzi* did convey a pervasive sense that the people are incapable of providing for their own material well-being, thus making the rulers responsible for their survival,[96] just as parents are responsible for their children;[97] that it was those cultural heroes (e.g. the Great Yu) who provided for them the food, clothing, shelter and everything else necessary for material survival;[98] that the people were too ignorant even to understand that it was their rulers' wise policy that accounted for the improvement of their well-being;[99] that when the government became oppressive, the people were utterly helpless and defenseless against oppression except to wait for another benevolent ruler to liberate them from the oppression;[100] that the people are ultimately material animals, hardly capable of any higher pursuit than basic material life, would be "wholly satisfied" if the means to peaceful survival was provided for them,[101] and would have no regret even when they died.[102] Regrettably, nothing in these parts of his work ever suggests that the common people have the moral capacity for self-government. And his remark that "the difference between humans and animals is slight; the common people lose it, but the gentlemen keep it,"[103] if taken literally, further identifies the people with inferior creatures since they failed to cultivate the unique virtues that would set human beings apart from other animals.

Having taken for granted that the ordinary people were essentially uncultivated animals—weak, incompetent, and dependent, Confucian scholars of all generations lost a bulk of their moral ground for demanding that the rulers respect humanity. They could not say, "Treat your people with humanity because, like you, they are human beings endowed with potential for humanity and righteousness, and ought to be treated as such"; instead, they said, "Treat your people with compassion and benevolence because these poor creatures rely on you in order to survive (and, incidentally, doing so will also help to make your regime more stable)." Had Mengzi stopped with condemnations of government excesses as Mozi did and refrained from too many negative remarks on the capacities of the common people, he would have been able to develop more powerful arguments for practicing benevolent government and, more importantly, to ground this notion on a more solid moral basis. Benevolent—or, more precisely, humane—government is not just about providing benefits and welfare to the people; it is also about the provision of enough opportunities for people to fully develop their innate virtues, the full development of which would ultimately enable them to govern themselves and provide for their own needs. Although the social reality at Mengzi's time was anything but favorable to self-government, Mengzi could have advocated for other alternatives. Perhaps the proper solution was not taking the people's weakness for granted and appealing to the ruler's compassion, but holding the state responsible for developing the people's moral and intellectual qualities. Perhaps the state should busy itself not so much with the provision of welfare as with the establishment of a fair education system, which would provide equal opportunity for moral and intellectual development to all children, irrespective of their family backgrounds in status and wealth. Although Mengzi did talk about education and the establishment of schools,[104] a new point of departure firmly rooted in his moral theory of humanity would have moved his political persuasion to a fundamentally different and morally more forceful direction. Regrettably, the unnecessarily negative view of the capacities of the common people prevented Mengzi from taking that direction.

The root of the problem, then, lies in the inconsistency between the two conceptions of *Ren* applied in Confucianism. While Confucian scholars, in their ethical theory, endorsed the ideal of humanity, they reduced it to the narrow notion of benevolence in political theory, where they gave up their recognition that everyone is born with sufficient capacity to lead a unique human life. In effect, they renounced in the practice of government what they had defended in the theory of human nature. Having believed that the common people were low and helpless, they were left without any ground upon which they could build a sound moral foundation for the state; all they could rely upon was the benevolence of a kingly government, which was necessarily beyond the ordinary people's control. Unable to transcend the limits of historical conditions, Confucian scholars mistook the existing form of government to be the invariable law of nature, and found themselves in a position where the only hope was to persuade the kings by appealing to their compassion and self-interest. Having allowed the ultimate purpose of government to deviate from the original ideal of humanity, no wonder they failed to establish a valid political theory.

RULE OF PROPRIETY IN XUNZI AND ITS LIMITATIONS

If Mengzi fell short of developing a consistent political theory based on the moral conception of *Ren*, can we find help from the other major classical school of Confucianism—Xunzi (ca. 313–238 B.C.)? After all, Xunzi begins with the apparently opposite assumptions about human nature, and may provide fresh insights not found in Mengzi. Xunzi speaks sparingly of both *Ren* and *Renzheng* and seldom appeal to compassion, even though he may have implicitly assumed its presence in certain situations. While Mengzi assumes that a person is endowed by Heaven with a heart-mind that makes him naturally good, Xunzi believes that a human being is born with insatiable desires that make him naturally bad,[105] and that the only hope lies in his intellectual capacities by which he can consciously improve his nature through continuous learning and reformation.[106] "The human nature is bad," he says, and "his goodness is only acquired training."[107] To correct their bad nature, human beings cannot rely upon amoral Heaven, which for Xunzi was simply the natural order of things; instead they must rely upon their own cognitive capacity of making distinctions between what is proper and improper, just and unjust.[108] Despite major differences in their theories of human nature, however, both Xunzi and Mengzi appear to agree on the fundamental purpose of government.[109]

Human Nature and Moral Transformation

Unlike Mengzi, who believes that every human being is equally endowed with the heart-mind for humanity and righteousness, Xunzi believes that everyone's nature is equally bad to begin with:

> *In natural talent, inborn nature, awareness, and capability, a gentleman and a petty man are one. In cherishing honor and detesting disgrace, in loving benefit and hating harm, a gentleman and a petty man are the same.... All men possess one and the same nature: when hungry, they desire food; when cold,*

they desire to be warm; when exhausted from toil, they desire rest; and they all desire benefit and hate harm. Such is the nature that men are born possessing. They do not have to await development before they become so. It is the same in the case of a Yu and in that of a Jie.[110]

Yet, mankind is not doomed by its bad nature, since everyone also possesses the innate capacity for transforming his nature. At least the ancient sage-kings and the gentlemen have demonstrated that it is possible to fundamentally transform their nature and become good:

As far as human nature goes, the sages Yao and Shun possessed the same nature as the tyrant Jie and Robber Zhi, and a gentleman possesses the same nature as a petty man... The reason people honor Yao, Shun and the gentlemen is that they are able to transform their nature, apply themselves to conscious activity, and produce rules of propriety and justice.[111]

Since these rules are knowable to the common people, everyone can apply them to transform his nature. Indeed, just like Mengzi, Xunzi believes that even an ordinary person in the street can become Yu, a legendary sage king after Yao and Shun.[112] Of course, such an effort is anything but easy,[113] and this is probably why Xunzi thinks that although it is possible for everyone to become Yu, most people fall short of fully transforming themselves because they are unwilling to undertake the hard effort.[114] Thus, like Mengzi, Xunzi thinks that everyone is rather equal by nature, but the posterior efforts (or their lack) and circumstances give rise to the individual differences.

Whether a person can become a Yao or Yu or be a Jie or Robber Zhi, whether he becomes a workman or artisan, a farmer or merchant, lies entirely with the accumulated effect of circumstances, with what they concentrate on in laying their plans, and on the influence of habits and customs.[115]

So why have most people failed to become Yao, Shun, or Yu? "I say that it is because they remain uncultivated; even Yao and Yu were not born wholly what they became, but rose up by transforming their old selves, brought them to perfection through cultivation and conscious exertion, and only after first putting forth the utmost effort did they become complete."[116]

It is interesting to note that Xunzi arrived at these conclusions that are remarkably similar to those of Mengzi from the apparently opposite point of departure. Xunzi seldom talks about *Ren* and almost never appeals to the human feeling of compassion for his arguments, which are mostly carried out in cold, coherent, and deductive logic based on some public good purposes. It is perhaps not surprising from this perspective that Xunzi's test for distinguishing an uncultivated petty man and a cultivated gentleman is not the compassionate principle of humanity, but the Golden Rule: the petty man always expects to receive more than he gives, for example, he conducts himself like an animal, yet wants others to think well of him; to the contrary, "the gentleman is trustworthy and so desires that others should trust him as well. He is loyal and so wants others to have affection for him. He cultivates rectitude and makes orderly his management of situations, and so desires that others should think well of him."[117]

Origin and Functions of Li

Unlike Mengzi who thinks that the primary human defects lie in his moral and intellectual incapacity, Xunzi argues that bad human nature derives from the multitudinous passions and desires inherent in his life.[118] Yet, Xunzi does not simply condemn human desires (as Mengzi might do), perhaps because they are just part of our nature; he merely thinks that it is necessary to control excessive desires for the obvious reason to avoid disastrous social and personal consequences. Human beings need to control their desires in order to better satisfy them. It is precisely for this purpose that the complex system of propriety (礼 *Li*) is created:

> *What is the origin of propriety? I reply: man is born with desires. If his desires are not satisfied for him, he cannot but seek some means to satisfy them himself. If there are no limits and degrees to his seeking, then he will inevitably fall to wrangling with other men. From wrangling comes disorder and from disorder comes exhaustion. The ancient kings abhorred such disorder, and therefore they established principles of propriety in order to curb it, to train human desires and to provide for their satisfaction, so that desires did not overextend the means for their satisfaction, and material goods did not fall short of what was desired. Thus, both desires and goods were looked after and satisfied. This is the origin of propriety.[119]*

For Xunzi, it is the unique malleability and intellectual capacity of human beings that makes them superior to other animals and enables them to form associations among themselves, through which they unite their strength to engage in various types of cooperative activities. Yet, without distinctions imposed by a system of laws and propriety, the human organization would be beset by internal strife that eventually saps its strength. A primary function of propriety is to make distinctions among people and assign them with different status.[120]

Thus, Xunzi, like Hobbes, teaches that both the danger and hope of mankind lies in its ingenuity. Foreseeing the dire consequences in the state of nature, human beings are able to save themselves by instituting a government that brings order to human community. After all, human beings are born to seek after profit.[121] Without a government, the uncontrolled pursuit of desires and rapacious seeking of gain would goad human beings to fight against one another, thereby bringing great disorder to themselves. The function of government is precisely to prevent such a human calamity. For this purpose Xunzi emphasizes rewards, punishments and penal laws as a necessary means to social order, peace, and prosperity. But unlike Hobbes, Xunzi believes that human beings can improve their nature and become good through conscious moral cultivation. For this reason he puts propriety above everything else and takes it to be the foundation of laws and justice. His ideal, the "rule of propriety" (礼治 lizhi), is a system of social norms formulated by the sages who, having perfected themselves through learning and self-cultivation, come to save the human world from its own destruction.[122]

This difference accounts for the fact that Xunzi's toleration of human desires does not make him more liberal than Mengzi. It is commonly acknowledged that Hobbes was the first to develop a systematic theory of modern liberalism, which essentially made the classical Aristotelian teleology stand on its head. For Hobbes the moral "end" of mankind is not to be metaphysically presupposed, but to be determined by the practical needs of the multitude of individuals living under certain natural conditions. Like Xunzi, Hobbes posits a negative human nature—one which would not in itself make human beings social animals suitable for amicable cohabitation,[123] but the Hobbesian solution is fundamentally different. Unlike Xunzi, Hobbes takes the negative nature for granted and does not appear to think it necessary (or possible) to improve it. Although an individual is still supposed to observe the "fundamental law of nature,"[124] these laws are scarce and minimal, and Hobbes would never have thought it feasible or desirable to prescribe such a complicated moral system as *Li* for moral transformation. Xunzi, on the other hand, did not give up hope in transforming human nature, and believed that the institution of propriety is necessary for social order and prosperity. In this respect, he decisively follows the Confucian path for moral cultivation, and shares with Mengzi in putting a high moral premium on human beings.

The result is, not surprisingly, the Confucian elitist emphasis on moral achievements and, particularly for Xunzi, the class distinctions drawn along the lines of one's social and moral status. Arguably, the Confucian insistence on moral improvements tends to make society more autonomous and less dependent upon an all-powerful state (so Xunzi has never proposed to establish anything even close to a Leviathan), yet it also tends to make the state depend on elites rather than the multitude of common people. After all, despite their common nature shared with the sages, most people failed to become sage-kings like Yu. More importantly, there *are* a few who succeeded in cultivating moral virtues. So, why not simply entrust them with the governance? If the state is (at least partly) responsible for providing moral education for its people, then it seems to be absurd to allow the uncultivated petty men to put hands on the government before they become adequately cultivated. Thus, it is only natural for Xunzi that the entire body of moral rules and principles (*Li*) was to be made only by the ancient sage-kings, and it is never to be touched by the ordinary people who failed to completely transform their bad nature and who should be transformed, if possible, precisely by these rules—will you ever allow criminal suspects to make rules about crimes? Since the people are to be educated and transformed by the state, the state cannot possibly emanate from these objects of transformation through, say, the making of a covenant by which they mutually consented to certain type of government; it must come from a morally superior source—the few cultivated sages and gentlemen who inherit the moral authority from their ancient counterparts: Yao, Shun or Yu, who had completely cleansed their bad nature through studious moral efforts that are beyond the ability and tenacity of the common multitude.

Limits in Xunzi's Political Persuasions

Unlike Mengzi, Xunzi hardly talks of "benevolent government" (*Renzheng*), but there are passages that do suggest that they essentially agree on the ideal type of government.[125] Xunzi also shares with Mengzi the same utilitarian persuasion of benevolent government that presupposes the unity of interests between the king and the people. If a king honors propriety and justice and loves his people, then his state will be well-governed, making himself powerful and secure; otherwise, he will suffer from ruin and destruction.[126] Thus,

He who cultivates propriety will reign; he who governs properly will become powerful; he who gains the allegiance of the people will be secure; he who accumulates wealth by exploitation will come to ruin.[127]

One who uses the state to establish justice will be king; one who establishes trust will be a lord-protector; and one who establishes a record of expediency and opportunism will perish.[128]

One who loves the people will be strong; one who does not will be weak.... Rules of propriety are the highest expression of order and discrimination, the root of strength in the state.... Kings and dukes who proceed in accord with their requirements obtain the whole world, whereas those who do not bring ruin to their altars of soil and grain.... If they proceed in accordance with the Way of propriety and justice, they will succeed; if they do not, they will fail.[129]

As I pointed out with respect to the Mengzian arguments, the Xunzian arguments in terms of the ruler's interest share the same tendency to compromise the moral force of his persuasions and equivocate the ultimate purpose of government. After all, if he is primarily concerned with the people's interest, then the ruler's interest is not so relevant, and it is impossible to argue for a complete coincidence of the ruler's personal interest and the general social interest. Of course, Xunzi is aware of the latter difficulty, as he clearly sees the possibility that the practice of humanity and justice may not always lead to personally beneficial results, and bad conducts may sometimes go unpunished.[130]

Even though Xunzi merely argues that the ruler should be led by the regularity and not exceptions, however, the fact that there are exceptions means that an opportunist ruler may well take the risk and deviate from the regular course of humanity and justice. In that case, Xunzi seems to have reached the end of his persuasion, and can only wish that the evil deeds be punished and corrected through natural course of things. Like Mengzi, he was limited by the political framework of his time, which prevented the Confucians from making the straightforward moral demand that the rulers should observe the principles of humanity and justice, and respect the basic interest of the common people. In fact, compared to Mengzi, Xunzi might find it even more difficult to put forward such a demand. For Mengzi, the common people, although morally weak, are still born good and deserve some compassion—if not respect—from the rulers; for Xunzi, however, the common people are born morally bad and would have remained a group of rapacious animals preying upon one another, had they not been educated in propriety and constrained by penal laws imposed by the government. It seems that the people should tolerate even an evil ruler because, without him, they would have plunged into the greatest evil: individual warfare and social disorder. Other than the dubious utility to his own reign, the ruler would seem to have even less reason to promote the people's common welfare, much less to treat them as human beings as such.

It is therefore hardly surprising that Xunzi never suggested as Mengzi did that the people would have any right of rebellion against an oppressive tyrant. Since the uncultivated people would fall into chaos and conflicts without a government positively enforcing the penal laws and rules of propriety, it seems to be only consistent to insist that the people should remain obedient in all circumstances. Indeed, at various places in his work, Xunzi does make frequent analogies that put the people in the position of infants—even horses—to be protected by the kingly government.[131] Although Xunzi does not necessarily mean that the gentleman should rule over the people in the same way as riding on horses, the parallels drawn here clearly indicate the lack of respect for the common people. Therefore, it does not seem plausible that the Xunzian doctrine on the rule of propriety can offer much help in resolving the problems found in the Mengzian theory of benevolent government.

It should be acknowledged that the Xunzian assumption of human nature is not necessarily a fatal impediment toward a decent political theory; quite to the contrary, it offers us genuine hope. Western political philosophies since Hobbes all assumed, more or less, bad human nature to some degree, and the common question is how to design good institutions given a variety of weaknesses and limitations in the nature of ordinary individuals. Xunzi, to be sure, was strongly oriented toward institutional building, and he made many insightful remarks in that regard. In fact, he taught two prominent disciples, Han Fei and Li Si, who were exclusively concerned with establishing effective institutions for the strength and prosperity of a state inhabited by self-interested individuals. As a Confucian, however, Xunzi was primarily occupied with defending the existing system of propriety, which he saw as an effective instrument for transforming the bad nature and restraining excessive desires. So far as the political system goes, he seemed to be content with the moral preaching that a ruler should practice rules of propriety and justice for his own good, and kept silent about the situations in which the ruler proved to be willful or inept. And when his students took the Legalist turn and abolished all the class distinctions and humanistic elements in his teaching, they did help a militarist ruler to unite China—not with benevolence, justice or propriety, but with sheer military power and political tyranny. The sudden rise followed by the violent death of the Qin dynasty agitated tremendous social turmoil, all at enormous cost of human lives and sufferings.

One might argue that such an example tends to prove that Xunzi (and Mengzi) are correct in insisting on the principles of humanity, righteousness and propriety, but it also illustrates the limits of their moral persuasions and the unreliability of the rulers in taking care of their own interests. Even though they might very well be right about the consequentialist preaching that the ruler would do himself good by treating the people well, the instances of Qin recurred nevertheless, perhaps at less grandiose scales. Unable to rely upon the moral and intellectual capacities of the common people, Confucian scholars of all generations are compelled to count on the goodwill of kings, the reliability of which has been constantly brought into question by the reality of Chinese political history.

BEYOND BENEVOLENCE

The Chinese political tradition has been one of *Renzheng* without *Ren*. While the theory of *Ren* recognizes that everyone can reach moral perfection through self-cultivation, the theory of *Renzheng* presupposes that the ordinary people are incapable of governing themselves, so that an active government must be imposed on them in order to provide them with basic goods. It is difficult to reconcile the two notions of *Ren* since they are based on dramatically different emphases on the aspects of innate human capacities. The ability of moral cultivation implies an ability of self-government and, correspondingly, a version of minimal government, but this has not been the working assumption of Chinese political practice throughout history, in which the government, (supposedly) benevolent and omnipotent, always retains its moral superiority by providing goods and benefits to its subjects. The "three-represents" doctrine, claiming that the ruling Communist Party is supposed to represent the "advanced productive force," the "advanced culture," and "the most basic interests of the most people," is only the official recapitulation of the benevolent government tradition, as it still stands for a government *for* the people, but decidedly not *by* the people,[132] and not surprisingly, its main rationale is that the people are not morally and politically mature enough to govern themselves.[133] Up to this day, direct election of the representatives of the People's Congress is still limited to the lowest levels of government, partly because it has been thought that ordinary Chinese, especially peasants in the "backward" rural areas, are not ready for general elections. We still live in the shadow of *Renzheng*, a political tradition that is far from *Ren* and has been preventing us from improving our political and moral conditions. As I argued above, this confusion of two conceptions of *Ren* was not the result of deliberate or ignorant misreading of the Mengzian and Xunzian teachings, but it has been with us since the very beginning of the Confucian scholarship.

Some contemporary neo-Confucians, however, attempt to find liberal democratic resources in traditional Confucianism. In 1958, for example, four prominent neo-Confucians published a "Declaration of Chinese Culture to the World," claiming that Chinese thoughts contained "seeds of democracy."[134] To be sure, all classical schools object to the abuses of public power, and the Confucians believe that "everyone can become Kings Yao and Shun," and require the emperor to "favor what common people favor and disfavor what common people disfavor." Yet, "seeds" are not ripe fruits, and would remain seeds if they fail to find favorable intellectual and social environments, just as the heart-mind for *Ren* may never turn into a mature moral character. Although the traditional Chinese culture does imply ideas not repugnant to democratic ideals, that does not mean they will necessarily develop into democratic institutions.[135] As Tu Weiming points out: "Democracy as a fully developed political system is the modern phenomenon; it had never appeared in China, and it cannot be developed from the Confucian thought itself, even though we can find some democratic elements when reviewing Confucian ethics."[136] Thus, even though it may be true that the Confucian tradition did not hamper China from accepting western democracy, and might even have served as catalysis for its development,[137] the efforts to merely confirm its potential for adapting itself to the prevailing contemporary ideas seem to be less helpful than uncovering the true impediments that had kept the Confucian moral teachings from going beyond the political realities of the imperial time.

Historically, the Confucian moral and ethical theories proved to be more transcendent than its political theory. This is hardly surprising, since political ideas are fundamentally limited by the tradition of political practice and social reality. In China's long history, not only had the governments been unfriendly to the moral ideal of *Ren*, but the practice of *Renzheng* had created a mass uniquely suitable for despotic governance, the legitimacy of which the Confucians seemed to have taken for granted without critical reflection. But as soon as they returned to their private sanctuaries and reflected deeply in themselves, less disturbed by the worldly affairs and apparent social necessities, they recovered their moral sublimity. This is perhaps why we observe this conceptual rift: while *Renzheng* is applied to govern the multitude, *Ren* as a moral ideal is acknowledged as theoretically applicable to all and indeed urged upon all, but in reality it is entertained as a cultivated virtue only by a few Confucian gentlemen who succeeded in acquiring it. For better or worse, the Confucians did not believe that what was achieved by the few could or should be applied to the many, and the moral implications of *Ren* were not to be extended as a whole to the political sphere. Today we still witness the multifarious consequences of such rift as well as the danger that the reformulated notion of *Renzheng* is gradually losing its hold on the individual minds while the moral appeal of *Ren* has not. The contemporary Chinese are heir to the Confucian moral and political tradition, but they are obviously not obligated to inherit, much less to defend, it as an indiscriminate whole and continue to be handicapped by limitations in the Confucian political perception characterized by the political practices of its time.

The Confucian Political Tradition and Beyond

In making the above critiques I obviously do not mean that the Confucian political philosophy is completely anachronistic and bereft of merits; I suggest only that its political theory need be seriously reflected and reformulated in its moral framework. The works of Mengzi and Xunzi do contain passages that can legitimately be taken as seeds for rule of law and democratic (perhaps even liberal) ideas.[138] After all, the government is created for the people and is thus obligated to further their welfare. "Heaven bears the people not for the king; Heaven establishes the king for the people."[139] To set a "secure foundation of the state," Xunzi says:

> *A humane person will organize his state in order to proclaim principles of propriety and justice to all and will allow nothing to impair them. He will not perform even a single act that is unjust or that would result in the execution of even one blameless man, although he might gain the empire by doing so.... The laws and punishments to be promulgated to the nation must be of a legal model that is just. What he eagerly tries to instill in all his various officials is the paramount importance of aspiring for justice in everything.*[140]

The above passage seems to indicate that an innocent individual should never be treated as means to any end other than himself—not even if the sacrifice of one life would enable a ruler to obtain the entire empire.

Mengzi would go even further. Like Kongzi, he did not simply accept the natural law doctrine of the early Zhou dynasty, which claimed that the mandate of Heaven was granted only to the virtuous, but developed direct linkages between the government and the people without Heaven as a mediator. While Kongzi points to the people's trust as the foundation of a state,[141] Mengzi claims that a ruler must also receive—albeit implicitly—the people's consent, before he could legitimately begin to exercise his power.[142] This seems to imply that the common people should play some role in the government. Even though practical participation was made impossible by the social conditions of the time, Mengzi nevertheless insisted on the idea that important government actions must acquire the people's content: "When all your immediate ministers say that a man is worthy, it is not sufficient. Nor is it sufficient when all your great officers say so. When all your people say so, look into the case and employ him if you find him worthy."[143] And the same should be done when the king wants to execute someone or dismiss someone who is no good, so that eventually it is the people who made the decision. "Only in this way can a ruler become parent of the people."[144] The progressive thought of Mengzi culminated in his famous passage, which seems to have transcended the limit of "benevolent government": "The people are the most important; the gods of the land and grain is the next; the king is of slight importance."[145]

To be consistent with his moral theory, however, Mengzi would have to give up the notion of benevolent government and, instead, take true humanity as the very foundation for a legitimate government. In this respect, his moral doctrine does offer practical advantages. The most immediate advantage is that it provides an ontological basis for humanity and moral autonomy, thereby firmly repudiating the misconception that identifies *Ren* with mere benevolence. Since a person is endowed with humanity in his heart-mind, he is supposed to be capable of leading a decent human life through moral strength gained from within. If one fails to live the moral life that is unique to human beings, one cannot blame Heaven (for fate) or others; he can blame only himself for having failed to attain what is by nature attainable. To attain such a moral end, it is true, one must engage in continuous learning and self-cultivation, in order to ward off the pernicious influences from outside which alienates one's good nature; but it is entirely up to one's own will to make such an effort. Training and chastisement are perhaps necessary, especially for the young, yet the final purpose of education is for human beings to attain moral maturity, by which they can live up to what humanity requires, even when they are alone. Ultimately, everyone *can* and, thus, *should* be responsible for his own actions and way of life; a person is required to live morally, precisely because he is endowed with the inherent capacity for a moral life. Had Confucian scholars consistently extended the implications of their moral theory to the political realm, there would be little room for paternalism.

This also helps to clarify the meaning of absolute benevolence as the Way of Heaven and its earthly counterpart. It is true that Heaven must have intended mankind to live a good and comfortable life; being absolutely good and omnipotent, it created a material world for human beings to enjoy. Yet this does not necessarily mean that human beings are obliged to imitate Heaven in every respects because, as limited beings, they often find themselves lacking in certain powers required for such efforts which, if made strenuously, might results in more evil than good. For example, to continuously confer material benefits upon others certainly requires an ability that often is beyond most human beings; all that can be required is the goodwill to be benevolent. The requisite power to implement benevolence can be found only in human organizations of massive scale, such as a public power established for a commonwealth, which unites individual human strength by various means. Thus, to imitate the benevolence of the omnipotent Heaven, a human society often finds it necessary to confer equally omnipotent power to its government. Practically, however, it must be understood that the eagerness to do good might produce evil consequences instead. While we can suppose that Heaven is necessarily good, we cannot suppose the same for a human government, especially in light of the fact that the rulers may be influenced by selfish passions and desires, who will reign freely over all without any institutional checks against the arbitrary exercise of power. The notion of benevolent government, then, is a self-contradiction because to maintain such an omnipotent power on the earth is inconsistent with its supposedly good purpose. And the contradiction is based on the misunderstanding that the Way of Heaven is one of material benevolence, an imperfect benevolence which mankind is supposed to imitate.

Such a difficulty is avoided altogether by the Mengzian moral theory. Heaven is not benevolent merely in that it created an external environment comfortable for human living; it is benevolent absolutely in the sense that it has made human beings themselves to be good. It should be both unnecessary and inadequate to confer upon a person all sorts of material benefits—unnecessary because the people have the abilities and skills necessary to acquire basic goods for their own living, and inadequate because to give them no more than material goods would suggest a paternalistic attitude that is contrary to their moral autonomy. Endowed with the inherent capacity for humanity and justice, everyone is a son of Heaven, an end in himself rather than merely a means to his pleasure and needs, the satisfaction of which depends on the imperial patronage. Every person deserves the respectful treatment that is only proper for a moral being as such. To the common people, then, mere benevolence does too much for their material lives and, as a result, too little for their moral lives. This inconsistency is avoided only by the proper understanding of *Ren* as humanity—the principle of perfect Heavenly benevolence, which commands human imitation: to treat every human being as the end and not merely as a means, because this is the way by which he is created. The Way of Heaven commands nothing that is practically impossible for the human world; on the contrary, it guides mankind to adopt rational precepts that enable it to consistently achieve a good life. The moral ideal of *Ren* requires not so much the provision of material benefits as respect for the people as moral agents—a task that is well within the capacity of any human society and government.

Modern Implications

For these reasons I believe that it is time now to take more seriously the Confucian moral conception of *Ren*, and to reconstruct Chinese political philosophy on the basis of this moral foundation. At a minimum, to take *Ren* seriously means to take human life seriously and avoid causing harm to oneself and others. It is true that Confucians would have strongly condemned the official misconduct in tragedies like the Tang Fuzhen incident. The problem with traditional Confucians is that they failed to recognize the root cause of such tragedies. The incident was not an isolated mistake; it was a reflection of the customary mode of handling the rights of the common people to their person and property, to which the imperious rulers routinely showed scorn and contempt. Having assumed their moral inferiority, Confucians might feel justified in such contemptuous treatment of the uncultivated masses, as long as they were given enough material goods and a peaceful environment for living, since this was quite close to the political ideal of *Renzheng*. Yet, the Tang Fuzhen tragedy and the like cases show clearly that *Renzheng* is not to be achieved without

Ren. So long as the people are not trusted in their moral and intellectual abilities, the government will assume too much power, which is bound to be abused and to bring damage to the people's welfare.[146] Without *Ren*, the pursuit of *Renzheng* will only condone if not positively inculcate tyranny. To avoid such a self-defeating loop, we must take issue with the fundamental aspects of the Confucian political culture and formulate a new relationship between the people and the government based on a fuller understanding of *Ren*.

Thus, to take *Ren* seriously means to trust and respect the people's innate abilities, usually sufficient for attaining a decent life, and leave them free to deal with most matters that affect their welfare. This implies a demand for implementing and adhering to a list of basic rights and freedoms to be respected and protected by the government.[147] Under normal circumstances, the government is not to interfere with the people's beliefs, speech, publications, assemblies, associations, or freedom of pursuing economic activities, nor should it restrict the people's freedom of movement, unless such restriction is supported by genuine public needs. These requirements seem to be implied by the traditional notion of *Ren*, even though "rights" and "freedoms" are alien to the traditional Chinese vocabulary.

And this is not to say a government based on *Ren* should abstain from providing material goods, as *Ren* does mean to provide material support in needy circumstances; indeed, even Western liberal governments are deeply committed to welfare provisions today. And the government is certainly instrumental in providing the proper institutional environments (e.g. protection of property rights, which is also part of the existing Chinese constitution through the most recent amendments) as well as a sound education system (especially compulsory education for children), which is a precondition for developing innate human potentialities. This essay argues only that the mere provision of material benefits is not enough to meet the moral requirements of *Ren*. If benefits are distributed without respect for people's innate abilities, from which rights and freedoms are derived, then we are back to the state of *Renzheng* without *Ren*.

The reformulated Confucian teachings on humanity and government are relevant today to the developing and the developed nations alike. For most of the developing countries like China, personal lives are undergoing radical transformations and the government is bound to play active roles in the modernization process. It is a process fraught with disturbances, abuses, even tragedies. Both the people and the government must be under some moral guidance, so that society can hopefully progress with more harmony and less frustrations. The Confucian theory of *Ren* can fulfill this role; indeed it was created for that purpose. For the Confucians, poverty itself is not to be feared; it can serve rather as a source of inspiration for hard efforts or a test for one's moral integrity.[148] Abject poverty, of course, does handicap development, and this is why the Confucians like Mengzi appealed to the notion of benevolent government. We do need a benevolent government, but this time "benevolent government" is to be solidly founded on the principles of humanity and righteousness, so that the innate potentials of the common people are equally respected. The government is "benevolent" not because the people are weak and incompetent, but precisely because they are potently good and able, and their natural capacities should not only be protected against abuses, but also be provided with adequate opportunities for a full development.

This is obviously not the place to begin a fresh discussion on modern welfare states, but I hope the Confucian implication for the developed nations is just as clear. The postwar welfare state is very much the Western version of *Renzheng*, which may be identified with the insurgence of so-called positive rights, that is, rights that not so much prevent the government from infringing certain basic "inborn" rights ("negative" rights) as require it to create, maintain and distribute benefits to certain needy groups. Although positive rights are criticized for their tendency to encourage paternalism, overreliance, and abuse of power, which characterized all the former socialist states,[149] they remain an important feature of Western liberal democracies. As Margalit rightly points out, welfare society is a necessary condition for decent society, since "[h]uman dignity is described as being created in God's image, and this dignity has been destroyed" by poverty, and "only the welfare society has the power to eradicate the institutional humiliation."[150] On the other hand, the welfare society itself can be debasing and its humiliation is institutional because it is founded on pity. Here we see Mengzi coming back with his well example, in which our feeling of compassion will be naturally induced by seeing a helpless creature in danger. As this chapter illustrates, however, the Confucians can tell us much more than compassion. Mengzi did advocate for a minimal welfare society, but its purpose is not to hold people as the object of pity, but to provide for their basic needs and opportunities, so that everyone can pursue a meaningful life in which he will rediscover true humanity.[151] Providing protection and nourishment for the people's physical lives *is* one level of benevolent government, but it is meant to be the means to achieving higher end(s) rather than the end in itself. At the very least, the government is also supposed to provide adequate general education,[152] so that the people are enabled to pursue their happiness and govern themselves according to such fundamental precepts as humanity and righteousness. Otherwise, if the welfare state meant nothing but paternalism, then such a benevolent government would not only run counter to humanity, but with all likelihood turn against benevolence in the end. Restored to its authentic understanding, the Confucian theory of *Ren* can help us to transcend such moral and political predicaments that are ultimately responsible for social crisis at the time of Kongzi and of our own.

Notes

1. For a vivid depiction of peasant lives in China, see the outlawed bestseller Chen Guidi and Chun Tao, *The Chinese Peasant Investigations* (2004).

2. Just as I was making the final revisions to this book, massive explosions set off in the harbor of Tianjin municipality, hitherto a shining model for speedy economic development, killing hundreds of inhabitants and firefighters and causing serious property damage. The explosions took place in a chemical storage plant located near the residential area, the permission of which apparently involved corruption or malfeasance. Yan Yingzhuan, "The 24 Hours Following the Tianjin Explosions," *New Beijing Daily*, August 14, 2015, http://news.163.com/15/0814/00/B0UHO09A00014SEH.html.

3. "A Relocatee in Chengdu Died of Self-immolation after Resisting the Urban Demolition Team for 3 Hours," http://news.163.com/09/1202/10/5PH8QC3K00011229.html, December 2, 2009.

4. All of these news can be located on internet rather easily, see, for example, http://news.163.com/05/0712/13/1OFC81240001122B.html (neighbors switched their handicapped children in order to kill them); http://news.163.com/05/0820/01/1RIGCP56000 1122B.html (father killed his wife and son simply because of the latter's bad exam performances); http://news.163.com/05/0826/04/1S29KE930001122B.html (patricide). These should be enough to convey a sense of moral chaos in China today.

5. The *pinyin* for a Chinese character is usually in small letters, but here *Ren* is used in capital to be distinguished from another word with the same romanization for person (人*ren*).

6. The ideographic structure of the word *Ren* interestingly illustrates its implication. The word is composed of two parts. The left half represents a person standing aside, the right half stands for "two," indicating the plural form of the left. Taken together, *Ren* is understood to express the moral principle that governs human relationships.

7. See Immanuel Kant, *Grounding for the Metaphysics of Morals* (3rd Ed.), trans. J.W. Ellington (Indianapolis/Cambridge: Hackett Publishing, 1993) 429. This (second) formulation of the categorical imperative is logically related to the first (universal law) and the third (autonomy) formulations.

8. Sandra A. Wawrytko, "Confucius and Kant: The Ethics of Respect," *Philosophy East and West* 32 (1982): 237–257.

9. *Analects*, 7.22; see Wing-tsit Chan, *A Source Book in Chinese Philosophy* (Princeton, NJ: Princeton University Press 1963), 32.

10. *Mengzi*, 7A4.

11. Kongzi says only that "By nature human beings are alike. Through practice they have become apart" (*Analects*, 17.2; see Chan, *A Source Book in Chinese Philosophy*, 45). He did claim, however, that "a person is born with uprightness." (*Analects*, 6.17; trans. Chan, *Source Book in Chinese Philosophy*, 29) Although there are other interpretations of this sentence, Zhu Xi (朱熹) seems to represent the dominant opinion when he cites Cheng Hao (程颢) as saying "the principle of life is uprightness." Zhu Xi, *Collective Annotations of the Four Books* (Ji'nan: Qilu Books, 1992), 56.

12. *Doctrine of the Mean*, Chapter 20; trans. Chan, *Source Book in Chinese Philosophy*, 104.

13. *Analects*, 12.22.

14. The general love in Confucianism is not to be confused with the Mohist notion of undifferentiated, universal love. The Confucian concept of love is graded, requiring an order of hierarchy according to a system of propriety, with different rules for treating one's family members, friends, and members of society. For a comparison of Confucian *Ren* and feminist "care" in this connection, see Julia Po-Wah Lai Tao, "Two Perspectives of Care: Confucian *Ren* and Feminist *Care*," *Journal of Chinese Philosophy* 27 (2000): 221–227.

15. *Mengzi*, 7B1.

16. *Mengzi*, 7A45.

17. *Analects*, 3.3.

18. *Analects*, 4.15. Qingjie Wang argues that reciprocity is more important among the two, so that the Confucian "thread" is primarily the Golden Rule, the practice of which is the way to acquire humanity. Qingjie James Wang, "The Golden Rule and Impersonal Care: From a Confucian Perspective," *Philosophy East and West* 49 (1999): 421–422.

19. *Analects*, 17.6; see Chan, *Source Book in Chinese Philosophy*, 46; James Legge, *The Four Books* (Hong Kong: Wei Tung Book Co., 1971), 154.

20. *Analects*, 13.19; see Legge, *The Four Books*, 112.

21. Kant similarly holds that goodwill is the only absolute good and worthy of respect, irrespective of the results. It constitutes the very basis for the moral law and for humanity. *Grounding for the Metaphysics of Morals*, 393.

    On one occasion, Kongzi did agree that a man who can "extensively confer benefits on the people" would surpass even the standard of humanity. *Analects*, 6.30. Yet, it would be unreasonable to interpret him as allowing one to abandon the mental and behavioral requirements of humanity. Kongzi seemed to have taken for granted here that a person so noble as to be willing to assist everyone in the world must have necessarily possessed a goodwill and respect for the others.

22. The first formulation states that "I should never act except in such a way that I can also will that my maxim should become a universal law." Kant, *Grounding for the Metaphysics of Morals*, 402. As a formal condition that limits one's subjective material maxims, it is related to the second formulation (the principle of humanity) by forbidding one from treating others merely as means to the satisfaction of any material end.

23. *Analects*, 15.24; see Chan, *Source Book in Chinese Philosophy*, 44. Some would categorize general love and the Golden Rule as two different formulations of *Ren*, and view the second formulation as reaching higher level of generalization, see, for example, Roetz, 1993: 133–148. Yet these two formulations are not inconsistent with one another, and in particular the positive (versus the mere negative) expression of the Golden Rule is closer to the first formulation as it requires us to do to others what we like others to do to ourselves; presumably we all like to be loved, so reciprocally we should love others (of course, in a differentiated fashion depending on the others' relationships to us).

24. In Kant's moral philosophy, this is only an imperfect duty which, though dependent upon one's own capacity in obtaining the means, ought to be taken as a goal throughout one's life.

25. *Analects*, 6.30; see Legge, *The Four Books*, 46; cf. Chan, *Source Book in Chinese Philosophy*, 31.

26. Kant also points out that the material needs of human beings depend on particular circumstances, and thus cannot serve as the basis for unerring morality, which must be an absolute command universally applicable to all human beings.

27. Weiss points out that, for Golden Rule to produce good effects, it has to meet three conditions: we know what we want, what we want is identical to what we ought to desire, and what is good for us is also good for the rest. Paul Weiss, "The Golden Rule," *Journal of Philosophy* 38 (16): 422. Although the third condition is theoretically relevant (my good is not necessarily your good, sometimes it is even possible that one's food is another's poison!), the problem it poses is least serious and thus is not discussed here.

28. Kant, *Grounding for the Metaphysics of Morals*, 37, n. 23.

29. For arguments that the Confucian Golden Rule has several advantages over the western Christian version of the same rule, see Wang, "The Golden Rule and Impersonal Care," 423–425.

30. Heiner Roetz, *Confucian Ethics of the Axial Age* (Albany: State University of New York Press, 1993), 137–140.

31. *Mengzi*, 4B3, trans. Chan, *Source Book in Chinese Philosophy*, 76.

32. *Analects*, 12.1–12.3, 12.22, 13.19.

33. *Analects*, 12.7, 12.11, 12.18–12.19, 13.1–13.3, 13.17.

34. *Analects*, 20.2.

35. *Mengzi*, 7B16; see Chan, *Source Book in Chinese Philosophy*, 81.

36. Chinese philosophers had long believed that a person's goodness originated in a physical entity—the heart (*xin*), even though goodness clearly refers to the quality of mind. The notion of "heart-mind" here refers the physical entity that is responsible for a person's moral character.

37. *Mengzi*, 6A6, trans. Chan, *Source Book in Chinese Philosophy*, 54.

38. *Mengzi*, 2A6.

39. Mengzi argues that the current corrupted state of human mind does not prove the absence of humanity in the inner nature of human beings. Like many other arguments, he cannot offer a direct proof since most assertions are of transcendental nature, but resorts to

analogies. For example, the Ox Mount was previously filled with green plants and became barren only after prolonged destruction, yet one cannot justifiably maintain that the mountain is barren by nature. *Mengzi*, 6A8.

40. *Mengzi*, 2A6, trans. Chan, *Source Book in Chinese Philosophy*, 65.

41. As Ivanhoe points out, Mengzi in this hypothetical thought experiment suggests merely that the falling scenario would produce the feeling of alarm and distress in everyone, but one may or may not take any action. Philip J. Ivanhoe, *Confucian Moral Self Cultivation* (New York: Peter Lang, 1993), 29–30. While this is true, it nevertheless seems reasonable to interpret the entire passage as implying that such a feeling naturally produces an urge for action, even though the person may well be deterred from actually taking any action for a variety of reasons, for example, fear, expectation of or reliance on actions to be taken by others, or even sheer shyness to act like a good Samaritan before a crowd; otherwise, the rest of the passage would seem to be quite irrelevant—if I simply sat there feeling alarmed, why should I ever worry about seeking rewards from the child's parents or praises of neighbors and friends? The difference between his reading and mine is minor, however, since we agree that the feeling that emanates from one's heart-mind does not necessarily produce action. Indeed, the intensity of such feeling necessarily varies from one individual to another.

42. *Mengzi*, 4B32; see Chan, *Source Book in Chinese Philosophy*, 77.

43. Ivanhoe, *Confucian Moral Self Cultivation*, 34.

44. Immanuel Kant, *The Metaphysics of Morals*, trans. Mary Gregor (Cambridge University Press, 1996), 214–216.

45. Kant, *The Metaphysics of Morals*, 237.

46. Indeed Mengzi seems to approve King Xuan of Qi's switch of a shivering ox with a sheep for ceremonial slaughter. *Mengzi*, 1A7. This is another example to demonstrate the presence of *Ren* in an ordinary person who had not consciously engaged in moral cultivation, and Mengzi does not explain whether there is a hierarchical order in the animal kingdom for human affection. It does show, of course, that if human compassion has been extended even to an ox, how much more will it be for the *Homo sapiens*!

47. *Mengzi*, 6A14.

48. *Mengzi*, 6A17.

49. *Mengzi*, 2A2.

50. *Analects*, 7.30.
51. *Analects*, 12.1.
52. *Mengzi*, 2A8, 2A10.
53. *Mengzi*, 7A37.
54. As Margalit points out, compassion may well arise out of pity rather than respect for the indigents: "The poor are given charity out of pity." Avishai Margalit, *The Decent Society*, trans. Naomi Goldblum (Cambridge, MA: Harvard University Press 1996), 231. And the feeling of pity is premised on the inferior status of those who receive assistance. Mengzi's writings seem to be mixed in this respect. On the one hand, he does seem to suggest that the uneducated poor is a pitiful mass to be benefited from a benevolent government, a point to which we will turn shortly; on the other hand, there are passages which suggest that even common people can become sages through continuous self-cultivation. At least there is nothing to prevent Mengzi from arguing that compassion is out of regard for innate human good rather than haughtiness assumed by a self-appointed superior; even though the condescending psychology is quite common and such psychology may actually play a part in alms, he can still argue that such be the inadequate side-effect of compassion as a natural feeling. His well example does not involve this potential problem since hardly anyone will take a baby as inferior (perhaps precisely because she is in a naturally inferior position, but such inferiority is to be overcome as she grows up).
55. Chan, *Source Book in Chinese Philosophy*, 50.
56. The word "material" refers broadly to all things related to the satisfaction of human needs and pleasure or avoidance of pain.
57. *Mengzi*, 3A4, 3B9.
58. *Mengzi*, 2A5.
59. *Mengzi*, 3A3.
60. *Mengzi*, 3A4.
61. *Mengzi*, 3A3.
62. *Mengzi*, 1A3.
63. For example, when the adulterated milk powder killed several and harmed many infants at the Fuyang city of Anhui province, the chief of the local Quality Supervision Bureau committed suicide during investigation, apparently under the pressure that he might be found responsible for failing to prevent the incident. See http://news.sina.com.cn/z/milkpowder.

64. *Mengzi*, 7B1.
65. *Mengzi*, 6B9.
66. Mengzi, 4A14.
67. *Mengzi*, 5B9.
68. *Mengzi*, 1B8, trans. Chan, *Source Book in Chinese Philosophy*, 62.
69. Locke's famous notion "appeal to Heaven" corresponds quite closely to the Chinese "practicing the Way on behalf of Heaven" (替 天行道 *titian xingdao*), see his *Second Treatise*, Sec. 20, in John Locke, *Two Treatises of Government*, ed. Peter Laslett (Cambridge: Cambridge University Press, 1988), 282.
70. *Mengzi*, 1A5, 1A7; trans. Chan, *Source Book in Chinese Philosophy*, 61.
71. *Mengzi*, 2A5.
72. *Mengzi*, 4A9.
73. *Mengzi*, 1B1, 2, 4.
74. *Mengzi*, 2B1.
75. *Mengzi*, 4A9; see Legge, *The Four Books*, 165.
76. *Mengzi*, 2A6, trans. Chan, *Source Book in Chinese Philosophy*, 65.
77. *Mengzi*, 1A7.
78. *Mengzi*, 4A1.
79. *Mengzi*, 4A3.
80. Mengzi, 2B4.
81. Even Mengzi's famous notion of people being "nobler" than the king (君轻民贵 *junqin mingui*) is to be understood as taking the people's welfare as the basis of the state, which is essentially the same notion as benevolent government. It simply expresses the idea that the people's welfare is a higher priority than the king's.
82. Since the notion of benevolent or compassionate government is metaphysically founded on the heart-mind for compassion (不忍人 之心 *burenrenzhixin*), one wonders whether it is better to take the Golden Rule as the primary interpretation of *Ren*. After all, compassion is so closely associated with pity that once one begins the arguments along that direction, it is too easy to end with an ethics of pity and forget about the true source giving rise to compassion. This is partly why I used the Golden Rule in Chap.2 to argue that Confucian moral philosophy is really centered on human dignity, and leave out compassion altogether when interpreting humanity.
83. *Mengzi*, 6A8.
84. In this connection, it seems unfair to charge Mengzi for being too optimistic about human nature. The Confucian of the Han dynasty,

Dong Zhongshu, for example, compares good and nature with rice and rice stalk or with silk cocoon and silk, and argue that human nature cannot simply be said to be "good," but merely has the potential to become good when properly cultivated with training and education. See *Luxuriant Gems of the Spring and Autumn Annals*, "Profound Examination of Names and Appellations," Ch. 35, see Chan, *Source Book in Chinese Philosophy*, 273–278. But in a way he is merely disputing what "nature" means rather than the basic tenet of the Mengzian human nature theory, which is rather careful in distinguishing the potential from what is actually acquired.

85. *Mengzi*, 3A4; trans. Chan, *Source Book in Chinese Philosophy*, 70.

86. *Mengzi*, 4B19.

87. *Mengzi*, 3A3. Kongzi would agree with Mengzi on this point since he also emphasized the importance of education before the application of criminal punishments. See *Analects*, 20.2.

88. Guo Jian, "*Ren* in Confucianism and the Chinese Legal Culture," in ed. Research Committee on Chinese Confucianism and Legal Culture, *Confucianism and Legal Culture* (Shanghai: Fudan University Press, 1992), 102–107.

89. *Mengzi*, 1A1.

90. *Mengzi*, 1B2.

91. Mengzi is, of course, not alone in lack of effectiveness. Just recall how Kongzi traveled from one kingdom to another and how his advices were politely rejected in every case. And Mozi advanced essentially the same type of arguments as that of Mengzi, and experienced the same ineffectiveness. He was actually unable to dissuade King of Chu by his utilitarian arguments, until he demonstrated that the king's aggressive plan would actually fail. *Mozi*, "Gongshu", Ch. 50. More details in Chap.4.

92. Just imagine, say, you have a swimming pool in your private backyard. You might feel good about inviting a few friends to share with you occasionally, but will you be convinced that you should make it accessible to the general public? There is no reason to expect that King Xuan would think differently, since they all took for granted that they owned the whole kingdom in the same sense as we own our swimming pools.

93. This points to a difficulty in the naturalistic arguments in general, which purport to establish the causal connection between moral worthiness and its consequences (rewards or punishments). To some

extent the Confucian and the Mohist schools all share the naturalistic difficulty.

94. *Hanfeizi*, "Five Vermin", Sec. 49.4.

95. *Mengzi*, 7B2.

96. *Mengzi*, 1A3.

97. *Mengzi*, 2A5.

98. *Mengzi*, 3A4, 3B9.

99. *Mengzi*, 7A13.

100. *Mengzi*, 1A5, 3B5.

101. *Mengzi*, 7A23.

102. *Mengzi*, 7A12.

103. *Mengzi*, 4B19.

104. *Mengzi*, 3A3.

105. As P.J. Ivanhoe points out, although the literal translation of *xing'e* is "evil nature," it would be misleading to adopt such translation since Xunzi does not believe that we *knowingly* act badly or *enjoy* doing what is wrong. Rather, we simply act without moral knowledge and in this sense we are bad or unsavory by nature, but we are not evil in the same sense that Christianity holds human beings to be evil for intentionally deviating from God's command. Philip J. Ivanhoe, "Human Nature and Moral Understanding in the Xunzi," in *Virtue, Nature, and Moral Agency in the Xunzi*, ed. T.C. Kline III and Philip J. Ivanhoe (Indianapolis: Hackett, 2000), 237, 243–245. Thus, it is translated as "bad nature" instead. Also see in that volume Eric Hutton, "Does Xunzi Have a Consistent Theory of Human Nature?", 220–221.

106. To retain that hope, Xunzi cannot consistently deny all natural good in human beings for, if they were merely bad, they would be beyond any hope of self-improvement; instead, he must have implicitly assumed that a person is born at least with some capacity and will to become good in later life. Xunzi anticipated this challenge in his work (*Xunzi*, "Human Nature is Bad," Ch. 23), but he might not have offered an entirely adequate defense. Chung-ying Cheng, *New Dimensions of Confucian and Neo-Confucian Philosophy* (Albany: State University of New York Press, 1991), 69–70. The neo-Confucian of the Song dynasty, Zhu Xi, would go so far as to say that Xunzi already lost his ground as soon as he took human nature to be bad, though that statement could be attributed to Zhu's strong Mengzian disposition. See, for example, Zhu Xi, *Collective Annotations of the Four Books* (Ji'nan: Qilu Books, 1992), 4.2.

107. *Xunzi*, Ch. 23; see Homer H. Dubs, *The Works of Hsuntze* (Taipei: Cheng-wen Publishing, 1966), 301.

108. Chen Fei-long, *Studies on Xunzi's Theory of* Li (Taipei: Wenshizhe Press, 1979), 42–55.

109. See Henry Rosemont, Jr., "State and Society in the Xunzi: A Philosophical Commentary," in *Virtue, Nature, and Moral Agency in the* Xunzi, ed. T.C. Kline III and Philip J. Ivanhoe (Indianapolis: Hackett, 2000), 5–6.

110. *Xunzi*, "Of Honor and Disgrace," Ch. 4.8–4.9, trans. John Knoblock, *Xunzi: A Translation and Study of the Complete Works* (vol. 1) (Stanford: Stanford University Press,1988), 190–191.

111. *Xunzi*, "Human Nature is Bad," Ch. 23, see Burton Watson, *Hsün Tzu: Basic Writings* (New York: Columbia University Press, 1963), 164–165.

112. *Xunzi*, "Human Nature is Bad," Ch. 23.

113. In fact, Ivanhoe interprets Xunzi's notion of "bad nature" to mean that human beings, born without any moral faculty, need to engage in moral learning and practice at the first place before they acquire any moral sense. Ivanhoe, "Human Nature and Moral Understanding in the Xunzi," 240–245.

114. *Xunzi*, "Human Nature is Bad," Ch. 23.

115. *Xunzi*, "Of Honor and Disgrace," Sec. 4.9, trans. Knoblock, *Xunzi*, 191.

116. *Ibid.*, trans. Knoblock, *Xunzi*, 192.

117. *Xunzi*, "Of Honor and Disgrace," Sec. 4.8, trans. Knoblock, *Xunzi*, 190.

118. Benjamin I. Schwartz, *The World of Thought in Ancient China* (Cambridge, MA: Harvard University Press, 1985), 290–320.

119. Xunzi, "On Propriety," Ch. 19, trans. Watson, *Hsün Tzu*, 89. See also "On the Regulations of a King," Ch. 9.

120. *Xunzi*, "On Enriching the State," Sec. 10.1, 10.4.

121. *Xunzi*, "Human Nature is Bad," Ch. 23.

122. *Xunzi*, Chs. 10, 19. For the explanation of Xunzi on rule of propriety, see Chen Da-qi, *The Theory of Xunzi* (Taipei: Huagang Press,1971), 144; Chen Fei-long, *Studies on Xunzi's Theory of* Li, 96–127; Weng Hui-mei, *Xunzi on Studies of Man* (Taipei: Zhengzhong Books, 1988), 183–187; Jin Bingcai, "The Modern Meaning of Xunzi Philosophy," in *The Modern Interpretation of Traditional Confucianism*, ed. Zhou Boyu (Taipei: Wenjin Press,1994), 167–174.

123. No one can forget his vivid depiction of pathetic conditions in the state of nature, where human life is supposedly "solitary, poor, nasty, brutish, and short." Thomas Hobbes, *Leviathan*, ed. C.B. Macpherson (New York: Penguin, 1985), 187.

124. Hobbes, *Leviathan*, 190.

125. *Xunzi*, "On Enriching the State," Sec. 10.3b.

126. *Xunzi*, Ch. 15.

127. *Xunzi*, Ch. 9.

128. *Xunzi*, "Of Kings and Lords-Protector," Sec. 11.1a, trans. Knoblock, *Xunzi*,150. See also "On Strengthening the State," Ch. 16.

129. *Xunzi*, "Debate on the Principles of Warfare," Sec. 15.1c, 15.4, trans. Knoblock, *Xunzi*, 222, 229.

130. *Xunzi*, "Of Honor and Disgrace," Sec. 4.8.

131. *Xunzi*, "Of Kings and Lords-Protector," Sec. 11.9a; "On the Regulations of a King," Sec. 9.4.

132. Theoretically, the current regime is one *of* the people, since the 1982 Constitution stipulates that "all powers belong to the people." (Art. 1) Without adequate mechanisms for the people to exercise their powers, however, such statements remain empty.

133. The immaturity thesis, of course, has been taken for granted throughout Chinese political history, but only in the late Qing (清) dynasty, when the imperial government was forced to undertake institutional reforms, was it put forward as a theory by such prominent scholars as Liang Qichao and others as an argument against immediate democratization. Since then both the supporting and opposing arguments were repeatedly raised during the Nationalist government, see, for example, Hu Shih, "The Question of Constitutionalism," *Independence Review* 1 (1932) 1. For an argument against the conventional wisdom that elections require high levels of education and literacy, see Cai Dingjian ed., *A Survey Report of the Chinese Elections* (Beijing: Law Press, 2002).

134. Mou Zongsan, Xu Fuguan, Zhang Junmai, and Tang Junyi, "Declaration of Chinese Culture to the World: Our Consensus on Chinese Scholarly Research and on the Future of Chinese Culture and World Culture," in *Tang Junyi's Collection*, ed. Huang Kejian et al. (Beijing: Qunyan Press, 1993), 475–525.

135. See Lin Yusheng, "Dilemmas Confronting neo-Confucians in Pushing for Theories of Democracy and Science in China," *China Times*, September 7–8, 1988.

136. Tu Weiming: *The Challenge of Singapore* (Beijing: Sanlian Books, 1992), 151.

137. Remarks of Yu Yingshih, when he pointed to "an apparent fact" that the early Chinese who accepted western democratic ideas were nearly all Confucians. Yu Yingshih, "Modern Confucians and Democracy, Speech on Cultural China Conference," August 30, 2004, http://www.gongfa.com/rujia.htm.

138. I do not mean to measure the merits of Confucianism by modern western yardsticks, but I do argue that *Ren* as a moral concept is closer to the modern ideals and that, following the Aristotelian approach, the notion of a good government should be derived logically from a moral conception of good.

139. *Xunzi*, Ch. 27.

140. *Xunzi*, "Of Kings and Lords-Protector," Sec. 11.1a, trans. Knoblock, *Xunzi*, 150.

141. *Analects*, 12.7.

142. *Mengzi*, 5A5.

143. *Mengzi*, 1B7, trans. Chan, *Source Book in Chinese Philosophy*, 61.

144. *Mengzi*, 1B7, trans. Chan, *Source Book in Chinese Philosophy*, 62.

145. *Mengzi*, 7B14; see Chan, *Source Book in Chinese Philosophy*, 81.

146. Of course, the whole enterprise of traditional Confucianism is to reduce official abuses to a minimum, mainly through moral education, but Chinese history shows at most mixed success in this grand political project. This is a broad topic by itself, which I shall discuss in more detail elsewhere.

147. It is noteworthy that the new amendment to the 1982 Constitution, ironically together with the "three-represents" doctrine, stipulates that "the State respects and protects human rights." What is lacking so far is, of course, an effective mechanism to protect concrete rights and freedoms.

148. "A gentleman can stick to poverty, a petty man in poverty would do anything." *Analects*, 15.1.

149. For China, it suffices to say here that apparently negative rights are somehow even harder to enforce than positive rights. It is therefore not surprising that China has ratified the International Covenant for Economic, Social, and Cultural Rights—a convention of positive rights (preserving an exception to the negative freedom to form labor unions), without ratifying (though having signed) the International Covenant for Civil and Political Rights, which protects basic negative rights.

150. Margalit, *The Decent Society*, 224–226.
151. For the relevance of Xunzi today, see Rosemont, "State and Society in the Xunzi," 27–30.
152. *Analects* 13.9; *Mengzi* 3A3.

CHAPTER 4

Propriety, Law, and Harmony: A Functional Argument for Rule of Virtue

INTRODUCTION

While humanity and righteousness are lofty ideals, they cannot be achieved without the concrete practice of social norms and rules of propriety embodied in the classical system of *Li*, which the Confucians thought are vitally important for maintaining harmony (和*he*), peace, order, and prosperity of the traditional society. Although these are obviously salutary social ideals cherished by all classical schools of Chinese thought, the ways to realize these ideals differ profoundly.[1] Where the Legalist school exclusively relies on rule of law and punishments, Confucianism places heavy emphasis on the moral principles of humanity (*Ren*) and righteousness (*Yi*), and the practice of rules of proper conducts. In the very opening dialogue from which the above passage is taken, Mengzi points out the contradictions inherent in rational egotism, which has been widely taken as the philosophical foundation of liberal democracy today.[2] To the narrowly self-interested question raised by the King Hui of Liang, what can be done to benefit his kingdom, Mengzi answers that the formulation of the question itself would defeat its solution:

> *Why must your Majesty speak of profits (li)? All you must have are simply humanity (Ren) and righteousness (Yi).[3] If your Majesty asks: "what is to be done to profit my kingdom?", each superior officer asks: "what is to be done to*

© The Author(s) 2016
Q. Zhang, *Human Dignity in Classical Chinese Philosophy*,
DOI 10.1057/978-1-349-70920-5_4

profit my fief?", then every inferior officer and common people would also ask: "what is to be done to profit my person?" Now superiors and inferiors all fight for profits against one another, and the kingdom is in danger.... If interest is placed above righteousness, then superior officers would never be content until they snatch away all properties from of their king. But there is never a single man of humanity who would ignore his parents, nor a single man of righteousness who would disrespect his king. Thus, your Majesty has only to speak of humanity and righteousness, and why even mention profits?[4]

Thus, so long as the king continues to place his focus of consideration on the interest, he would eventually find his own interest be defeated; in unexpected ways, exclusive concerns over oneself, "rational" as it may seem, often, if not always, lead to consequences opposite to what was originally desired. Paradoxically, to benefit the state and the king himself, who supposedly "possesses the state" (有国 *youguo*) in the sense that he is in charge of running it and can legitimately derive benefits from his successful governance, he must shift his focus from self-interest to something broader, namely, the observance of such fundamental moral rules as required by humanity and righteousness. The only consistent solution, according to Mengzi, is to follow the moral principles, by which one's self-interest is only to be achieved as a sort of "by-product."[5]

The view of Mengzi, which had since become a prominent branch of Confucianism, was squarely countered by the rising Legalist school at his time. According to prominent Legalist theorists and statesmen, most notably Lord Shang (商鞅) and Han Fei (韩非), human beings in (what was by their standard) modern societies are primarily driven by material interests and self-regarding desires. Moral preaching are useless, they assert, for governing a large society; rational law, which supposedly shapes the people's motives by prescribing adequate rewards and punishments, is the only device on which a ruler can rely to maintain the harmony and strength of his kingdom. Joining romantic Daoists and pragmatic Mohists, the Legalist particularly opposed the Confucian emphasis on following traditional rules of propriety (*Li*) and developing personal virtues as socially ineffective means of governing a state. The Confucian tradition was attacked with renewed vigor by the radical intellectuals during the May-Fourth Movement of 1919, whose relentless effort to replace the Chinese tradition with western ideals contributed to the demise of the traditional moral order and the ensuing social and political disorder. Arguably the common thread unifying the Legalist and the May-Fourth intellectuals is the rational choice thinking,[6] which finds its systematic expositions later in the "core versions" developed in the USA after the World War II.[7] Following the social contract tradition of Hobbes and Locke, these schools have made various efforts to find purely rational basis for liberal individualism, democracy, and constitutionalism.[8] What has commonly been ignored, however, is the inherent contradictions in a narrowly self-interested society, as revealed by the modern rational choice literature itself.[9] Consistent rational choice reasoning, as I shall argue below, by and large confirms the validity of Confucian wisdom expressed by Mengzi above.

This chapter focuses on the relationships between moral commitment and rule of law and their relevance to social harmony. It has long been acknowledged that rule of law is insufficient for governance without some moral support,[10] but most works seem to rely on general arguments without solid positive proofs. Rather than elaborating on general ideas, this chapter examines particular aspects of the moral debate from a social, historical, and theoretical perspective in the Chinese cultural setting. Specifically it focuses on the Confucian-Legalist lines of arguments about the relevance of basic moral norms to social prosperity and harmony. By reviewing the dilemmas of narrowly rational society—primarily the Prisoner's Dilemma and the related collective action problem,[11] I seek to provide a defense for the crucial functions of traditional social rules and norms as embodied in the Confucian system of *Li*.[12] Following Mengzi, I argue that a harmonious society presupposes a set of basic and widely subscribed rules and norms governing the behavior of its members, which I broadly designate here as the "constitution of society," written or unwritten, and that *Li was* such a constitution that was "engraved... in the people's hearts,"[13] as it were, and served its unique functions of holding the traditional Chinese society together.[14] Far from unconditionally suppressing individual freedom, a charge commonly made against the Confucian propriety, the traditional *Li* had historically preserved a limited degree of local self-government against the tyranny of the central state, a trap into which the Legalist regimes had repeatedly fallen—and for good reasons.

I label my arguments "functional" (but not necessarily "functionalist")[15] in the sense that justification for a social norm is to be sought in its serving useful social functions (in the Chinese term, 用 *yong*). It should be pointed out at the outset that, although the scope of the article is limited to the study of the "outer" aspects of *Li*, that is, its social and political functions, it does not preclude that *Li* can also be justified on its "inner" moral dimension.[16] More recently, following Mengzi and the neo-Confucian tradition,[17]*Li* has often been defended as an expedient means to achieving the highest moral ideal, humanity (*Ren*).[18] No doubt harmony, which means here a good social order, can find its ultimate, meaning only in its efficacy of promoting humanity and individual good life. Yet, as it is often criticized,[19] the neo-Confucian tradition seems to have a tendency of retreating into the "inner self" and, as a result, neglecting the "outer" sphere of *Li*, which embodies its social, political, and cultural functions. Nowadays, under the broad influence of individual liberalism, it is fashionable to dismiss the roles of social rules and customs, and to associate them with such unfavorable terms as "social control," "manipulation," or "cultural programming." It would be a mistake, however, to overlook the social, cultural, and political functions of *Li*. Indeed, just as *Li* would be made blind and arbitrary without the guiding principle of *Ren*, and reduced merely to a device that defends the status quo and impedes social progress (as both the Legalist and the May-Fourth intellectuals argued), *Ren* would become empty and mysterious without the concrete manifestation of *Li*.[20] After all, just as the moral virtues and dutiful obedience to law on part of citizens are the very guarantee for social harmony, a harmonious social order is an institutional prerequisite toward the achievement of learning and cultivation of virtues (*de*). It is precisely by the neglect of this "outer" aspect of *Li*, as marked by its social functions in maintaining order and harmony, that both the Legalist political programs in imperial China and the radical modernization effort around the May-Fourth Movement had failed.

My arguments are presented in two parts. First, I evaluate the Legalist arguments against the necessity and desirability of *Li* for social order. The history of traditional China has refuted the Legalist belief that a narrowly rational state can be sustained solely by laws and punishments tailored to human interests. The social dilemmas revealed by the contemporary rational choice theory further discredit Legalism as an infeasible political program. Second, aiming to resolve these social dilemmas, I argue that the cultivation of personal virtues through the common practice of *Li* is necessary for holding a society together and bringing about requisite cooperative actions. In particular, public education is necessary to prepare the way for an ordinary child to become righteous and trustworthy gentlemen (*Junzi*). Here I bring in the views of Dong Zhongshu (c. 179–c. 104 B.C.), who reconciled the human nature disputes between the rival schools within Confucianism by arguing that innate human virtue is only a potential rather than completed reality; it requires the positive guidance of society for a complete development, and this indispensable need was fulfilled by practicing the Confucian moral rules defined in *Li*. In fact, Confucian *Li* had become such a vital part of the Chinese culture that, by seeking to abolish the entire body of *Li*, the radical modernization efforts that culminated in the May-Fourth Movement necessarily undermined and eventually destroyed the binding force of the constitution of the traditional Chinese society, and created decades of war and turmoil rather than progress, development, or harmony. Overall, I find that the Confucian argument, with a more sophisticated and plausible assumption of human nature, prevail over the Legalist argument. While the latter shares with the western rational choice theory in the effort to build public institutions based on the egocentric view of human beings, the Chinese experience suggests that seemingly non-rational commitment to basic moral norms is nonetheless necessary for sustaining a harmonious, cooperative, and prosperous society.

LEGALISM, RATIONAL CHOICE, AND THEIR LIMITATIONS

China used to be a *"Li-*governed" (礼治*lizhi*) society. For several thousand years, the traditional Chinese society was regulated by an extremely complex and concrete system of social customs, conventions, and ceremonies. Opening the dense volumes of the *Book of Rites* (礼记*Liji*),[21] we find that these customary and conventional rules touched upon almost every aspect of ordinary human lives: child training, ethical education, marriage, communal activities, state ceremonies and, not the least, lengthy and tedious procedures of mourning for deceased relatives. Of course, not every rule recorded in the massive *Book of Rites* was meticulously observed.[22] Over the time, some of the rules did change; and near the end of every dynasty, as many Confucians observed, the observance of *Li* was at any rate relaxed to the breaking point. Notwithstanding periodic disruptions of social and political continuity, however, the main body of *Li* as well as its guiding ideas did manage to sustain the Chinese tradition for over 25 centuries, maintaining the cohesion of society, while at the same time protecting it from potentially disruptive progresses and, in the case of sudden and violent eruptions in political leadership, playing the pivotal roles of reintegrating the society and rebuilding the social networks on the model of the traditional order. Without exaggeration, as late as the nineteenth century, it was Confucian *Li* that visibly and continuously embodied the Chinese cultural tradition.[23]

In the Chinese intellectual history, however, the Confucian preoccupation with *Li* was by no means uncontested. Now and then, the validity and the desirability of the entire system of *Li* were subject to challenges of this or that rival school that the Confucian orthodox would label as "heretic." Besides the Daoist who would laugh at the Confucians' apparently dogged commitment to traditional practice (Chap. 6) and the Mohist who had long questioned the utility and economy of the elaborate ceremonies provided by *Li* (Chap. 5), the Legalist had furthered probably the most systematic and pointed critique of Confucian *Li*. They forcefully challenged the Confucian assumption that rule of propriety was the best or a feasible way at all of governing a state and society.[24] Does society really need an overarching moral system, as one embodied in Confucian *Li*, to help inculcate personal virtues in order to maintain a stable order? Or was *Li* indeed a system of antiquity, totally unsuitable to and useless for modern society, and laws and punishments alone are enough to bring about social stability? Based on opposing assumptions of human nature, the Confucians and Legalist arrived at entirely different answers.[25] As a result, although both schools share the primary concern over social order and prosperity (or, in the Legalist term, the "strength" of the country), they fundamentally disagreed in the ultimate purpose of the state and in the most efficient methods of governing the state. While the Confucians put great emphasis on the function of *Li* as a social constitution in cultivating personal virtues and in maintaining the social order, the Legalist school consistently opposed *Li* as an ineffective instrument for running a large society and as a fetter of social progress. While the Confucians believed in the innate virtues (for Xunzi, at least the ability of self-transformation) in every human being, the Legalist were convinced of the incorrigibility of bad human nature. The Confucians were committed to a stepwise program as prescribed by *Li*, aiming to make virtuous individuals as the governors of society; the Legalist, believing the Confucian approach to be totally useless and counterproductive, proposed to do away with all these niceties and adopt a blanket political program founded upon universal laws tailored to the rational human interests. Put simply, the Legalist believed only in rule of law; the Confucians, while not denying the need for law, believed that morally decent human beings were also indispensable to a good society, and placed the practice of *Li* and cultivation of virtues above law because they regarded them as better means for achieving long-term order, stability, and prosperity.[26]

In examining these debates, this section points out the major limitations in the Legalist arguments. It first presents the Legalist program of the statecraft that challenged the traditional Confucian belief in *Li*, and then explores the presuppositions and inconsistencies implied in the Legalist arguments. The Legalist presuppositions of narrowly rational human nature and the state policies built thereupon are further undermined by their undesirable social effects as exposed in the modern rational choice research. The latter suggests that rational self-interest alone cannot sustain a cooperative society; seemingly irrational commitment to social norms is necessary, negatively, to maintain social order and, positively, to inculcate social cooperation and collective actions. Reduced to the core, my arguments merely confirm the traditional Confucian wisdom that a unified moral system like *Li* is necessary to hold a society together, and that it is impossible to sustain law and order in a group of completely egocentric persons without an all-powerful government, which would be only a step away from total tyranny.

Classical Legalism and Its Limitations

The Legalist theory of the statecraft is simple, elegant, and modern. It shares the basic assumptions of human behavior with what we now know as the theory of rational choice, coupled with a primitive version of behaviorism prevalent today.[27] Unlike the Confucians, who believed in the capacity of moral improvement, the Legalist held that human beings are purely self-interested and governed by self-regarding desires. Everyone invariably seeks to pursue honor and material pleasure, and avoid pain and disgrace. The desires of the multitude, if unsatisfied, inevitably give rise to strife and chaos; but human desires also provide the means by which the multitude can be governed. As Lord Shang (d. 338 B.C.) succinctly puts it, "the human nature is this: those who are hungry seek food; those who are belabored seek leisure; those who are distressed seek pleasure; those who are disgraced seek honor.... Thus, whither honor and profits are gathered, whither the people are directed."[28] If the ruler can discern the true needs of the people and monopolize the means toward the satisfaction thereof, then he is able to keep the entire state under control. The best way to achieve social order is by designing a mechanism of rewards and punishments which manipulates the motive of human conducts in such a way that, upon the calculation of losses and gain, everyone will rationally choose to obey the laws laid down by the ruler and refrain from those conducts that the ruler has clearly indicated as "deviant" or "dys-functional" through the prohibitions of his laws. As long as the penalties are made sufficiently severe, and the punishments sufficiently certain, then no one would have the rational incentive to deviate from the ruler's order and violate his laws; harmony would be achieved, perhaps even without actually using any punishment.

Of course, this presupposes that ordinary people must at least be made aware of the prohibitions of the laws and the penalties for the violations thereof. Thus, laws must be promulgated and made open to all. Also, the people must be assured that the state will enforce the laws consistently and relentlessly. The idea is eloquently expressed by Han Fei, a prominent student of Xunzi:

> *An enlightened monarch will make sure its laws steep and penal punishments severe. While common men will not give up ordinary cloth and silk, even Robber Zhi dare not take a hundred pounds of shining gold. If harm is uncertain, then man will not give up even ordinary things; if harm is certain, one dare not take a hundred pound [of gold]. Thus an enlightened monarch will make certain his executions.*[29]

Besides the ruler's own resoluteness, however, neither Han Fei nor other Legalists quite explain how punishments are to be made certain and reliable.

As the laws and punishments are regarded as the sufficient means for maintaining harmony, the Confucian teachings of humanity and other vir-tues are thought to be superfluous, even counterproductive, for governing a large state. Unlike Confucians who laid emphasis on the exemplary role of a minority of moral elites, the Legalist are primarily concerned with the techniques for keeping mass behavior under control. The self-evident law of nature seems to suggest that most people are motivated not by moral virtues, but by satisfaction of material needs and self-interests. It is simply impractical to wait for everyone to become virtuous before the state is governed. Nor is it possible to make everyone virtuous by promulgating the system of *Li*. After all, the cultivation of virtue is a difficult process, destined to be achieved only by a few, thus seemingly useless for restrain-ing the desire of the multitudes. And the governance of the mass is the sole business of the state. As Han Fei puts it: "A ruler makes use of the majority and neglects the minority, and so he does not devote himself to virtue but to law."[30]

It is questionable, however, whether the Legalist rational thinking, which posits that the people obey the law not for its own sake, but out of their self-interest, can be made consistent with itself. Tough laws can be made and promulgated, but they need not necessarily be followed and executed. The Legalist doctrine contains several assumptions that prove problematic. Besides the obvious problem in supposing smooth transitions of imperial regimes, absent any moral constraint, and highly enlightened rationality in a single hereditary ruler (despite the avowed effort to create an institutional scheme supposedly within the competence of a mediocrity), the Legalist postulate of egocentric human nature, though arguably supported by modern behavioral theories, can be self-defeating. If everyone is solely governed by their own self-interests, there is nothing to prevent officials of all levels from abusing, and the ordinary people from evading, legal punishments, especially when they become so familiar with the law that they can make full use of the loopholes in the legal text.

In order to keep the people in check, the Legalist had resorted to numerous draconian mechanisms characteristic of a totalitarian state and the extreme of personal rule rather than rule of law. In practice, none of these measures turned out to be effective or long-lasting in the course of Chinese history. Indeed the time when the Legalist gained power was invariably accompanied with large-scale persecution within the court and often deep suppressions of society at large. Persecution invited retribution, excessive oppressions led to violent revolts: the human strives induced by the Legalist policies very much contradicted the original ideal of law and order with respect to which they were designed.

In a historical perspective, it is fair to say that the Legalist program had enjoyed short-term success but suffered from long-term failure. The dramatic story of the Qin (秦) Dynasty illustrated the occasion where the Legalist assumptions failed to meet reality. Although the Legalist policies could at times bring a state to quick success in military adventure, it was much more difficult to defend and sustain it in peace. The Legalist success was short-lived for a variety of reasons. Rationally selfish calculations of consequences and balance of rewards and punishments alone are not sufficient to oblige ordinary people to abide by the law; it is precisely by weighing potential losses and gains that intelligent human beings seek to evade punishments and, ultimately, to resort to violent and overt uprising against excessive oppression. The factual inconveniences in the Legalist arguments were caught by the Confucians in the official debates about the state salt and iron policies during the Han dynasty.[31] As they pointed out,

> *In the past the laws of the state Qin were more minute than autumn reeds, and the net [of punishments] was finer than condensed fat. Yet the superior and inferior cheated each other, and treacheries and deceptions were numerously generated. The legal prosecutions of officials, like saving the rotten and extinguishing the burnt, could not prohibit the wrong-doings. That the net became so loose and crimes eventually went unpunished was precisely due to the abandonment of propriety and righteousness and the preoccupation with criminal punishments.*[32]

Thus, although laws and institutions are necessary conditions for harmony and good governance, they alone are not sufficient. However rational an institution may seem to be in terms of self-interest, people almost always find it more expedient—if only for the present moment—to disregard and act against the supposedly established rules. In reality, given the complexity of human interactions in asocial system, the possible consequences of any particular human action are so numerous, human foresight so limited, and the ruler's capacity of surveillance and enforcement often so circumscribed, that a person will almost always find some "rationality" in disobeying laws. At the very least, there is nothing to prevent individual members of society from calculating and recalculating the net payoffs of violating some laws, and this process itself implies the lack of stability and predictability of law enforcement. Thus, a policy purely based on the ground of rational self-interest, if followed consistently, would seem to defeat its own purpose: the rationality of a social system presupposes some stability and predictability in human actions, yet the very nature of interest-based policies allow or even encourage human beings to attempt at constant recalculations in order to maximize their perceived self-interest, with the inherent tendency to disregard those basic social norms, the common observance of which make a stable society possible.

Despite its fearsome and costly consequences, the draconian Legalist devices had proved to be ineffective and short-lived. Contrary to the Legalist expectations, tough laws and heavy punishments failed to deter crimes and appeared powerless against an already crime-ridden society. In the case of the Qin Dynasty, instead of saving the regime from downfall, the Legalist policies merely encouraged the power holders to abuse their powers and accelerated its decay. This has been proved true generally for all historical revivals of Legalist practice, during which the Legalist in power almost always end up with large-scale persecution and social suppression,[33] inviting societal retribution in turn against the Legalist cruelty and personal tyranny.

Prisoner's Dilemma and Insufficiency of Statist Solutions

The failure of classical Legalism in bringing about social harmony and its general tendency toward political tyranny are not unexpected. The Legalist, exclusively focusing on law and punishment, sought to establish a society entirely free from reliance on moral virtues and social trust (as they were thought to be unreliable).[34] The Legalist mission has proved to be practically impossible, and its relentless pursuit necessarily leads to heavy reliance upon the monitoring and sanctioning power of the highest ruler of the state. The practical impossibility is borne out by the development of rational choice theory, which highlights the contradictions inherent in the framework of rational choice assumptions. Above all, every society of rational human beings is confronted with the Prisoner's Dilemma and the related free-rider problem, which it must resolve in order to maintain basic order and prosperity.

The so-called Prisoner's Dilemma occurs in those situations where, given the choices either to cooperate or to defect in a common enterprise, social actors always find it individually profitable to defect, regardless of others' choices, even though universal defections make everyone worse off (hence the "dilemma").[35] The dilemma is frequently found relevant in daily social life because voluntary cooperation usually involves some cost, either in the form of time (attending to the discussion of public issues), effort (coming to ballot box to cast vote) and, often simply, material expenses (union membership dues, all forms of donations). By choosing to defect, however, one can enjoy others' contribution for free. This is what Mancur Olson famously notes as the "free-rider" problem,[36] which applies generally to all collective actions which create non-exclusionary benefits to society at large, but in particular to the former socialist countries for its contribution to their low economic efficiency and, ultimately, the demise of their political systems. In liberal democracies the collective action problem, with its rational choice underpinning, is found in occasions as simple as voluntary blood donation and citizens' turning out to vote in general elections.[37] Other instances include voluntary control of externality effects. For example, a polluter will not voluntarily choose to clean up the air or water waste they created and, without coercive solutions imposed by the state and society, environment would deteriorate to such an extent as to endanger the health and survival of entire human species. People also tend to overuse natural resources held as common properties (e.g. the common land for grazing) to the point of their complete depletion, a phenomenon often called the "tragedy of the commons"[38]—a "tragedy" because, although each individual makes what to him the most rational decision, the collective outcome is next to the worst: the ruin of the common property that could have been moderately enjoyed by everyone.[39]

The common pattern behind these social conundrums is the Prisoner's Dilemma: although it is rational for each individual to decline cooperation, it is collectively irrational (suboptimal) because, without anyone choosing to contribute to (or voluntarily refrain from depleting) public goods, no one can enjoy the very basic social good, including peace, security, and order; at the end, everyone is made worse off by their narrowly rational choices. Thus, everyone benefits from a harmonious society, but many may find it even more profitable to engage in opportunist activities that would in a long run corrode harmony.[40] In the extreme form, human beings living in the same territory may come to distrust one another to such an extent that it becomes individually irrational to obey law whenever violations appear more profitable after weighing the risk of getting caught and punished. Everyone now becomes a potent criminal to his neighbors. Such a human condition is nothing other than the Hobbesian state of nature, where every person engages in a "war of all against all," the same situation as that Mengzi depicts in our opening discussion when the principles of humanity and righteousness are ignored. Once a society is trapped in the Prisoner's Dilemma, then universal defections and mistrust become the rational (and thus dominant) strategy, and its people would be permanently plagued by war, disorder, and poverty.

The Prisoner's Dilemma presupposes narrowly rational actors without previous interactions, mutual trust, and the perspective of future encounter. Self-interested strangers, lacking mutual trust and expectation for future interactions, would customarily not cooperate with one another even if they are brought closely together by occasions—unless they are forced to do so by an external authority. Before the Legalist solution is examined once again, however, it should be pointed out that there *are* non-political solutions to the dilemma. Researches in game theory show that, in repeated interactions, social actors who care reasonably about future rewards and punishments might rationally choose to cooperate with others at the present stage, even though the short-term payoffs at any particular time are still characterized by the Prisoner's Dilemma.[41] Through dynamic interactions, mutual trust can be established, and individual reputation consolidated. And once people begin to trust each other, they might rationally choose to refrain from defection because they know that everyone is to be made worse by shirking and believe that others will make due contributions rather than simply take advantage of their cooperation. Mutual trust is the indispensable resources that help society to resolve the pervasive Prisoner's Dilemma.[42] This point is made persuasively by David Hume,[43] who argues that law and government were not established in a fictitious contractual moment when strangers were supposed to make fundamental promises to each other, but through a long process of mutual interactions in which members of community came to be acquainted with one another and eventually agree upon certain basic rules and norms for governing their conducts.[44] Hume also rightly observes, however, that such a process operates only during the initial stage of human communities, in which small size, close proximity, and limited number of human actors makes effective mutual surveillance and norm enforcements possible.[45]

Yet, as the Legalists might contend, although repeated interactions help to explain the origin of rules and conventions, they do not provide a feasible solution to the dilemmas of modern society where, owning to the mobile and diverse nature of human interactions, personal contacts are likely to be so loose and unstable that no one can reasonably expect to encounter the same stranger twice (e.g. one can commit hit-and-run, and expect that he will never run into the same victim again). Repeated interactions might have initially enabled rational individuals to come to cooperate with one another, but such an avenue is limited to only a few (and mostly economic) situations in which actors have extensive personal dealings, or to small communities where members are acquainted with each other. As communities grow in population and territory, repeated interactions become limited to small clusters of close acquaintance (e.g. families, clans, closely supervised factories). And, as Olson observes, only in relatively small groups, where each group member can derive sizable benefits, that collective actions will voluntarily take place.[46] The prospect for voluntary collective action is further enhanced by the presence of a subgroup within the group, which has such disproportional stake in the action that it is willing to undertake the entire cost to make the collective action possible, thus allowing the rest of the population to be free riders of the benefits (hence Olson's notion of "exploitation of the great by the small"). Russell Hardin derives the threshold size of the subgroup that would have the rational incentive to do so because the disproportional benefits it will obtain from the collective action sufficiently compensate for its costs.[47] These types of collective actions are limited to particular situations, however, and do not seem to apply to society in general. Without developing a minimal degree of mutual trust, an undifferentiated population at large would remain rationally selfish strangers, each confronted with the same Prisoner's Dilemma; the threat of universal defections alone would make the basic social order elusive.

To be sure, if *voluntary* collective action is not forthcoming, rational human beings can choose to establish coercive institutions to induce cooperation. They can design laws that reward the social cooperation and punish defections, thus hopefully motivate the common people to act in a socially productive direction. Hume proposes, for example, that a large community may find it in the interest of public good to create a privileged elite group (the executives) with rational incentive to enforce the laws of the state.[48] This would essentially create a subgroup within society with the rational interest to induce collective actions by coercive means. A rational institution operates, however, only if there are good law-makers and effective executives who are themselves willing and able to follow institutional rules. But do they necessarily have the incentive to do so? The Legalist, to be sure, never ignored this problem. Indeed, to prevent various sorts of deviations, they devised extremely intricate schemes to keep the people mutually in check. They employed, for example, tightly organized quasi-military governments at the local level and the infamous "connected imprisonment" (连坐 *lianzuo*) institution, which legally required relatives, friends, and neighbors to expose each other, or otherwise suffer from the same penalty as the offender would if it was found that they failed disclose the offense to the authority. But the severe Legalist solutions, owning to their inherent defects, had proved to be practically ineffective in preventing defections against legally prescribed rules. Here we may distinguish two types of deviations from the rules, neither of which, I argue, the Legalist have succeeded in preventing.

To begin with, the Legalist assumed that ordinary human beings cannot be trusted to obey laws voluntarily because they are by nature rationally selfish and would take advantage of the political and social arrangements whenever they find profitable to do so. If the law against larceny is not tightly enforced, then thieves would abound to avail themselves of stolen properties. But even taking for granted the Legalist assumption that the ruler at the very top of the political pyramid is "good" (mindful of public needs) and intelligent (able to choose the right means to implement the desired ends), we will still find the cost of social sanctions to be so prohibitive as to make them entirely impracticable.[49] Can we imagine a viable society where everyone is a potent criminal, who is ready to offend his neighbors, and refrain from doing so only out of fear for legal punishments? Is it possible for any legal institution to survive and function in such a crime-ridden society? Laws, as the Confucians sensibly argue, have their own limits; every law is designed and established with the assumption that its violation would remain exceptions rather than the norm, and once offenders become so numerous as to embrace the whole population, one begins to question both the rationality and the feasibility of enforcing such a law. As many Confucians have observed, the laws during a tyranny like Qin never failed to be severe, specific, and publicly known; they nevertheless failed to deter frequent crimes. Before punishments can be constructively carried out to constitute effective deterrence, deviations from the laws must first be ferreted out and verified. This presupposes, of course, the ability and integrity of the executive officers. But even if we assume a competent, responsible, and meticulously rule-following executive, it may nevertheless lack the resources to meet its task once the violations become too numerous and the people decide to cheat the government together. To bind a crowd of potential thieves and robbers solely by law, then, the only hope is to institute an all-powerful and pervasive government—indeed, so powerful and pervasive that such a government has never and perhaps will never be found in human history.

But if a society needs be heavily guarded by punitive laws, who is to guard against the Legalist guardians? What will happen if the guardians themselves are corrupt and, upon weighing the risk, they find it more profitable to accept bribery than it is to enforce the law? There is certainly no reason to expect a sage-like stratum of political elites to arise from a universally corrupted population. Indeed, the Legalist themselves assume that the imperial officers of all levels are rationally self-interested and ready to take advantage of their king and the kingdom. Here, we encounter the famous principal-agent problem in business, where the agent (the manager) and the principal (the owner) possess divergent and conflicting interests. To resolve this problem, the Legalist designed many tactics aiming to put officials under effective control of the king. Again, we may doubt the validity and the practicability of the Legalist solution owning to the perceptible limits in the monarch's resources, competence, and foresight. But, more fundamentally, rather than solving the problem, the Legalist merely relegate it to a higher level. If the officials at all levels cannot be trusted to uphold the state institutions, then the ultimate hope is to be found in the monarch, who hopefully has the rational incentive to take measures reasonably aimed to better his own kingdom (which he supposedly "owns"). The Legalist presuppose here that the interest of the monarch is always identical with society at large—despite ample evidence to the contrary in the Chinese history, and the situation could have become much worse if the Confucian moral education provided to the king were entirely ignored (as the Legalist would recommend). Even if the ruler wants to promote harmony, cooperation, and prosperity (by which his own position can hopefully be secured), he may nevertheless lack the personal and institutional competence to do so. In either case, whether the monarch himself is inept or corrupt, the Legalist would run out of recourse altogether, and society as a whole is left to ruin.

Thus, following the rational choice logic, the Legalist begins with rule of law, but ends with the extreme of rule of man, in which the good will and competence of a single ruler alone would decide the vicissitudes of whole society. By ignoring the moral resources and the potential of voluntary cooperation that lie within society itself, which the Confucians proposed to bring about by socialization and moral education, the Legalist is compelled to relegate all social responsibilities and power of control to the government. Finding that the officials themselves cannot be trusted, it further shifts everything to the single man at the crown, thus paving its way toward veritable personal tyranny. Fundamentally, the Legalist ideal society is plagued by universal defection of rationally selfish and distrustful individuals, who find themselves hopelessly mired in the Prisoner's Dilemma. To resolve the Dilemma, purely legal or political solutions based on rational choice are not enough. A group of anomic individuals cannot be bound together to refrain from taking advantage of—much less to cooperate with—each other without establishing a Leviathan, which creates more problems than it solves. Human life in an oppressive government, often including the life of the monarch himself, is as "nasty, brutish, and short" as it is in the Hobbesian state of nature. To afford long-term harmony, security, and prosperity, members of society cannot rely *only* on the rationally designed rewards and punishments as provided by the laws and enforced by the state, but must somehow establish mutual trust, obligations, and stable incentives to observe the laws. Once again, we are back to the teaching of Mengzi.

SOCIAL FUNCTIONS OF CONFUCIAN LI: A PRELIMINARY INQUIRY

To resolve the social dilemma revealed by the rational choice theory, the Confucians basically picked up the solution that the Legalist discarded: the making of decent and trustable moral characters through the common practice of *Li*. Confucians like Mengzi and Xunzi share the belief that a person is trustable only if he is committed to follow the basic principles of humanity and righteousness. Thus, if the Legalist was preoccupied with designing a rational institutional structure to make ordinary individuals conform to social order by their own interest, the Confucians, while not denying the importance of legal institutions and rules, laid heavy emphasis on the moral quality of persons in control of these institutions. After all, the laws are to be carried out by human beings. As Mengzi famously put it: "Virtue alone is insufficient for ruling; laws cannot carry themselves into effect."[50] In the traditional Chinese society, if the power holders became corrupt at the very top of the political pyramid, nothing could obligate them to execute the laws, however rationally designed; nor would there remain anything short of a successful rebellion to prevent the power holders from abusing their powers to aggrandize their own interests at the expense of the common interest. Thus, conceding that laws are the bridle and criminal punishments the oars of the state, without which the state could not be well-governed, the Confucians in an official debate before the Han court nevertheless contended that.

> *The bridle is the instrument for driving horses, and is attuned only by good workman; the laws and the power are the instruments of governing, and are employed only by virtuous men. If the bridle-holder is not good, then the horse will run away; if the helmsman is not good, then the ship will flip and be damaged.... Now to abandon the way of humanity and righteousness, and to leave discretion to those who are preoccupied with penalties and names [of the crimes] (xingmingzhitu), is to repeat the stories of the states Wu and Qin.*[51]

The historical failure of the Legalist regime arguably lends merit to the Confucian solution which, despite its elitist nature, did not ignore the moral education of common people. To ensure good governance and social harmony, neither personal quality nor institutional quality can be ignored. While to drive a horse requires the bridle, it also requires an experienced driver. A state cannot become governed without laws, but nor without a virtuous people. Systematic cultivation of virtues would make people follow laws on their own behalf, thus reducing the need to actually use material rewards and punishments (as both can be materially expensive) and making it possible to enforce laws at an affordable cost. Thus, the Confucian program is committed to the making of virtuous gentlemen (*Junzi*) with moral integrity and somehow putting them in office.

A society can sustain harmony only when the personal moral status is matched with the political status. To ultimately transcend the trap of the Prisoner's Dilemma, society must make sure that its rulers and, if possible, ordinary members possess a stable moral incentive structure different from that of a narrowly rational individual. The social function of Confucian *Li* lies precisely in its offering a unified moral code (a "constitution") for the traditional Chinese society, which served to socialize every young generation and make trustworthy adults through conscious cultivation of virtues.[52]

The Confucian Solution to Social Dilemma: Rule of Virtue

Perhaps the best argument for the significance of moral virtues still comes from Xunzi. Although Xunzi shares with his Legalist disciples the assumption that human nature is essentially bad (but more below), he also recognizes the innate potential of moral transformation in every individual and its necessity for social harmony. He believed that a good government must be capable of taking a variety of measures, and must not only imposes laws, but also positively engage in the transformation of human nature. The sage-kings, he asserts, "created the propriety (*Li*) and righteousness (*Yi*) to transform them, instituted laws and governmental measures to rule them, and made punishment severe to restrain them, so that all will result in good order and be in accord with goodness. Such is the government of sage-kings and the transforming influence of propriety and righteousness."[53] Thus, laws and punishments are but one way of governing a state; the other condition, equally indispensable, is the cultivation of virtues to become a Confucian gentleman through the influence of *Li* and *Yi*. Indeed, for Xunzi, Confucian gentlemen play a pivotal role in a harmonious society:

> *Heaven and earth are the beginning of life generations; propriety and righteousness are the beginning of good government; the gentleman is the beginning of propriety and righteousness.... Without gentlemen Heaven and earth would be out of order, propriety and righteousness would be without rulership; there would be no [order among] kings and teachers above, and fathers and sons below. This is the extreme of chaos.*[54]

Thus, just like Mengzi quoted at the beginning of the chapter, Xunzi also sees a rationally selfish society as one filled with conflict, strives, and violence. Unlike his Legalist students, Han Fei and Li Si, Xunzi clearly understood that order in society could not be guaranteed solely by the laws; legal order would be short-lived without a secure moral foundation. For him, precisely because human nature is flawed, moral practice, learning and education, and cultivation of virtues are all the more necessary to transform a natural person in order to live a decent social life.

If it is impossible to secure basic harmony through the Legalist approach based on rational choice, still less is it possible to secure collective actions for the well-being and prosperity of any large society. As Popkins observes,[55] even in relatively small Southeast Asian villages, it was exceedingly difficult for rational peasants to undertake collective actions—especially on large scale—for promoting the common good of their communities.[56] The problem of size is especially acute for the Chinese society ever since its great unification achieved by the Qin dynasty over 2000 years ago. Although voluntary collective action was still feasible through repeated interactions in traditional villages of relatively small size, it would practically be impossible in a vast empire unified under a single monarch who was equipped solely with legal force without moral legitimacy. Equally subject to the fear for punishments to be administered from the top of the ruling pyramid, mass subjects in a large society could not find a single group that has the rational incentive to organize collective actions for the good of all. Indeed, everyone would rather seek to act against laws and evade punishments whenever propitious time seems to have arrived. As Mengzi eloquently points out to the King Hui of Liang at the very beginning of the chapter, states governed by the principle of self-interest would soon be filled with violence, deceptions, treacheries, and patricide. And such episodes did break out, sometimes frequently, in Chinese history. Yet, although social peace was periodically erupted by violent riots and repressions, harmony and a degree of prosperity were nevertheless not uncommon in the Chinese history. Collective actions and, more generally, cooperative social activities did seem to take place routinely in traditional China after its grand unification,[57] a fact contrary to the gloomy prediction of rational choice theory made for a large egocentric society.

How had the traditional Chinese society managed to resolve the Prisoner's Dilemma and maintain a basic degree of harmony and prosperity? The answer lies, again, in the teaching of Mengzi: long-term peace and harmony arrive only in those societies which are governed by the guiding principles of humanity and righteousness. But human societies are not endowed with these principles as birth rights; they must be acquired through conscious human efforts and, in traditional China, these efforts culminated in the practice of Confucian *Li*, which prescribed a uniform program for moral development with the aim to maintain a harmonious social relationship. For this purpose, as we have seen, the political and legal unifications are insufficient—indeed they would aggravate the problem by enlarging the scale of community. What the Confucians had contributed was the moral unification which allowed the Imperial administration to be carried out at the local level and, at the same time, enabled the numerous localities to cohabit peacefully together on the vast territory. Consistent with the rational choice argument, collective actions in such a large society are made possible not by the uniformity of laws, but by breaking down an indistinguishably egocentric population into numerous local conclaves where a small leading group would have the incentive—rational and moral—to initiate actions that will benefit (though perhaps unequally) every member of the community. In the meantime, the uniform practice of *Li* as a social constitution and the common belief in the basic values contained therein had, for the better part of Chinese history, held the different units of society together and maintained a harmonious relationship among them. In other words, the Chinese unification *was* achieved by military force and facilitated by the uniformity of laws, but it was sustained peacefully over time only by a common moral system prescribed in *Li* and supported by the Confucian gentlemen who had succeeded in acquiring moral virtues through the practice of *Li*.

Although the Confucian gentlemen might be at all times a minority, it can plausibly be argued that society does need this minority as the nucleus, as it were, whose unifying force binds the different components that would otherwise fall apart. Without them, a society of egocentric individuals would become totally demoralized, and everyone would plunge into "rational" calculations of his self-interest, leading to myopic and self-destructive behaviors that render long-term cooperation impossible. As Elster observes,[58] the chance for collective action is significantly enhanced if society contains a core of few privileged members subscribed to the altruistic norm, with the effect of encouraging the average population who submit to the fairness principle (basic reciprocity) to join and thus enlarge the scope of cooperation. To create such a normative core by which social cooperation can take place at a larger scale, the Confucians made a further step along the rational choice direction: they did not leave the acquisition of virtues to solitary individuals alone and for its own reward, for that would be beyond the average human ability; rather, they maintained the system of *Li* to engage every member of society in the common practice of what they saw as virtuous activities beneficial to society, and established social and political institutions which would positively reward virtues and punish vices.

As a prominent example, the traditional state examination system established the earliest civil service based on merit in the world, permitting only those familiar with Confucian classics to attain high political status and social privileges. In this way the Confucians created a group of gentlemen distributed all over the empire, who were united by the common Confucian values and norms, and were in various ways motivated to enforce these norms throughout the empire. It was this same group of gentlemen, both constrained and motivated by the Confucian norms, that took charge of local administrations and enabled the Imperial court to keep a distance from the daily details of local affairs while maintaining its theoretical supremacy.[59] In this way, the vast empire was no longer an undifferentiated whole composed of egocentric parts, each trapped in the Prisoner's Dilemma. Rather, the core of morally united gentlemen had both moral (virtue as its own reward) and material (social and political privileges) incentives to uphold *Li* as a constitution for entire society. The ordinary people were likewise motivated to follow these common norms, both for internal (gratification or suffering derived from the internalized norms) and external (material rewards and punishments arising from the coercive enforcement) reasons. The norms common to all inhabitants, which constituted a social constitution, gave rise to stable expectation and formed effective constraints to the social behaviors of all, whether the upper or lower class. Only such a society, I argue, can sustain mutual trust among its members and make large-scale cooperation possible. It was precisely the common value and norm structure, enforced by the practice of *Li* as a constitution of society, that had united a numerous and geographically scattered population and enabled it to transcend the Prisoner's Dilemma.

It might be objected, as the Legalist had done earlier, that the process of moral education is lengthy, cumbersome, costly, and inefficient. To be sure, this objection is valid to an extent. The Confucian program of *Li* involved "expenses" and could not guarantee success in every individual case. Indeed, avowed adherents who meticulously followed the procedures prescribed by *Li* might turn out to be hypocrites, who pretended to follow *Li* only to better pursue their own interests. It was quite likely that only an indefinite portion of the practitioners of the *Li* would become genuine gentlemen who truly acquired moral virtues in the process. Nor was there guarantee that the small minority of gentlemen would always succeed in keeping society in a high moral standard and maintaining social cooperation without being overwhelmed by the destructive forces coming either from a corrupted court above or from the apathetic self-interested mass below, both driven by purely private desires. Yet these possibilities do not defeat the argument that the cultivation of virtue serves a positive social function. After all, having shown the insufficiency of stringent laws and punishments, it seems impossible to sustain a society in which everyone behaves purely out of self-interest against (at least indifferent to) the needs of others. Comparatively, "rule of virtue" led by a group of gentlemen, sharing the same moral conviction and spreading it throughout society, offers much more durable bond than the Legalist regime which relied upon a single despot isolated in the center of the court. The program of "virtue-making," however lengthy and socially expensive, might prove ultimately indispensable to the order of traditional Chinese society. At the very least, while the degree of enlightened rationality of a monarch is left entirely to chance factors, whether hereditary idiosyncrasy or vicissitudes of court struggles, the making of Confucian gentlemen is guaranteed to have a constant, albeit small, yield.

Thus, it seems that the Confucian stepwise program—from the acquisition of knowledge and cultivation of personal virtues, to the establishment of family, and finally to the governing of the state and entire society—as described in the *Great Learning* (大学 *Daxue*), a prominent chapter of *Liji*, created a self-regulating, decentralized social order permeating the separate levels of individuals, families and the state. Otherwise, given the state of technology and communication at the time, China would never have been able to maintain a unified civilization over such a diverse population on such an extended territory and for such a long time. Far more than uniform laws and edicts, it was shared moral ideas and practices, embodied in *Li* as the common "constitution" of society, that made a durable civilization possible. The Qin dynasty, founded upon rule of penal law and terror of punishment, did create the first political and legal unification and, with it, the material conditions for a unified civilization (including, e.g. a uniform written language and weights and measures). But, relying on material incentives alone and without a common moral constitution shared by society, it proved incapable of sustaining itself. This also explains why the Legalist revivals in the Chinese history were always ephemeral and why Confucianism had dominated Chinese tradition for so long.[60] Measured by the criteria of social harmony and cooperative capacity, the decentralized Confucian society, led by the rule of virtue and harmonized by the uniform practice of *Li*, possessed some decisive advantages over the Legalist centralized state based on the egocentric ideal of impartial wisdom from above and the fear of punishments from below. Despite many potential weaknesses, the basic tenet of the Confucian position is overall easier to defend because it is more moderate and closer to human nature. The Confucian belief in the innate ability of moral transformation and improvement in every human being had made it possible (and meaningful) to devise a moral system aimed to systematically produce gentlemen who, committed to the moral principle of humanity and righteousness, constitute a necessary ingredient for every cooperative society.

Human Nature, Li, and Education: The Making of Gentleman

Few if any are born gentlemen of virtues. If one takes a survey on the philosophical views of human nature, the mean is likely not far from the Hobbesian position that human beings are born unfit for society.[61] Left alone and morally uneducated, they would remain egocentric and mutually distrustful animals, who are permanently trapped in the Prisoner's Dilemma and universal defections, fighting a war of "all against all" which endangers such basic social good as peace, security, and harmony. East and West, philosophers widely agree with the Aristotelian definition that moral virtues are primarily acquired habits rather than natural faculties endowed at birth. Socrates wondered early on, for example, that the virtues of great Athenian generals did not pass on to their offspring.[62] Put in modern "scientific" language, moral virtues, unlike intellectual faculties, are not genetically inheritable; if anything, they are socially transmitted from one generation to another to guarantee the basic continuity of social life. In the long process of social interactions, human beings discover those basic moral norms indispensable to harmonious and prosperous living, and seek to internalize these norms as an integral part of human habit. As every human generation cannot afford the cost of rediscovering such knowledge anew, it is passed on to younger generations, often as rules and commands that require unreflecting subscription. The Chinese system of *Li* was but one example, upheld by the Confucians as a necessary means of making good individuals and a harmonious society. Human being is to be made virtuous, it was believed, through continuous learning, education, and conscious practice of activities prescribed by Confucian *Li*.

Although Confucians agree generally on the importance of *Ren*, *Yi*, and *Li*, they are divided into two major schools on the basic assumptions of human nature and, as a result, on the ways to inculcate human virtues. While Mengzi assumes that a person is born with a heart-mind (*xin*) that makes him naturally "good" (*shan*), Xunzi believes that a person is born with insatiable desires that makes him naturally "bad" (*er*), and the only hope lies in his innate ability to improve his nature through continuous learning and reformation. "Human nature is bad," he says, and "his goodness is only acquired training."[63] Based on this assumption Xunzi asserts that the institution of propriety (*Li*) is necessary for social order and prosperity. On the other hand, the more optimistic view of human nature furthered by Mengzi *can* be interpreted in such a way as to denigrate the elaborate system of *Li* as a superfluity that distract mankind from a sincere internal search, the proper method to rediscover and regain one's good nature. But under the reconstruction of Dong Zhongshu, the great Confucian during the Han dynasty, the Mengzian view was made compatible with that of Xunzi on the necessity of *Li*.

The apparent difference between the two rival theories about human nature arises partly from the confusing notion of "nature" (性*xing*) itself, and the contribution of Dong Zhongshu was to clarify such a confusion. Although he concedes to Mengzi that human being has the innate potential to become "good," Dong criticizes Mengzi for confusing what is merely potential with the actual, and agrees with Xunzi that "the nature of all people depends on training, which is external, before it becomes good. Therefore goodness has to do with training and not with nature."[64] He proceeds further by analogical reasoning: "the silk cocoon contains [potential] silk but it is not yet silk, and the egg contains the [potential] chicken but it is not yet a chicken."[65] To put in another way, human nature is essentially dormant, and before it is awakened, "it may be said to possess the basic substance to become good but it cannot be said that it is already good."[66] Thus, while Mengzi speaks of human nature in terms of unique human potentiality absent in lower animals, Dong's notion of "nature" (consistent with that of Xunzi) refers to the developed and matured good character as manifested in the sage. Mengzi failed to make this distinction, he argues, as "human nature may be compared to the rice stalks and goodness to rice. Rice comes out of the rice stalk but not all the stalk becomes rice. Similarly goodness comes out of nature but not all nature becomes good."[67] Although Dong may be unnecessarily harsh on Mengzi, who insists only that human beings have sprouts (*duan*) for humanity and righteousness, and does acknowledge the role of moral cultivation and education,[68] his observation seems to be in order in the sense that the Mengzian view of human nature, if understood too optimistically, *can* lead to neglect of moral education. Once the conceptual confusion about "nature" is removed, however, the two views are essentially consistent. Both schools do acknowledge the malleability and transformative ability of human nature and the necessity of moral education, differing perhaps only in the degree of significance attached to *Li* as the means for cultivating virtues.

In the Confucian view elaborated by Dong Zhongshu, a person is born an incomplete animal, who possesses the innate potentiality to be good, but falls short of being actually good. In other words, nature did not provide everything for mankind; it leaves to human beings to complete themselves through their own efforts.

The activity of Heaven extends to a certain point and then stops. What stops within the operation of Heaven is called human nature endowed by Heaven, and what stops outside the operation of Heaven is called human activity. Human activity lies outside of human nature, and yet it is inevitable that [through training] human nature will become virtuous.[69]

It is precisely the need for the reformation of an unformed character that makes the practice of *Li* so indispensable to a human society. This is why we need a government that honors the virtuous gentlemen and actively inculcates the virtues among the people. "The people receive from Heaven a nature which cannot be good [by itself], and they turn to the king to receive the training which completes their nature. It is the duty of the king to obey the will of Heaven and to complete the nature of the people."[70] Otherwise, "if the nature of all people are already good, then what duty is there for the king to fulfill when he receives the mandate from Heaven?"[71]

Measured against the criteria of modern science, Dong Zhongshu's view of human nature might appear rudimentary and underdeveloped, but it does find empirical support from the cultural and anthropological studies, which received the first inspiration from Rousseau. Rousseau believed that human rationality is the result of socialization and that primitive human beings, being presocial, were also "pre-rational"; human rationality was developed only along with the development of associative activities which constituted human cultures and societies.[72] The modern

from weakness can emerge strength

expositions of this idea have been summarized by cultural anthropologists and sociologists. Geertz points out, for example, that we are "incomplete and unfinished animals who complete or finish ourselves through culture."[73] As "incomplete and unfinished" animals from bare genetic inheritance, human beings are made complete only by learning from and participating in cultural activities. The same point is made by Berger and Luckmann, who observes that, for other higher animals, the world has already been "programmed,"[74] as it were, properly for each species; for *Homo sapiens*, however, the world is yet to be made. Unlike bees and birds that are born with the knowledge to build their nests, beavers to erect dam, and baboons to organize themselves, human infants are endowed with little knowledge and few capacities to enable them to lead a mature and self-reliant life through a complex variety of social interactions. While non-human animals acquire highly specialized and firmly directed drives at their births, a human being is *not* born with a instinctual structure proper to his species-specific environment, and such a structure does not become mature and fixed until the child has fully interacted with the external world and "internalized" the values of the society.[75] In a word, genetically speaking, human being is an unfinished animal, only to be finished by his social activities which he shares with the other members of society.

There appears to be an "information gap," then, between the human genetic endowment and the mature capacity that the necessity of rational social life requires every individual to possess. And this gap is filled only by such culturally invented social devices as customs, conventions and rules— the knowledge for practical social life transmitted from one generation to another through the cultural tradition. The built-in plasticity, immaturity and instability of individual human organism give rise to the social imperative to provide a stable cultural environment for human development.[76] Children are made mature and capable only by learning from the culture which carries the extra-genetic information for handling the organized social life; it would be impossible for human society to carry on were every generation obliged to discover and promulgate its own moral codes. To the contrary, basic rules and norms must be given to the children in order to prepare them for social lives. A key function of Confucian *Li* was precisely to provide the means for socialization of every young generation according to a uniform value pattern commonly accepted by society.

Since the moral training naturally begins in one's formative years, Confucian *Li* carried a detailed account of an elaborate program designed for the moral education of the young generations. The education of youth was doubtless an essential part of *Li*, as "Jade will not form a vessel without being cut; man cannot know the Way without learning. Thus the ancient kings, in building a kingdom and governing a people, place instruction and learning in the first priority."[77] From the Book of Rites (*Liji*) we find an admirably enlightened program of education designed to fit both the social needs and the developmental capacity of the child.[78] From very early on, children in virtually every family received training in the basic filial duty and respect for parents, which Confucians believed to be the very foundation of moral virtues. At early age children were taught with the popularized version of Confucian classics. Thereafter, children (presumably of well-to-do families) would follow a progressively developed program to study music, poetry, and basic social skills, by which the youth would be exposed to the preliminary influence of *Li*. The formal study of *Li* began at 20, the year of "capping" for male. Living at a school away from home, the students was supposed to discuss the meaning of *Li* closely with their teacher and colleagues, a process through which the teacher and the students would make progress together in moral learning and development.

Thus, through continuous learning and practices, and through the positive efforts of transforming human characters in order to achieve interpersonal harmony, *Li* made it practicable for all members of society to cooperate and engage in collective production of social goods. The socially integrative and morally transforming functions of *Li* turned out to be indispensable to an orderly and cooperative society, which cannot be sustained by law and punishment alone. As the French political philosopher Montesquieu observes perspicaciously:

> *Punishments will cast out of society a citizen, who, having lost his mores, violates the laws, but if everyone loses his mores, punishment will not reestablish them. Thus, when one abandoned the principle of Chinese government, when morality was lost there, the state fell into anarchy and one saw revolutions.*[79]

This observation was attested by the disruptive experience of modern Chinese history following heedless revolts against the traditional moral order.

THE MAY-FOURTH MOVEMENT AND BEYOND

Despite sporadic challenges from the Legalist reformers or otherwise, Confucian *Li* had remained the guiding moral system throughout Chinese history. This continuous cultural tradition was fatally disrupted, however, by the western ideas accompanied with its economic and military intrusions since the middle of the nineteenth century. China's repeated failure to respond in timely fashion to these challenges cast doubts on the sacrosanctity of its traditional values and norms embodied in *Li*, and forced Chinese intellectuals on all fronts to undertake critical reflections upon the cultural tradition from which they had hitherto derived much pride. Agitated by domestic crises and international failures, these reflections led to a series of modernization efforts that ultimately proved detrimental to the old political and social regime.[80] The elimination of the traditional examination system (1905) and the collapse of the Imperial court (1911) removed the political support for the moral hegemony of Confucian *Li*, and opened the possibility of systematic challenges against the traditional moral practices. Once again China was thrown back, literally, to the period of Warring States. Reviving the historical debates among the Confucians, Daoists, Mohists, and Legalists over 2000 years ago, and under the great awakening influence of the western ideas—whether liberal, Marxist, or social Darwinian, Chinese intellectuals of all convictions joined the debates about the desirability of the Confucian cultural tradition.[81] While the cultural conservatives took the maintenance of traditional rules and norms as necessary for social harmony and the general well-being of the people, the liberals challenged *Li* for suppressing personality, spontaneity and individual freedom, and the Marxists equated *Li* with nothing but the institutional device for class suppression in the interest of the ruling gentry and an impediment to modernization.[82] Only this time, the conservatives were on the losing side. First with the liberal democratic influence and then with the Communist infection spreading from the new Soviet Russia, the cultural debates decidedly took a radical left turn and culminated in the May-Fourth Movement (1919). Since then the traditional "teachings of *Li*" (*lijiao*) suffered from vehement attacks from the radical intellectuals. If *Li* was taken before to be the basis of an eternal and perfect order, indispensable to individual success and social harmony, now it became the ultimate scapegoat for every backwardness and impotence of China before the foreign powers, and was to be ruthlessly swept aside as the major blockade on the road to modernization. In the name of modernity the traditional norms, if not immediately thrown out, were gradually cast aside. As a result, the entire value system crumbled in the twentieth century, leaving virtually a moral vacuum in Chinese society, the effects of which are felt even today in the modernizing China.

The painful aftermath of the historical destruction of the traditional moral system had frustrated the radical expectation for Chinese modernization. In their effort to renovate the Chinese culture, the radical intellectuals overlooked the need for the continuity of cultural tradition as the prerequisite for establishing a social order and maintaining basic harmony; they attacked *Li* relentlessly and advocated a total westernization of Chinese society. While the old ideas were discredited and ceased to govern the people's mind, motley of new ideas were yet fighting among themselves to gain social currency. Without a common norm shared by society—at least by the elites of Chinese society, the vast empire could no longer sustain itself, and warlords were quick to announce their reign over segmented territories. The destruction of the old regime was not followed by the establishment of a stable new order, and the nation, hopelessly divided by a myriad of conflicting interests without a common identity, plunged into a long series of wars that shattered the original dream for radical progress. Amid the chaos of foreign invasions and civil wars, China was to be reunited only under a totalitarian principle. The moral vacuum left by the May-Fourth Movement had accrued enormous social cost in human lives, happiness, and material goods. In light of the past failures of Imperial reforms, the painful aftermath of repudiating the traditional normative system, and the contemporary decline in the strength of the Marxist ideology concomitant with the recognition of the urgent need for unifying values, a debate over the practical desirability for maintaining Confucian values and norms as embodied in *Li* is as relevant today as it was 90 years ago.[83]

The Chinese experience following the May-Fourth Movement suggests, once again, that social harmony and progress could not be maintained without a minimum sharing of social values and norms. It is consistent with the traditional Confucian wisdom that a harmonious and cooperative society cannot, as the May-Fourth Marxists and the Legalist of the Warring State had commonly supposed, exist in a moral vacuum. The Legalist experiments with rule of law failed, of course, partly for failing to incorporate democracy, but I believe that my basic conclusions still hold for modern societies committed to democracy and rule of law since such regimes are premised on the same rationalist foundation on which traditional Legalism is based. The historical efficacy of Confucian *Li* lied Lay in its integrative functions by which it held the immense Chinese society together. It was no less than a social constitution commonly upheld, at least by the privileged elites, throughout a numerous people residing in a vast territory, making it possible to maintain local autonomy and resist centralized tyranny without formally incorporating modern democracy. It embodied the moral consensus of society on the fundamental values primarily reflected in the Confucian teachings of humanity and righteousness. It contained an admirable education program, which provided the primary means of socialization for the children and by which the basic moral values were internalized in the minds of the younger generations. It prescribed regular ritual activities at both the national and the local levels, in order to continuously reassert the original meaning of cultural symbols among ordinary members of society. By producing the gentlemen of Confucian virtues in every generation, who were committed to the basic moral principles of humanity and righteousness, by which they were able to transcend the narrow rationality centered on self-interest, the traditional Chinese society resolved its own Prisoner's Dilemma, which would have otherwise imprisoned itself in the interlocking miseries of mutual defections, antagonism, poverty, and civil wars.

This chapter is written partly as a defense for the historical social functions of Confucian *Li*. My purpose is not, however, to attribute praises and blames, but to highlight the lessons that our society today may find useful to remember. In the age of internet, it would be a truism to say that the bulk of Confucian *Li* had long been antiquated. In a world where fundamentally different values meet with and clash against one another, perhaps moral pluralism is the only tenable position that gains consensus among the human race brought up in so many different cultures. But even in our global (or globalizing) village, where technological improvements confer new outlook to the world every day, do we not need, just as the Chinese did over two millennia ago, a harmonious and minimally cooperative society to pursue our daily productive activities? Do we not need some basic common rules and norms governing our behavior and attitudes toward others, which help to inculcate human trust and make social cooperation possible? Do we not need an education system that is capable of making individuals not only intellectually competent, but also morally committed to the basic norms shared by members of society?

The answer to these questions, I assume, is a resounding *yes*. If so, then the central question raised by the debates about *Li* is as relevant to our world today as they were to China 2000 years ago. For we then seem to need a global constitution, as it were, which embodies the common values based on mutual respect among various people, for the provision of the harmony and prosperity in a world whose different parts are increasingly brought together by expanding economies. Only this time, we have learned from the fate of Confucian *Li* and other moral systems of the world that unquestioned and unconditional submission to a dogma will end in its stagnation and, finally, its own demise, and that the moral vacuum it leaves behind would bring back the Prisoner's Dilemma and do havoc to social harmony. To maintain the moral force which can continue to bind our global society together, the global moral system must indeed be a "living constitution," constantly renewing itself in response to the fresh problems and insights arising from human experiences. Only such a living constitution of society can enable us to rise above the dilemmas in an inevitably dilemma-ridden society: harmony but not coerced peace, stability but not stagnancy, progress but not chaos, moral freedom but neither nihilism nor new dogmatism.

This chapter should not end with a wrong impression that I simply support Confucianism against Legalism. As explained in the beginning, my purpose is only to illustrate the Confucian theme that rule of law and a degree of harmony cannot be attained in a moral vacuum, and it is quite beyond the scope of this book to discuss the other half of the theme—how rule of law can contribute to the development of genuine moral commitments and social harmony. Yet, it should be quite obvious that the causal relationship is far from unidirectional, and that the moral and the legal aspects of social life are mutually reinforcing to make a more harmonious society. In fact, both harmony and rule of law are the overarching rhythms in China's political symphony today, and they are pursued in a political environment where *Li* had been replaced with the Chinese version of the Marxist ideology. China's experience has proved, however, that moral preaching alone hardly accomplishes anything, and may even become dangerous when it is done by the state. Besides its obvious danger for infringing one's moral autonomy and creating a dogmatic society blind to moral and institutional alternatives, the state monopoly of moral education, which the Confucians delightfully insisted for centuries, utterly failed in contemporary China. It has produced not "gentlemen" in any sense, but petty hypocrites who are good at taking full advantages of the political monopoly. Without a legal environment and institutional mechanisms that enable ordinary people to vindicate their legitimate interest and actually feel the benefits of rule of law, they simply cannot trust the words printed in laws and develop commitments to the moral ideals defined therein.[84] We need a more sophisticated understanding not only of rule of law, but also of rule of virtue. This simply means that Confucianism has not only a role to play in our world, but also plenty of rooms to improve and evolve in future.

NOTES

1. This is not to say, of course, that different schools would agree on the exact conception of harmony. These schools may well differ as to what constitutes a good society. For example, while harmony as a good social order may stand for a variety of goods for a Confucian, it may be reduced to bare peace for a Legalist. In fact, although the concept of harmony figures prominently in Confucianism, it is hardly mentioned in Legalist works, and what is viewed by the Legalists as good order under rule of law might not at all amount to Confucian harmony, in which the order defined in *Li* is to be fully realized. Yet, this chapter defines "harmony" generically rather than from any particular perspective, and limits its scope to most basic elements of a reasonably "good" society, including peace, order, security, adequate supplies for living and free from arbitrary abuses of the government. It seems reasonable to hold that all schools agree upon these basic ideals, and such a minimal reading of "harmony" is more likely to afford a common platform on which different schools may exchange and carry out arguments.

2. See, for example, Francis Fukuyama, *The End of History and the Last Man* (New York: Avon Books, 1992).

3. Here the word *li* (利) is equivalently translated as benefits or, more generally, self-interest. There are disagreements about the precise meaning and adequate translations of *Yi* (义). Compare Chung-ying Cheng, *New Dimensions of Confucian and Neo-Confucian Philosophy* (Albany: State University of New York Press,1991), 233–243; and David L. Hall and Roger T. Ames, "Getting It Right: On Saving Kongzi from Confucians," *Philosophy East and West* 34 (1984), 3–14. These debates are only tangentially relevant to this chapter since it focuses rather exclusively on *Li*. Here, these concepts simply serve as moral basis for social norms expressed in *Li*, which constrains human behavior against the temptation of self-interest.

4. *Mengzi*, 1A1.

5. The similar idea is expressed in his reply to a Mohist student, Song Keng, who was on his way to dissuade the kings of Qin and Chu from engaging in a war, with the utilitarian argument in mind that the war would be "against their interest" (不利*buli*) (*Mengzi*, 6B4).

6. This alliance may appear somewhat surprising, but it is not far from truth. The liberal wing of the May-Fourth Movement, represented by

Hu Shi and early Chen Duxiu, is very close to the rational choice school in its individualistic and utilitarian spirit. The Marxist wing, represented by Li Dazhao and later Chen Duxiu, is not reducible to rational choice individualism, but it shares with the Legalist school in its primary concern of material interest—class if not individual interest. The close proximity between Legalism and Chinese Marxism is further attested by the fact that, although the May-Fourth Marxists did not formally profess to be Legalist, their direct descendants—the Chinese Communists who eventually succeeded in taking over the political power—explicitly sided with Legalism against Confucianism in the political movement of the 1970s.

7. The "core versions" are represented by the Virginia and the Rochester schools, see Gabriel A. Almond, *A Discipline Divided: Schools and Sects in Political Science* (Newbury Park, CA: SAGE, 1990), 19.

8. For representative works, see James M. Buchanan and Gordon Tullock, *The Calculus of Consent: Logical Foundation of Constitutional Democracy* (Ann Arbor: University of Michigan Press, 1962); William H. Riker, *Liberalism Against Popularism: A Confrontation between the Theory of Democracy and the Theory of Social Choice* (San Francisco: Freeman, 1982); and Barry R. Weingast, "The Political Foundation of Democracy and the Rule of Law," *American Political Science Review* 91 (1997): 245–263.

9. See, for example, Kenneth J. Arrow, *Social Choice and Individual Values* (2nd Ed.) (New Haven, CO: Yale University Press, 1963); Mancur Olson, *The Logic of Collective Action: Public Goods and the Theory of Groups* (Cambridge, MA: Harvard University Press, 1971).

10. See, for example, Lon L. Fuller, *The Morality of Law* (New Haven, CO: Yale University Press, 1969), 33–41.

11. Olson, *The Logic of Collective Action*. I follow Russell Hardin in using the word "rational" in its narrow sense, that is, instrumental rationality with regard to one's self-interest, which includes those items usually desired by an ordinary person, such as honor and material gain. Russell Hardin, *Collective Action* (Baltimore: Johns Hopkins University, 1982), 9.

12. The word *Li* has been translated variously as rites, rituals, proprieties, etiquette, and ceremonies. As *Li* embraces all these meanings, no single translation is best or even adequate. Following Wing-tsit Chan, I translate 礼记 (*Liji*) as the *Book of Rites* (but 礼治 *lizhi* as "rule of propriety").

13. Jean-Jacques Rousseau, *On the Social Contract*, trans. Donald A. Cress (Indianapolis: Hackett, 1987), 48.

14. I argue elsewhere for the adequacy of formally characterizing *Li* as a social constitution. See Zhang Qianfan, "Rule of Virtue, Rule of Law, and Constitutionalism," *Studies of Law and Commerce*, 2 (2002), 34–39. For the limitations of self-interested individualism and the necessity for some moral commitments, see Robert N. Bellah et al., *Habits of the Heart: Individualism and Commitment in American Life* (Berkeley: University of California Press, 1985).

15. The view represented by Parsons and other functionalists is sometimes associated with the so-called functionalist fallacy, which essentially justifies a particular social arrangement by the integrative social functions it serves. Talcott Parsons, *The Social System* (New York: The Free Press, 1951); Talcott Parsons and Edward A. Shils ed., *Toward a General Theory of Action* (Cambridge, MA: Harvard University Press, 1954). For reasons not fully elaborated here, while I partly accept the Marxist critique of the functionalist approach in that it tends to overemphasize the role of social integration and neglect the pervasive social conflicts in reality, I nevertheless agree with the functionalist school that a minimal degree of social integration is necessary for sustaining a cooperative society, which is good for *all* rather than just particular segment(s) of society.

16. For the categorization of these two types of justifications as "negative" and "positive," see A.S. Cua, "Dimensions of *Li* (propriety): Reflections on an Aspect of Hsun Tzu's Ethics," *Philosophy East and West* 29 (1979):373–382; "*Li and Moral Justification: A Study in the Li Chi*," *Philosophy East and West* 33 (1983): 1–17.

17. *Mengzi*, 5B7.

18. For arguments justifying *Li* as a "process of humanization," see Tu Weiming, "The Creative Tension between Jen and Li," *Philosophy East and West*, 18 (1968), 29–38; Tu Weiming, "*Li* as a Process of Humanization," in *Humanity and Self-Cultivation: Essays in Confucian Thought* (Berkeley: Asian Humanities Press, 1979), 3–20.

19. See, for example, Jiang Qing, "From Heart-Nature Confucianism to Political Confucianism," in Liu Shu-xian et al., *Collection of Papers on Contemporary Neo-Confucianism* (Taipei: Wenjing Press, 1991), 153–178.

20. See Lin Yu-sheng, *Thoughts and Characters* (Taipei: Lianjing Press, 1983), 121–140 for an argument for the dialectical relationship between *Ren* and *Li*.

21. In this chapter, I take 礼记*Liji* and 荀子*Xunzi*, as the authoritative expositions of Confucian rites since these two works contain the most elaborate expositions on the nature of *Li*. To be sure, *Liji* is only the "exposition" (记*ji*) of *Li*, above which there are two "classics" (经*jing*): 仪礼*Yili* and 周礼*Zhouli*. For an overall introduction, see Li Ri-gang et al. ed., *A Collection of Studies on the Three Li* (Taipei: Cultural Enterprise Press, 1981), 1–12. But, while *Yili* is widely and justly seen as arcane and out-dated, the origin and authenticity of *Zhouli* are still debated. Xu Fu-guan, *The Time of the Writing of Zhouguan and Its Intellectual Characters* (Taipei: Student Books, 1980); Jin Chun-Feng, *New Examination of the Time of Zhouguan's Writing and the Culture and the Epoch It Reflected* (Taipei: Dongda Book Press, 1993). *Liji* thus seems to be the best source of authority on *Li*, because its scope is comprehensive, because it is most accessible and scholarly annotated, and because it contains most relevant arguments for the justifications of *Li*.

22. See Hu Shih, "The Natural Law in the Chinese Tradition," in E.F. Barrett ed., *Natural Law Institute Proceeding* 5 (1953): 142–144.

23. Montesquieu observes, with his usual perspicacity, that Confucian *Li* penetrated everything in traditional China: "Legislators of China confused laws, mores, and manners; this is because mores represent laws, and manners represent mores. The principal object of the Chinese legislators was to have their people live in tranquility.... Therefore, they extended the rules of civility to a great many people." Montesquieu, *The Spirit of the Laws*, trans. Anne Cohler et al. (Cambridge: Cambridge University Press, 1989), 317.

24. Thus, "if a sage can strengthen his state thereby, he will not imitate antiquity; if he can benefit the people thereby, he will not follow the established *Li*." *Lord Shang*, "The Reform of the Law," 1:3; see J.J.L. Duyvendak, *The Book of Lord Shang* (Chicago: University of Chicago Press, 1963), 169–170.

25. The Marxists would reduce all ideological debates to the clash of economic interests—in this case between the "feudal" gentry class controlling local administration and the central bureaucracy allied with the "capitalist"-spirited merchants. Although the realist elements in the intellectual debates cannot be entirely dismissed (the Legalist reforms, for example, would obviously undermine the socio-economic status of the court nobility and the gentry class), the realist reduction nevertheless ignored the philosophical underpinning of the debates

over the state's economic policies and the practical impact they necessarily had on the ordinary social lives, with a scope far broader than a mere court struggle relevant solely to the selfish interests of participating parties.

26. I do not mean to pit Confucianism against Legalism as two opposite and mutually repugnant schools of thought, for the validity of such exaggerated opposition would be clearly refuted by the imperial practice in Chinese history. As QuTongzu suggests, the Confucians at the early Han dynasty were actively absorbing the Legalist techniques in order to make Confucianism a practicable instrument for government. The result of such effort is that the Confucian norms became codified in formal codes (hence the "Confucianization" of laws). QuTongzu, *Chinese Society and Chinese Law* (Beijing: Chung Hwa Book Co., 1981), 328–346. The Chinese empire had been effectively governed, then, by the combination of Confucian morals and Legalist techniques. The question here is not the necessity (which Confucians did not deny), but their sufficiency (on which the Legalist seemed to have insisted), of rewards and punishments for maintaining a state. The Confucians duly recognized that laws, rewards, and punishments were necessary means that any government must employ; they denied only that laws and punishments should be taken as the exclusive means of governing a society, especially when they were used to achieve nothing but punishment and fear for their own sake.

27. See Benjamin I. Schwartz, *The World of Thought in Ancient China* (Cambridge, MA: Harvard University Press , 1985), 321–349.

28. *Book of Lord Shang*, "The Calculation of Land," 6: 4.

29. *Hanfeizi*, "Five Vermin," 49: 7.

30. *Hanfeizi*, "Prominent Doctrines"; 50: 8, trans. Chan, *Source Book in Chinese Philosophy*, 254.

31. See Esson M. Galetrans, *Discourses on Salt and Iron: A Debate on State Control of Commerce and Industry in Ancient China* (Taipei: Cheng Wen Press, 1967), "Introduction."

32. *Discourse on Salt and Iron*, "Punishments and Benevolence," Ch. 55.

33. Yu Ying-Shih, *The Modern Interpretation of Traditional Chinese Thought* (Nanjing: Jiangsu People's Press, 1989), 81–91.

34. For a more thorough analysis of trust and the "paradox of trust" in democratic governance, which has been described by scholars as the institutionalization of distrust, see Julia Tao's contribution in this volume.

35. The Prisoner's Dilemma is a classic case extensively studied in game theory initiated by John von Neumann and Oskar Morgenstern's now classic work, *The Theory of Games and Economic Behavior* (Princeton University Press, 1944). For an introduction, see Edna Ullmann-Margalit, *The Emergence of Norms* (Oxford: Clarendon Press, 1977), 18–73. It can be roughly stated as follows: Suppose two suspects, A and B, are caught and put into separable rooms. The authority makes the same options to each of them (as a part of their common knowledge): if both confess, each will serve five years in prison; if only one confesses, but the other does not, then the first will walk off scot-free (as reward for his confession), while the second will be punished by a ten-year sentence. But if neither of them confesses, then each will be kept in custody for some time before they are released for lack of sufficient evidence. Excluding altruistic motivation (which would have altered the basic payoff structure of the game), if A and B are purely self-interested players without trust toward each other, then both will choose confession, a "dominant strategy" which achieves better outcome for oneself whether the other choose to confess or not, even though both know that the net result (both to be put in prison for five years) is next to the worst results (one of them to be jailed for ten years) and far less desirable than the optimal result that they could have achieved by cooperating (i.e. both refusing to confess). The Prisoner's Dilemma can be extended to multiplayer situations, where each social actor has the choice of cooperating with others or defecting, with the same result: universal defection is a stable "Nash equilibrium," in which defection is the best response for everyone given that everyone else chooses the same strategy. See Jon Elster, *The Cement of Society: Study of Social Order* (Cambridge: Cambridge University Press, 1989), 1–16.

36. Mancur Olson, *The Logic of Collective Action: Public Goods and the Theory of Groups* (Cambridge: Harvard University Press, 1971).

37. Douglas C. North, *Structure and Change in Economic History*, trans. Chen Yu and Luo Huaping (Shanghai: Sanlian Books Press, 1981), 49–65.

38. Garret Hardin, "The Tragedy of the Commons," *Science* 162 (1968): 1243–1248.

39. Since this paper is primarily about the social functions of Chinese *Li*, I will not discuss the related problems in the west, but only mention that the pure rational choice theory of society is frequently challenged

for its difficulties in explaining the apparently non-rational human actions that often prove to be pervasive in society or crucial for certain significant historical developments. For an explanation of the rise of modern capitalism, see, for example, Max Weber, *The Protestant Ethic and the Spirit of Capitalism*, trans. Talcott Parsons (New York: Charles Scribner's Sons, 1958). If everyone is strictly rational and self-interested, as the pure rational choice theory tends to depict, then no one should offer to donate blood or turn out to vote since, in both cases, the cost simply overrides the potential gain. But, fortunately, we do see these and other forms of actions—whether altruistic in nature or not—still occurring at a large scale in liberal democratic societies. North, *Structure and Change in Economic History*, 101–124. Thus, descriptively, the pure rational choice theory seems to be neither accurate nor complete about the empirical aspects of human nature; normatively, it is not appealing because it would leave the basic social dilemma unresolved.

40. For this point, see Jean-Jacques Rousseau, *A Discourse on Inequality*, trans. Maurice Cranston (New York: Penguin Books, 1984), 147: n. 1.

41. See Robert Axelrod, "The Emergence of Cooperation among Egoists," *American Political Science Review* 75 (1981): 306–317; Michael Taylor, *The Possibility of Cooperation*, Cambridge University Press (1987). For an excellent review, see Elinor Ostrom, "A Behavioral Approach to the Rational Choice Theory of Collective Action," *American Political Science Review* 92 (1998): 1–18.

42. See Francis Fukuyama, *Trust: The Social Virtues and the Creation of Prosperity* (New York: Free Press, 1995), 23–32.

43. David Hume, *A Treatise of Human Nature*, ed. Ernest C. Mossner (London: Penguin Books, 1969).

44. See his *Treatise*, Book III, Part II, Sec. V. Thus, "a man, unacquainted with society, could never enter into any engagements with another"; "a promise itself arises entirely from human conventions, and is invented with a view to a certain interest." Hume, *Treatise of Human Nature*, 568, 601. Like the interest group political theorists before Mancur Olson, however, Hume seems to have taken for granted that the Prisoner's Dilemma can be easily resolved once every person perceives the common interest he shares with others and thus will faithfully performs his part of the contract. Unlike Hobbes, he assumes that human beings are generally far-sighted enough to cooperate with one another when they are made aware of their true long-term interest. See Hume, *Treatise of Human Nature*, 575.

45. Hume, *Treatise of Human Nature*, 590–594.
46. Olson, *Logic of Collective Action*, 34, 45.
47. Russell Hardin, *Collective Action* (Baltimore: Johns Hopkins University, 1982), 38–49.
48. It is "impossible for [human beings], of themselves, to observe those rules, in large and polished societies; they establish government, as a new invention to attain their ends...by a more strict execution of justice." Hume, *Treatise of Human Nature*, 594–595.
49. See North, *Structure and Change in Economic History*, 49–65.
50. *Mengzi*, 4A1, trans. Schwartz, *The World of Thought in Ancient China*, 322–323.
51. These two states perished, according to the Confucians, by systematic implementation of the Legalist policies. *Discourses on Salt and Iron*, "Punishments and Benevolence," Ch. 55.
52. Before proceeding further, I must answer one charge made by Francis Fukuyama against the Confucian culture. In *Trust*, Fukuyama characterizes traditional China, together with its peripheral areas under the Confucian influence, as a "low-trust" society, in contrast with the "high-trust" societies like Japan, Germany, and the prewar USA (in which the trust, according to him, has declined in the last few decades). Fukuyama's main argument is that the Confucian ethics had been primarily family- (rather than group-) oriented, and had failed to recognize general duties to society; mutual trust, expectations, and obligations were strictly limited to small circles within the family, beyond which these terms would even lose their meanings. Fukuyama, *Trust*, 61–82, 84–94. As a result, the Chinese businesses have been managed primarily either by wealthy families (as is the case in Hong Kong and Taiwan) or by the state (in the prereform Communist China). Fukuyama seems to suggest that, between the family and state, traditional China had no institutional and normative means for making a trustful and cooperative society, and that monarchical despotism had been the only power that held the anomic families together. Fukuyama, *Trust*, 56–57.

If this picture were true, however, Confucianism would only be an extended version of Legalism in which rational families replaced rational individuals. But from the discussions carried out so far, this was obviously not the case. Conceding the quintessential position of family in Confucianism, I nevertheless contend that Fukuyama has mistakenly characterized traditional Chinese society. Although duties to one's family override duties to other members in society and even to the state, these duties are far from mutually exclusive. Even a cursory reading of *Liji* would convey a more complex picture that Confucian *Li* prescribed a densely overlapping network of mutual obligations, with families situated at the nodes. Otherwise, it would have been impossible to hold together these narrowly rational families in such a vast empire. The Prisoner's Dilemma would have eliminated any chance of cooperation among the families no less than it did to cooperation among rational individuals. It seems, then, that mutual trust in traditional China extended far beyond the family circle—though perhaps with a decreasing order in degree—to the local community, to the state, and to entire society (天下 *tianxia*). The Confucian *Li*, which served as a constitution of traditional Chinese society, enabled individuals and families to forge a common cultural identity, which facilitated mutual trust in a large population.

53. *Xunzi*, Ch. 23; trans. Chan, *Source Book in Chinese Philosophy*, 131.

54. *Xunzi*, "Kingly Government," Ch. 9.

55. Samuel L. Popkin, *The Rational Peasant* (Berkeley: University of California Press, 1979).

56. For debates in empirical studies between "moral economy" and "rational peasants," compare two representative works: James C. Scott, *The Moral Economy of the Peasant* (New Haven: Yale University Press, 1976); and Samuel L. Popkin, *The Rational Peasant* (Berkeley: University of California Press, 1979).

57. Richard Madsen, *Morality and Power in a Chinese Village* (Berkeley: University of California Press, 1984), 6–8.

58. Jon Elster, *The Cement of Society: Study of Social Order* (Cambridge University Press, 1989), 200–205.

59. See John King Fairbank, *China: A New History* (Cambridge, MA: Harvard University Press, 1992), 428–432.

60. For the argument that the Chinese social system, economic and political institutions, and the Confucian ideology formed a mutually reinforcing "super-stable" structure, see Jin Guantao and Liu Qingfeng, *Prosperity and Crisis: On the Super-Stable Structure of Chinese Society* (Hong Kong: Chinese University Press, 1992), 158–180.

61. See Thomas Hobbes, *Leviathan*, ed. C.B. Macpherson (New York: Penguin, 1985), 185.

62. See *Meno*, where Socrates concludes with his usual skeptic position: "virtue would be neither inborn quality nor taught, but comes to those who possess it as gift from gods which is not accompanied by

understanding." Plato, *Five Dialogues*, trans. G.M.A. Grube (Hackett Publishing, 1981), 87.

63. *Xunzi*, Ch. 23; see Homer H. Dubs, *The Works of Hsuntze* (Taipei: Cheng-wen Publishing, 1966), 301.

64. *Luxuriant Gems of the Spring and Autumn Annals*, "The Profound Examination of Names and Appellation," Ch. 35; trans. Chan, *Source Book in Chinese Philosophy*, 276.

65. *Ibid.*, trans. Chan, *Source Book in Chinese Philosophy*, 277.

66. *Ibid.*, trans. Chan, *Source Book in Chinese Philosophy*, 275.

67. *Ibid.*, trans. Chan, *Source Book in Chinese Philosophy*, 274–275.

68. Philip J. Ivanhoe, *Confucian Moral Self Cultivation* (New York: Peter Lang, 1993), 34.

69. *Luxuriant Gems of the Spring and Autumn Annals*, "The Profound Examination of Names and Appellation," Ch. 35; trans. Chan, *Source Book in Chinese Philosophy*, 274–275.

70. *Ibid.*, trans. Chan, *Source Book in Chinese Philosophy*, 275–276.

71. *Ibid.*, trans. Chan, *Source Book in Chinese Philosophy*, 276.

72. Rousseau, *Discourse on Inequality*, 97–104, cf. 109–115. For a penetrating exposition of Rousseau's position, see Leo Strauss, *Natural Law and History* (Chicago: University of Chicago Press, 1953), 264–274.

73. Clifford Geertz, *The Interpretation of Cultures* (New York: Basic Books, 1973), 49.

74. Peter L. Berger and Thomas Luckmann, *The Social Construction of Reality: A Treatise in the Sociology of Knowledge* (Garden City, New York: Doubleday, 1966), 47.

75. Peter L. Berger, *The Sacred Canopy: Elements of a Sociological Theory of Religion* (Garden City, New York: Doubleday, 1969), 4–6.

76. Berger and Luckmann, *Social Construction of Reality*, 52; Berger, *Sacred Canopy*, 6.

77. *Book of Rites*, Ch. 18, "Records on Education"; see James Legge, *The Sacred Books of China* (vol. 28.) (Oxford: Clarendon Press, 1885), 82.

78. See, for example, *Book of Rites*, Ch. 12, "Internal Norms"; Ch. 18, "Records on Learning."

79. Montesquieu, *The Spirit of the Laws*, trans. Anne Cohler et al. (Cambridge: Cambridge University Press, 1989), 318.

80. The predicament of the late Qing is best expressed in the words of Montesquieu: "The mores and manners of a despotic state must never be changed; nothing would be more promptly followed by a revolution." Montesquieu, *The Spirit of the Laws*, 314. Although, as we have

seen, Montesquieu's characterization of traditional Chinese society as "despotic" is a bit simplistic, his prediction bears particular relevance to the impact of the May-Fourth Movement.

81. For a sample of arguments, see Chen Songed, *Selected Papers on the East-West Cultural Debates Around the May-Fourth Movement* (Beijing: China Social Science Press, 1983).

82. The two strains of attacks (often mixed with elements of Social Darwinism) are often joined together. See, for example, Chen Duxiu's article in *The Youth Magazine* (*QingnianZazhi*) in December 1915: "The Fundamental Difference between Eastern and Western Thoughts," in *Selected Papers on the East-West Cultural Debates*, ed. Chen Song Chen Song 12–15.

83. Here, I disagree with Lin Yu-sheng in assessing the major problem with the May-Fourth Movement. From the western liberal and pluralist view, Lin points to the tendency of ideological hegemony as the common defect in both Confucianism and the May-Fourth Movement. Lin Yu-sheng ed., *The May-Fourth Movement: A Pluralistic Reflection* (Hong Kong: Sanlian Books Press, 1989), 28–45. From the perspective of the practical necessity for social integration, however, I argue that the major mistake (if an inevitable one) of the radical modernization effort, culminating in the May-Fourth Movement, lied precisely in its failure to preserve the basic moral and ideological consensus of society. And, surely, norm consensus does not have to imply moral despotism. It can include (but is not necessarily limited to) procedural principles commonly agreed among the members of society. Yet, even an entirely pluralist and value neutral society, as sometimes claimed for liberal democracy, still has to observe at least the general principle of tolerance (i.e. "agree to disagree") in order to survive.

84. Zhang Qianfan, "Rule of Virtue, Rule of Law, and Constitutionalism."

CHAPTER 5

Equality and Universal Love: Human Dignity in Mohism

INTRODUCTION

In Chap. 2, I interpret Confucianism as a moral philosophy centered on the notion of human dignity. The theories of Kongzi, Mengzi, and Xunzi have given substantive content to the notion of dignity by establishing the moral ideals of humanity (*Ren*) and righteousness (*Yi*), as exemplified in the moral character of the Confucian gentleman (*Junzi*). A gentleman has acquired dignity by realizing his innate virtue through self-cultivation. He follows the Principle of the Mean (*zhongyong*), and abides by the principles of righteousness and reciprocity, which give rise to his moral independence. The principle of humanity would require him to always treat everyone as the ultimate end and never merely as means. In other words, he is to regard everyone as a moral being with intrinsic worth, just like himself, and never as a mere receiver of benefits or a passive object of his own needs and desires.

Such an interpretation is extracted, however, from a traditional doctrine in light of modern understanding. In reality, Confucianism had been limited by the social context to which it was applied, and these limitations created disparities between theory and practice. Although the ontological doctrine of Mengzi would confer inherent worth (*de*) and nobility to every human being, Confucians in general laid heavy emphasis on the extrinsic virtues actually acquired through education and cultivation, and displayed a pervasive despise on the "petty men" (*xiaoren*) who failed to acquire

© The Author(s) 2016
Q. Zhang, *Human Dignity in Classical Chinese Philosophy*,
DOI 10.1057/978-1-349-70920-5_5

the Confucian virtues. Most notably, in the political realm, both Mengzi and Xunzi basically inherited the assumption from the Zhou dynasty that common people were morally and intellectually too inferior to govern themselves. Having underestimated the possibility of self-government, they treated ordinary people as mere receivers of government benefits and as the subjects of social and political control, rather than potentially independent moral beings worthy of respect. Likewise, in the realm of family, they endorsed primarily subordinate relationships between parents and children and between husbands and wives, and subordination presupposes physical dependence and moral immaturity. The "vulgar Confucians" (*suru*) of later days consolidated these unequal relationships, in the family as in the state, into the unchangeable part of *Li* (propriety), which stands for social customs that the people were supposed to practice in order to acquire virtue. Although *Li* had played the pivotal role of morally binding the traditional society together, the blind practice of *Li* might well have prevented ordinary people from fully developing their innate moral capacity and achieving full dignity. Thus, although I find Confucianism has the most to contribute to the theory of human dignity, its limitations did make it appear unsatisfactory from the modern perspective, which generally assumes that liberty and equality are the primary ingredients that constitute one's dignity.[1]

The dogmatic insistence on the immutability of *Li* has been attacked by the Daoist and Mohist "heretics" of the classical period on different grounds. Although, like Confucianism, Mozi (墨子479–381 B.C.) supports the promotion of the worthy and the sustenance of a hierarchical government, his doctrine of universal love under the will of Heaven carries an inherent tendency of reducing social distinctions and equalizing subordinate relationships. In particular, he takes his utilitarian theory as the overarching principle to reform the obsolete, wasteful, and repressive parts of the traditional *Li*. On the other hand, Laozi (老子 c. 571 B.C.) and Zhuangzi (庄子369–286 B.C.) would abolish the entire system of conventional *Li* altogether and return to the primitive society in which the common people can live in natural freedom. Instead of making oneself the object and sacrifice of social obligations, the Daoist preaches a free life-style in which everyone lives with one's true self as a part of the Way (道Dao).

The next two chapters discuss the ways in which Daoism and Mohism can help, especially where Confucianism faltered in practice, to make human dignity a more tenable concept in classical Chinese philosophy.[2]

The two chapters share a common argument that both Daoism and Mohism, like Confucianism in theory, can be interpreted to imply the principle that one must treat oneself and others as ends and not merely as means to some other ends. The present chapter is to show how the Mohist teaching can be construed to correct some of the practical imperfections in Confucianism and to defend it against several objections raised against modern utilitarianism for potential violations of human rights. Requiring only the general sentiment of universal love for all human beings, Mohism has built in certain checks against the majoritarian abuses. Indeed, one author has gone so far as to compare the Mohist principle with the Kantian categorical imperative that demands the treatment of everyone as an end in itself.[3]

Mohism does have its own problems, however. Although it tends to equalize social relationships by subjecting everyone equally to the universal principle, Mozi ultimately fails to provide a moral basis for autonomous human actions owing to the lack of metaphysical foundation for human virtue and dignity. Thus, while Mohism is able to provide a consistent approach to building a moral and political theory congenial to the modern perspective, it cannot substitute Confucianism for the purpose of developing a coherent conception of human dignity. Of course, this does not diminish the inherent values in Mohism and its unique contributions to the conceptual development of human dignity.

BASIC TENETS OF MOHISM

The Mohist Challenge to Confucianism

In many ways Mohism presents itself as a challenge to Confucianism.[4] While the Confucian ideal of *Ren* (humanity) requires a gradation of love centered upon one's family, Mozi spends his lifetime propagating his doctrine of universal love (兼爱 *jianai*) under Heaven,[5] against any distinction that sets people apart in social relationships. If the highest moral ideal for Kongzi is *Ren*, for Mozi the central tenet of morality is *Yi* (righteousness).[6] The Confucian despised talks of profits, and relegated them to the category of inferior things that preoccupied the minds of those "petty men" (*xiaoren*), as opposed to gentlemen who cares only about righteousness.[7] The Mohist, on the other hand, identifies the very meaning of *Yi* with profits and benefits.[8] Measuring against the principle of utility, the Mohist vehemently attacked the insistence of the later Confucians in meticulously following the traditional *Li*. Extravagant ceremonies and prolonged mourning practices, for example, were taken as marks of virtue by many Confucians of his day; but to Mozi they were utterly wasteful activities, producing nothing but harm to society. The incisive Mohist critiques have served as useful antidotes to the unreasoning Confucian conservatism.

Mozi is by no means an anti-traditionalist, however. As the prominent Legalist Han Fei observes: "Both Kongzi and Mozi follow Kings Yao and Shun, but they differ in choices."[9] In fact, while Kongzi take the early Zhou dynasty as the golden age of Chinese society,[10] Mozi would go back even further—to the legendary Xia dynasty, before the elaborate ritual system of Zhou was developed. Mozi does respect the tradition and proposes to use the "three standards" for evaluating everyone's words and deeds, one of which is the sacred book inherited from the ancient kings, primarily the *Book of History* (尚书 *Shang Shu*), the veracity of which he seems to have taken for granted. He does not aim his objection at the general system of *Li*, but only particular provisions of it.[11] Nor does he attempt to discard the tradition altogether, but only to correct the unduly conservative attitude prevailing among many Confucians of his day, especially about the petty details of practical matters, and to reform the traditional system of *Li* according to a general principle of morality that ought to govern human society at all times and under all circumstances. Mozi finds this principle in the will of Heaven (天志 *tianzhi*), which commands universal love and mutual benefits among all human beings.

Thus, the numerous differences between the two strands of thought should not obliterate what they partake in common. Indeed, Mohism and Confucianism share the same orientation of basic values. Both Kongzi and Mozi agree that, among other social rules, there should be at least some *Li* for mourning, and the basis for such *Li* is not the ceremony itself, but the genuine feeling of grief for the loss of the beloved.[12] They both agree that it is a paramount good to have congenial relationships at all levels of society, from families to the state.[13] They both take for granted the monarchical form of government, but insist that the kings must serve the basic interests of the common people.[14] At the bottom, both Mozi and Kongzi are seriously concerned about the harmony and order of society, in which all human beings may lead decent lives they deserve. For this purpose, they both seek to formulate or rediscover some sort of constitutional principles,[15] that is, fundamental rules embodied in the form of *Li*, by which society is rationally governed.

The substantive principles underlying such a "constitution" do differ profoundly, however, and I argue below that Mohist utilitarianism as a relatively egalitarian doctrine can make a unique contribution to building a modern theory of human dignity. It overcomes the strong elite tendency in Confucianism, challenges the latter's uncritical assumptions about the inferior moral and intellectual status of common people, and makes it possible to establish a popular sovereign in which everyone's dignity can be equally guaranteed.

Mohist Utilitarianism, Universal Love, and the Will of Heaven

Unlike Confucianism, the highest ideal of Mohism is to promote societal benefits or utility, and this is the utilitarian principle to which every human action ought to conform. To be humane (*Ren*), righteous (*Yi*), or filial (孝*xiao*) is ultimately nothing but to provide benefits to others and to society in general. Thus, "the filial duty is to benefit the kin."[16] The central concept of *Yi* is reduced entirely to *li* (利profit), as "*Yi* is to benefit; the opposite of *Yi* is to harm."[17] And a person of humanity is simply "to promote what is beneficial to the world and eliminate what is harmful."[18] Thus, if there is an overarching principle that runs through the entire *Mozi*, it is a version of utilitarianism, which judges every individual or social action by the benefits or harms it brings to the world.[19]

Of course, utilitarianism as an abstract moral principle is to be interpreted in specific historical and social context. Not surprisingly, Mohism is quite different from the western utilitarianism originally developed by Jeremy Bentham and J.S. Mill.[20] While Benthamite utilitarianism is premised on free individual actions as the foundation of liberal state and market economy, Mohist utilitarianism is to be realized under strict state enforcement of uniformity; while J.S. Mill believes, under the Malthusian influence, that prosperity requires containment of population, Mozi, who lived in a violent era of Chinese civilization when the population was decimated by wars, famine, and natural disasters, was completely unaware of the problems challenging contemporary China and advocated for the very opposite; while Benthamite utilitarianism is rigorously secular, Mohism is perhaps the only religious philosophy among the "hundred schools" (百家*baijia*), and derives its ultimate moral authority from the personalized will of Heaven.[21] These formal and substantive differences should not, however, obliterate the utilitarian features that stand out prominently in Mohism, even though it is rather primitive and not nearly as systematic as modern western utilitarianism, sharing with the latter deep concern for public interest and welfare.[22] Indeed, as I shall argue later, the very primitiveness of Mohist utilitarianism helps Mohism to avoid certain dilemmas faced by the Bentham's (and to a less extent even Mill's) more systematic theory, which requires all state policies or acts to *maximize* the total net utilities.

One peculiar feature of Mohism is its religious notion of "the will of Heaven" (*tianzhi*). In Mohism the will of Heaven is the ultimate source of moral judgment.[23] Unlike Confucianism (especially the work of Xunzi), in which Heaven is identified with the impersonal Way that governs nature and the human world, Mozi brings back the primitive notion of personal God prevalent during the early period of the Zhou dynasty. Indeed, among the classical Chinese philosophies, Mohism is the only one that premises moral order upon the personal authority of God and, for this reason, has been compared with western Christianity.[24] God presides over the human world by personal will and feeling, rendering judgments in rewards and punishments made proportionate to the merits of human actions. The will of Heaven is the ultimate moral principle against which human actions are measured. To be good is to act in accord with the will of Heaven and thus to please God; to be evil is to act contrary to his will, making him angry.

To be consistent, the Mohist Heaven is a utilitarian God, who sanctions the principle of universal love among all human beings, and disfavors any man-made distinctions that undermine its effective operation in society. Thus, "those who love and benefit others, and obeyed the intent of Heaven (天意 *tianyi*),[25] are ones who win Heaven's awards," and "those who hate and harm others, and disobey the intent of Heaven, are ones who incur Heaven's punishments."[26] The same basic principle applies everywhere without exception, and governs every person just as it governs the entire state. Thus, "in the same way Mozi uses the will of Heaven to measure the government of the rulers and ministers above, and the writings and words of the multitude below."[27]

Finally, like Christianity but in contrast to Confucianism, Mohism advocates universal love (*jianai*) for all under Heaven,[28] and criticizes the Confucian notion of general love (泛爱 *fanai*) that differentiates among social relationships. The Mohist theory of universal love is consistent with its utilitarian and religious tenets in that, although Mozi never explicitly spells out that everyone's happiness be counted equally,[29] his theory is preoccupied with the basic livelihoods of common people, perhaps owning to the generally low social profiles of Mohist disciples at the time, and that all social distinctions are receding to insignificance before the limitless Heaven that loves everyone equally. As pointed out later, however, this does not make Mozi a strict egalitarian, since equal love simply means to be impartial in delivering benefits or punishments according to the merits of human actions.

EQUALITY AND (SOME) LIBERTY IN MOHISM

Mohism as outlined above can make fresh contributions to the theory of human dignity beyond the limits of Confucianism. Although the Confucian theories do imply equal worth in every human being, such equality is only latent in human nature and never realized in actuality.[30] This lends justifications for according unequal treatments to persons in different family and social positions, and the entire body of *Li* is to define a complex set of rights and obligations according to one's relative social status.[31] Although Mohism, like Confucianism, also accept a strict merit system for rewards and punishments and a hierarchical structure of governance, it is entirely free from the Confucian inequalities largely associated with one's birth, and is thus found more acceptable from the modern perspective. The Mohist preoccupation with the welfare of the low social classes also leads it to strongly condemn wasteful and harmful government activities or regulations, giving rise to the earliest expressions for small government in Chinese philosophy.

Equality Based on Merits

The Mohist doctrine about the will of Heaven and universal love makes Mohism the most egalitarian theory in the classical Chinese philosophy. In contrast to Confucianism, which tends to overemphasize the social distinctions between father and son(s), husband and wife, teacher and students, king (君 *jün*) and officials (臣 *chen*), and to reduce the subordinate party of the unequal relations to inferior positions, Mozi expressly requires a minimal equality of all human beings in the necessarily unequal social relations. "Now there is no difference between large states and small states, all of which are Heaven's cities; nor is there is difference among the young and the elderly, the noble and the ignoble, all of which are Heaven's subjects."[32] Every person, being equally under Heaven, deserves some basic common concern from everyone else. And the heavenly love is extended equally to all, even the slaves. "Male slaves are humans, so to love male slaves is to love humans; female slaves are humans, so to love female slaves is to love humans."[33] While both the Mohists and Confucians keep silent about the legitimacy of the slavery system, Mozi explicitly confirms that slaves are human beings and should enjoy universal love just like everyone else.

The Mohist doctrine of universal love helps to equalize the subordinate social relationships, and lays the ground for the minimum dignity to be accorded to every single human being. In fact, seeing that parents and kings are not always good, Mozi expressly rejects the position taken by the vulgar Confucians that they can serve as unerring examples for children and subjects to follow, much less to demand absolute obedience:

> There are many parents under heaven, but the benevolent (Ren) ones are few; thus, to take the parents as the precept (fa) is to take the malevolent (buren) as the precept.... There are many teachers under heaven, but the benevolent ones are few; thus to take the teacher as the precept is to take the malevolent as the precept.... There are many kings under heaven but the benevolent ones are few; thus to take the king as the precept is to take the malevolent as the precept. And a malevolent precept cannot stand as precept.[34]

The best way is to directly take Heaven as the precept. Here Mozi differs significantly from all Confucians in expressly challenging the authority of the superiors and claiming that parents, teachers, and kings can commit errors, perhaps just as easily as others. Thus, they are not naturally entitled to any social privileges simply because of their privileged status.

The egalitarian relationship is further shown in the Mohist way of attributing culpabilities responsible for causing social disorder. If the Confucians deem respect for parents and kings to be the very manifestation of good order, Mozi thinks quite the otherwise. It is true that the lack of mutual love causes social conflicts and chaos, but for Mozi such a fault is attributed equally to the parents and the children, the king and his officials.

> The father is not benevolent (ci) to the son, the elder brother is not benevolent to the younger brother, and the king is not benevolent to his subordinates: these are also the cause by which the world is in chaos. The father loves himself and not the son, so he benefits himself at the expense of the son; the elder brother loves himself and not the younger brother, so he benefits himself at the expense of the younger brother; the king loves himself and not the subordinate officials, so he benefits himself at their expense. Why? All these arise from the lack of mutual love.[35]

In the Mohist view, then, various social actors are equally prone to pursuit of selfish interest and neglect in extending mutual love to each other (in violation of the will of Heaven). In this respect the parents are not naturally superior to the children, and the king stands in the equal footing as his subordinate officials.[36]

Mozi is far from being an absolutely egalitarian, however, as he does not seem to object unequal distribution of social status and wealth among the people. In fact, somewhat like the Confucian counterpart, Mozi adopts a strict merit system for his state:

> *Assign status according to virtue, assign functions according to posts, determine reward according to work, and distribute salaries according to merit. Thus the officials are not to be always noble, and the people are not to be always ignoble. The worthy should be promoted, and the unworthy should be demoted.*[37]

And the Heaven is supposed to reward the good and punish the evil. The emperor as the Son of Heaven is rewarded with most privileges precisely for his performance of the utilitarian function as commanded by the will of Heaven.[38] Yet, for Mozi, the merit system is not necessarily inconsistent with the equality principle. From the modern perspective, he can be interpreted to be opposing equal outcome but supporting equal opportunity in that everyone is roughly equal in virtue and capacities, and should be given equal advantage to prove oneself in political or economic systems established and maintained by the state.[39]

Primacy of the Common People

Closely associated with the Mohist egalitarianism is its deep concern with the welfare of common people. Among all classical Chinese philosophers Mozi is the closest to the low social classes, and the Mohist Heaven is as benevolent to them as it is to the privileged classes: "Heaven loves the common people (*min*) deeply, and Heaven loves the common people generally."[40] As one indication, the words "people" (民*min*) and "multitude" (百姓*baixing*) appear more frequently in *Mozi* than any other classical works (see Table 5.1), *Mengzi* being the only work with comparable marks.[41] And when Mozi talks about people or multitude, he always refers to them in sympathetic and respective tune.

As Mozi closely associates himself with the popular mass, his perspective differs from the Confucians. Although the Confucians also talk about

Table 5.1   The frequencies of words *min* and *baixing* appearing in classical works, as compared to their total numbers of characters

Works	Analects	Mengzi	Mozi	Laozi	Zhuangzi
Min/baixing	49/5	208/19	330/90	33/4	110/9
Total characters	22540	42560	91410	6270	80100

(graded) love and show sympathy to common people, their identification with the elite class makes them almost naturally contemptuous to the low and uneducated classes. Read, for example, the remark of Mengzi, who believes that everyone is naturally and equally endowed with the heart-mind for humanity and righteousness that distinguishes a human being from mere animals, but nevertheless "the difference between humans and animals is slight. The common people lose it, the gentlemen keep it."[42] One cannot fail to feel the sense of superiority that the Confucians attach to themselves vis-à-vis the common people. For the Confucians the multitude are to be educated, transformed if possible, and kept in order by penal punishments.[43] In contrast, for Mozi, the needs of common people always take the central position. While rules of propriety and proper music are quintessential to the Confucians for education and transformation of the multitude, Mozi would abolish them if they threaten to disturb the basic lives of common people. In his attack on the elaborate Confucian music system, he says "the common people have three worries: those in hunger cannot get food, those in coldness cannot be clothed, and those belabored cannot have rest."[44] Indulgence in music not only fails to resolve these problems, but aggravates them by wasting scarce resources available to the common poor. Indeed, Mozi proposes to abolish music altogether and radically reform the system of *Li*. Although such proposals may seem to be unnecessarily radical, they do highlight the central Mohist concern for saving social resources in order to secure the basic living conditions for common people.

Equal concern for the multitude is consistent with the utilitarian logic inherent in Mohism.[45] If everyone is roughly equal and there is no legitimate ground for distinguishing among different classes, then it is only natural to focus one's care on the most numerous, whose welfare is most likely to be deprived anyway. Although Mozi never demands an egalitarian distribution of economic and social resources, given the extremely limited quantity of these resources for satisfying everyone's basic needs, the moral commitment to guaranteeing a minimum living standard does make Mozi explicitly oppose any gross inequality and extravagance. Any extravagant spending beyond the need for maintaining basic governance and good order, for example, is seen as violating the utilitarian principle and taking away from common people the basic means of survival. The utilitarian principle urges Mozi to advocate vigorously for equality in the enjoyment of basic needs, so as to guarantee a basic living condition for common people.[46]

Small Government

If wasteful music and proprieties will deteriorate the people's welfare, so much more will harmful government activities. The concern for the welfare of common people naturally leads Mozi to caution against the government's excessive exactions and expropriations, as he sees clearly that the wealth of the government is taken from the ordinary people. The following remarks prove to be strikingly relevant to China today, where property takings in the name of development and renovation are creating many social conflicts and tragedies[47]:

> *For normal conscription to repair the city, the people labor without being harmed; for normal expropriation of rents and taxes, the people pay without getting poor. The people are harmed not by these [normal takings], but by excessive takings. So the sage king builds the palaces to facilitate living, not for deriving pleasure from its outlook; makes clothes and shoes to benefit the body, not for satisfying eccentric tastes.... Today's kings differ from this in building palaces, as they are destined to take excessively from common people, violently expropriate their property for basic living in order to build massive palaces with extravagant outlook.... Today's kings differ from this in making clothes,... as they are destined to take excessively from the common people, violently expropriate their property for basic living to make elaborate clothes requiring expensive materials and extraordinary labor. This is not for facilitating warmth, and the property and labor are exhausted for useless waste.[48]*

And the same is with the extravagant ways of dining and transport, the debauchery concubine system, and the socially wasteful mourning rules. Of course, the most serious threats to the ordinary people are various wars waged by avaricious rulers craving for more treasures and territories, and they are what Mozi would do everything to prevent—in the words of Mengzi, even by "rubbing smooth his whole body from head to foot."[49] "The state wages a war, expropriates the people's utilities, and deny them benefits. This is so common, but why do it? The ruler answers: it is because I crave for the vain-glory of victory and profits deriving there from."[50] Mozi makes it clear that the vain-glory and selfish motives of the ruler are the greatest danger to social peace and order.

Thus, although government still plays an important role in Mohism,[51] bad government is the original cause for social calamities. For Mozi, it is the excesses and exploitation of the rulers that compel society to engage in activities wholly irrelevant to the survival of the members of the low class, making them incapable of meeting the basic needs of life and driving them to the verge of committing crimes. "Since the people feel both hungry and cold, they begin to commit sins and obliquity. When sins and obliquity multiply, the penalties and punishments become strict; when the penalties and punishment become strict, the state falls into disorder."[52] In this sense, courtly extravagance, rather than the people's incapacity or evil predisposition, is the true origin of crimes and disorder. In contrast to Confucian teachings, the evil with which Mozi is seriously concerned is not that the government may fail to do enough benevolent things to its people, but that it may do too much in hurting them.

Of course, like the Confucians at his time, Mozi did not provide for a democratic institutional mechanism to check against government misconducts (more below), but his strong condemnations of the government excesses do *imply* a liberal voice that call for limitation of government powers. If the government can be kept away from various abuses and be compelled to imitate the legendary sage kings in exacting only the proper amount as required by the public interest, the common people will be enormously benefited and left alone to provide for their own necessities. And, unlike Confucianism, nothing in the work of Mozi suggests that the people are incapable of providing for their own welfare.[53] Overall, the implicit Mohist assumption about human nature of ordinary people is more positive than that in Confucianism (e.g. Mengzi). Since common people are self-sufficient individuals and the chief culprit is the excessive government, the natural implication is that everyone has enough ability to lead a decent life if the government abuses can be effectively checked.

Mohism and Benthamite Utilitarianism: Distinctions and Common Limitations

It is thus plausible to interpret the Mohist teaching as requiring an equal, minimal dignity for every member of society, irrespective of his social status. Yet, utilitarianism as a moral philosophy has been challenged both for technical difficulties and inherent tendency of producing unjust results that degrade human dignity in certain situations.[54] Besides the inherent uncertainty and impracticality in the numerical maximization of overall social benefits, western (Benthamite) utilitarianism sometimes finds itself in a position opposed to individual rights and dignity, since it immerses individual rights in a lump-sum of social interests, making it possible to require an individual person to sacrifice himself against his will in order to benefit the whole. I argue, however, that these difficulties do not apply to Mohism.

As a unique doctrine, Mohism is not flawed by many of the objections made against ordinary utilitarianism. Unlike Benthamite utilitarianism, Mozi has never explicitly endorsed the doctrine of *maximizing* the total sum of social utility. Rather, he simply insists upon the way of universal love and mutual benefit, which is "to regard other people's countries as one's own, to regard other people's families as one's own, and to regard other people's person as one's own."[55] If the Mohist utilitarianism does involve any calculation at all, the scope of the calculation is always made so broad, and assignment of weight so even, as to afford proper concern for the lower classes of society. Since a good society is measured not by the maximization of total wealth or other single indicator,[56] but by the satisfaction of the basic needs of every person, Mozi is able to formulate his utilitarian principle as a moral device against those rulers who were making personal gains at the expense of common welfare.

Further, the Mohist doctrine of universal love may seem to require that every individual sacrifices his interest to serve the interest of others and society. A common objection made against Benthamite utilitarianism is that it can be construed to require the torturing of one person to please a crowd, so long as the total utility derived from the pleasure exceeds the pain. But this challenge can hardly be raised against Mozi, who explicitly repudiates such sacrifice. "To love others," he says, "does not exclude the love for yourself; you yourself are among the loved. As you are among the loved, love is also added to yourself."[57] Mozi himself, as a saint, may well have chosen to abnegate his own interest and even his life in some dire circumstances, but it is clear that he requires only that one adopt the general attitude of loving others as much as he loves himself (which *is* a stringent requirement by itself),[58] and has never come to such an extreme position as that society can require any person to sacrifice himself in order to benefit a great number of people. In fact, as mentioned above, Mohism does not even require the egalitarian distribution of social benefits, much less the sharing of personal goods. Thus, there is no room for Mohism to support any iniquitous social practice that demands extreme self-abnegation. The universal love is realized not in self-debasement, but in reciprocal, impartial concern for one another;[59] not in the love for a mysterious whole, but in the love for every individual human being, including the loving person himself.

Most remarkably, in interpreting the meaning of *Ren* (humanity), Mozi says: "The love of oneself is not for the sake of using oneself, not like loving a horse."[60] According to the plain meaning of the terms, true love (or humanity) requires us to treat ourselves as the ends, and never merely as means, that is, in the same way as we loves a tool or an animal. Since Mozi also requires us to equally love everyone else in the world as we love ourselves, he seems to be expressing the Kantian principle that we ought to always treat everyone as the end and never merely as means to any other ends. Although it is perhaps too quick to identify Mozi with Kant from this single statement, it does seem reasonable to interpret Mohism as to require the guarantee of basic concern for *every* individual person.

Of course, Mohism as a version of utilitarianism does share the problems inherent in every utilitarian theory. For one thing, like Mengzi and Xunzi, who likewise adopt utilitarian arguments to support the notion of benevolent government, Mozi has failed to show how his utilitarian ideal can effectively influence the rulers of his time.[61] A more serious incoherence arises from the root of Mohist utilitarianism itself.[62] Unlike Confucianism, Mozi does not provide an explicit account of human nature, leaving a pervasive sense that human being is nothing but an empty shell of body driven by pleasure and pain. Despite the ambiguity, the source of morality for Mohism seems to lie entirely outside the individual person. A person wants to be good not for the sake of the good itself, but apparently for the hope to reap benefits from acting in accordance with the will of Heaven and for the fear of suffering from punishments if he acts to the contrary. At the bottom, human beings seem to be selfish and appear to love the others ultimately for their own interests. This understanding, derived naturally from Mohism, fails to recognize any dignity inherent in a human being, and is inconsistent with the Mohist teaching itself that a person is to respect himself and others as ends, not merely as means of his material feeling of pleasures and pains. Thus, although Mozi has formulated a clear overarching principle and seeks to apply it consistently to practical situations, the Mohist principle seems to lack a solid foundation in human nature.

MOHISM AND DEMOCRACY: POLITICAL IMPLICATIONS

The Mohist doctrine of Heaven, however simple on the metaphysical dimension, does contain practical merits when applied directly to the political realm. Here, we have something like a constitutional principle that reigns above the supreme head of the state. This ultimate principle is righteousness which, to be consistent with his utilitarian position, is identified with benevolence. It arises from Heaven, the supernatural authority that puts the highest human ruler under moral control. "Heaven is pure eminence and pure wisdom. Therefore, righteousness in fact originates with Heaven."[63] At the highest level, even the Son of Heaven (天子 *tianzi*) must identify himself with the will of Heaven; however powerful is an emperor over men, he is beneath Heaven and must act in accord with its will. "If the Son of Heaven does the good, Heaven has the power to reward him; if he commits violence, Heaven has the power to punish him."[64] Since Heaven wills the government to be righteous, it must take righteousness rather than brute force as the governing principle: "To obey the will of Heaven is to use righteousness as the method of control; to oppose the will of Heaven is to use force as the method of control."[65] The government, then, is compelled by the will of Heaven to follow the principle of righteousness, under which it should protect innocent lives against serious harm—at least avoid committing any harm by itself. Although the rule of righteousness does require that the worthy be put in a hierarchical government as proportional to their merits, Mozi has never adopted the Confucian position that the right to rule should be inherited and that the rulers should enjoy special privileges and honors by right. Rather, the government posts should be filled according to one's merit and the government ought to promote welfare for everyone alike.

Is Mohism Democratic?

Despite his egalitarian teachings, Mozi has never explicitly endorsed any version of democracy, as he clearly sees the necessity for a top-down, hierarchically organized government based on the merits and worth of the officials in order to unify the people's conceptions of right and wrong. As he says unequivocally, "righteousness is the standard. It is not to be given by the subordinate to the superior but must be given from the superior to the subordinate."[66] "Righteousness does not arise from those ignorant and ignoble, but from those who are noble and wise."[67] The Mohist meritocracy does tend to promote authoritarianism, especially when the central government is required to prescribe moral standards for right and wrong in order to prevent social chaos.[68]

It is interesting that Mozi identifies the chief evil of the lawless state of nature with the lack of agreed conceptions (*Yi*) about right and wrong,[69] and the unique function of constituting a structured government is to unify these individual conceptions that would otherwise lead to serious social conflicts and disorder. "There is order in the empire because the emperor can bring about a unified and agreed concept of right in the empire."[70] So, here is the original purpose of creating a relatively complex top-down system of government:

> *Heaven wished to unify all concepts of right in the world. The most worthy was therefore selected and made an emperor (i.e., tianzi, the Son of Heaven). The emperor, realizing his inadequate wisdom and ability to govern alone, selected the next best in virtue and appointed them as the three ministers. The three ministers, realizing their inadequate wisdom and ability to assist the emperor alone, divided the empire into states and set up feudal lordships.... When order prevails in the empire, the emperor further unifies all concepts of right as one in the empire and make it agree with Heaven.[71]*

The crucial question in the above passage is, of course, exactly how different levels of officials, with the emperor at the top, are to be selected. According to Fung Yu-lan, the last passage suggests that the Son of Heaven is to be directly elected by the people,[72] but such a dramatic conclusion is apparently unsupported by the text. For the very purpose of the government is to unify people's conception about right and wrong, and before this occurs common people may well differ as to the criteria of selecting the emperor. How, then, can people rationally and peacefully "elect" the emperor in the chaotic state of nature? The answer, as others suggest, is necessarily that he can only be selected by "Heaven," as the text literally suggests.[73] "Thus Heaven and ghosts reward him, and establish him as the Son of Heaven and as the parents of the people."[74] This obviously does not resolve the mystery, but it does suggest that the highest ruler is not elected by the people, and the rest of the text makes it clear that the selection processes for all levels of subordinate officials are to be carried out from top to bottom.[75]

Lacking individual freedom of judgment, the Mohist government can be even more authoritarian than the Confucian counterpart. At least in theory, Mengzi would allow the subordinates to deviate from and even rebel against the superior who is found in default of his primary obligations. Thus, "if the king commits a major error, the high officials in his family should advise him; if he refuses to follow after repeated advices, then they should replace him with someone else."[76] If the king fails to abide by the principles of humanity and righteousness, then he will eventually lose the qualification to maintain power and virtually become a lone usurper, who can be deposed without violation of any Confucian principles; as Mengzi states, "He who injures humanity is a bandit. He who injures righteousness is a destructive person. Such a person is a lone man. I have heard of killing a lone man Zhou, but have not heard of murdering of a king."[77]Although Mengzi never explains how to replace a king short of a bloody court plot or violent uprising, these courageous words virtually create a right of rebellion espoused by Locke in the West two millennia later.[78] Preoccupied with uniformity, however, Mozi never accepted such a right. In one passage he says instead, "if someone sees or hears about anyone who is good, he must report to his superior; if he sees or hears about anyone who is evil, he must also report to his superior. He must affirm what the superior affirms [as right], and negates what the superior negates [as wrong]."[79] Absolute uniformity in effect unifies the whole state with the ruling will of the emperor (Son of Heaven), and makes his abuse of power all the more dreadful. To be sure, ultimately the people are to unify with Heaven rather than the highest ruler on earth, and the Will of Heaven is to love everyone universally. Yet, Mozi has never specified how to effect such a supernatural identification and what to be done when the emperor or his subordinates apparently deviate from the Will of Heaven. As Mozi pins too much hope on the supernatural Heaven and not sufficiently on ordinary human beings, he runs the serious risk of rendering the latter entirely powerless before the abuse of public power.

Relentless pursuit of uniformity further deprives freedom of thought and speech, and lends powerfully to despotic centralism (or even totalitarianism). This is of course not intended by Mozi, but his simplistic institutional design, if implemented, will necessarily lean toward to such outcome. And in this aspect Mohism does share with the Legalist, whose policies were implemented during the short-lived Qin dynasty ending with a violent death.[80] Unfortunately, like the Legalists and Confucians, Mozi has never conceived a democratic government.

Merits in the Mohist Principles of Government

The root problem with the Mohist promotion of uniformity (尚同 *shangtong*) is, of course, that he fails to explore the institutional mechanism to carry out benign ideals without producing evil side effects. Such problem is not with Mozi alone, however, but widely shared by virtually all Chinese thinkers in his times, and its seriousness should not be exaggerated. Although the Mohist design of political system is oversimplified, thus prune to abuse of despotic power, the principle of promoting uniformities is premised upon and thus limited by the principle of elevating the worth (尚贤 *shangxian*). After all, the Son of Heaven is supposed to be the best sage selected to unify everything under Heaven, and the three ministers, lord kings, and likewise the local officials should be good and wise. For Mozi, worthiness is the only criterion of selecting all levels of officials, including the emperor himself, without any regard to such exterior factors as one's poverty, social status, or relative relationships. "Even Heaven makes no distinction as to rich or poor, noble or ignoble, far or near, or closeness in relationships; the worthy will be recommended and elevated, and the unworthy (不肖 *buxiao*) will be disfavored and demoted."[81] As the prominent historian Gu Jiegang points out:

> *The principle of promoting uniformity and the principle of elevating the worthy are complementary to each other: if elevating the worthy without promoting uniformity, then the politics cannot be unified and there will be chaos from below; if promoting uniformity without elevating the worthy, then politics will be corrupt and there will be chaos from above.*[82]

Since Mozi has to reconcile the principle of promoting uniformity with the principle of elevating the worthy as well as its generally egalitarian underpinning, there *are* some passages suggesting limits to identification with and subordination to the superior. "If the superior commits any fault, his subordinates shall remonstrate with him."[83] This seems to presuppose the existence of an objective standard for judging whether the superior commits any fault. On one occasion, Mozi suggests that an enlightened superior must rule according to the conception of right and wrong of the subordinate people.[84] On another occasion, Mozi makes a hypothetical case for his utilitarian argument, in which the poor and the belabored are imagined to select between two kings, one following the principle of universal love and the other to the contrary.[85]

Most importantly, though Mozi does not make it explicit, there is nothing in his theory to prevent him from designing an electoral scheme, by which the worthy are chosen collectively by the common people—especially if his utilitarian principle requires such a mechanism in order to make human beings better conform to the will of Heaven.[86] This prospect is made all the more appealing by the formal similarities between utilitarianism and democracy. In fact, an electoral scheme might seem natural and convenient to Mozi, since in the ancient time that he admired, "no official was necessarily assured of an exalted position for life; nor was any member of the common people necessarily condemned to remain forever humble. Those with ability were promoted, those without it were demoted."[87] The passage indicates that common people should have some opportunity to obtain positions in the state once they have acquired the commensurate abilities, and there is nothing to prevent timely promotions and demotion from being carried out in the form of popular consent. Perhaps owning to the low profile of most followers, Mozi, unlike Mengzi and Xunzi, has never suggested in his work that the common people are incapable of self-government. Thus, although Mohism never explicitly endorsed democracy, it is comparatively the most egalitarian school among all, and is perhaps most likely to accept a democratic political scheme.

Finally, it should not be overlooked that promotion of uniformity by itself does have a positive side, regardless whether it is carried out in a democratically elected regime or not. It can help to prevent local officials from abusing their power and violating the people's basic interests as guaranteed by the central government. After all, Mozi design the centralized system of government to facilitate governance and information exchange. The Son of Heaven is only one man, and he obviously cannot rule the whole state by himself, nor can the three ministers and handful of officials in the central government. This is why local governments must be established, but to prevent chaos the subordinates must obey the superiors and ultimately the emperor, so that the central commands can be enforced without impediments. Unlike the Legalists,[88] Mozi has not developed any elaborate theory on checks and balances among officials, but he does insist that everything the governments do must conform to the Will of Heaven, which ultimately protects the basic interests of and commands universal love for everyone under Heaven. If Heaven wills that every human being, no matter how low in social status, be provided with basic rights and livelihood, and such a will is to be carried out by the emperor, the three ministers, and different levels of governments in turn, then who can deny that "promotion of uniformity" can be quite desirable? In fact, if China can truly promote uniformity of this sort today, its people will be freed from all kinds of discriminations and deprivations imposed by the local governments in violation of the Constitution and laws made by the national legislature.[89]

MOHISM AND DIGNITY

It is a tragedy for the Chinese civilization that Mohism only enjoyed an ephemeral prominence in its early history. During the violent unification of Qin (229–221 B.C.), Mohism suffered from a great decline and became extinct in the seventh century, and was not revived until it was rediscovered nearly a millennium later, when the Chinese finally found the utility of Mohist utilitarianism in facing foreign challenges.[90] Since the Mohist decline, the common people had lost their spokesman, and the elite oriented Confucianism became the only viable moral philosophy that guided the Chinese society. In many ways, the Confucian *Li* had served as a moral constitution, as it were, of the traditional Chinese society, maintaining a degree of order and harmony.[91] But when the particular rules of *Li* were mistaken for permanently fixed principles mandated by the laws of nature, and the subordinate relations in families and in the state were taken to be naturally legitimate, they became the fetter of social and moral progress; by treating human beings merely as the subjects of social control in the interests of order, they deviated from the high principle of humanity (*Ren*), and could no longer serve as the "process of humanization."[92] For those who were disheartened by the social and political realities, the only alternative left was the passive Daoism, which preached the virtue of "doing nothing" (无为 *wuwei*) and returning to the primitive paradise esteemed in their imagination. But if this mysterious route proved to be futile for society as a whole, the prejudices of and deficiencies in the prevailing philosophy would stand untouched. The Chinese (at least its intellectual) after the Mohist decline was thus limited for a long time to two polar choices: he was to be either a pragmatic Confucian, who had by and large consented to playing his part in a complex web of social relationships according to the established rules; or a romantic Daoist, who retired completely into the private sanctuary where he was to enjoy a solitary life. Gone was the brave individual who had enough guts, talent, vision, and good will to positively challenge the existing way of life and make a change for the better. Ironically, when the system remained ossified and stagnant for lack of meaningful challenges, it was to be ousted altogether when it was suddenly found so useless for meeting the pressing needs of the day.

Mohism could have been a good corrective to both Confucian conservatism and Daoist pessimism. Its ideal personality, Mozi, is an active (perhaps, to some, a bit hyper active) social reformer, completely free from the negative attitude toward worldly affairs as prevalent in Daoism. And when he acts, he is free from all sorts of prejudices implicated in the unequal relationships imposed by the dogmatic Confucian system of *Li*. Mozi advocates a universal utilitarian principle that governs everyone equally, thus effectively alleviating the subordination of children, women, and subjects of the rulers.[93] Under the crushing burden of unequal social obligations, a person is turned into either a bigot or a cynic, and can hardly lead a dignified life by maintaining moral autonomy. Mozi would preserve the moral rules and norms but rid them of the unequal terms, and exercise efforts in order to maintain peace and a minimal standard by which everyone can quietly enjoy a self-sufficient and decent private life.

Mohism is, of course, far from being perfect. As noted above, it is philosophically much less sophisticated than either Daoism or Confucianism, and its naïve belief in uniformity lends itself to despotic influences. All these shortcomings are overcome and made secondary, however, by the close identification with common people and deep concern with their welfare. After all, we are all result-oriented to some extent: if a moral philosophy invariably leads to conclusions unacceptable to the prevailing views today, then no matter how well developed it is in its metaphysical foundation, it will be ruthlessly ignored if not consciously discarded, perhaps save only for some academic archaeological interest. And such has happened to the Confucian system of *Li*. Mohism experienced the opposite process; it revived when China was harboring upon modernity. This was no accident because, despite its scantiness in metaphysics, Mohism appears to be a much more familiar to modern society than the bulk of Confucianism. It is free from so many strange shackles that the Chinese were so eager to eliminate from their cultural tradition in the painful modernization process. One cannot help imagine that, had Mohism survived among the Chinese throughout the history, whether they would still be compelled to borrow democracy and science from elsewhere, as there is a good chance that these "western goodies" might have grown out of these plebian-oriented heretics they had for long suppressed.

Like the Confucian and Daoist rivals of his time, Mozi was not prescient enough to foresee the dawning of liberal democratic institutions that are crucial to the full development of individual dignity. He either took for granted the old form of government (e.g. the emperor, three ministers, etc.), or harbored on ideas of which the feasibility of implementation remained dubious (e.g. how the Son of Heaven is to be selected by the criterion of worthiness). These deficiencies prevented Mohism from being outwardly liberal or democratic, but it seems hard to deny that all the seeds have been there, even though they may never turn into fruits without some dramatic events to serve as catalysis. From his generous concern with the welfare of the multitude, his conviction that everyone (including slaves) is fundamentally equal under Heaven, and his mistrust of the superiors—whether kings, parents or teachers, it takes only one step to realize that some kind of elections is necessary to effectively guarantee the majority's interests.[94] And his knowledge about ubiquitous government excesses should constantly remind him that it is indispensable to introduce some mechanism in the system to hold the government powers in check. Compared to the Confucians and the Daoists, Mozi would be most likely the first to realize the necessity of both maintaining an active government and keeping it under popular and institutional controls.[95]

Finally, Mozi is primarily a practitioner, not a preacher. Unlike most Confucians, he does not *speak* so much about how to become a gentleman or acquire humanity, but he personally illustrates his moral principles by his deeds. He wears shabby clothes to advocate the ideals of simplicity and thrifty, he travels all around to stop wars in order to propagate pacifism and universal love, and he is a great craftsman because he deeply believes in the utilitarian principle of contributing tangible goods to society. Although we do not find many words on ideal moral personality in his work, Mozi himself has been a living example of the moral principles he relentlessly advocates.[96] In him, we find a healthy moral personality quite familiar to our own age: intensely sympathetic about the fate of common people who are usually poor and disadvantaged, firmly committed to the egalitarian principle based on merits, and strongly indignant to government excesses and abuses. And this is quite a different character from a typical Confucian or Daoist. For these reasons I believe that the conceptual development of human dignity cannot be complete without the Mohist contributions.

NOTES

1. See, for example, Alan Gewirth, "Human Dignity as the Basis of Rights," in *The Constitution of Rights: Human Dignity and American Values*, ed. Michael J. Meyer and William A. Parent (Ithaca: Cornell University Press, 1992), 10–28.

2. In one occasion Professor Nick Bunin suggested Legalism as a candidate for the fourth school that might contribute positively to the dignity theory. As indicated in Chap. 4, however, I have not been able to find enough positive contributions from Legalism to this subject to merit a separate chapter. To be sure, the Legalists during the Warring States were concerned with establishing a state ruled by law, but their point of departure was always the interest of the ruler, not of the ruled. The Legalist theory invariably took individuals as mere subjects of political control for the purpose of maintaining order and a strong army, which would enable the king to enlarge *his* territories and secure *his* regime. To put in short, the notion of human dignity is to be built on a decent moral ground, which is simply absent in Legalism as a purely instrumentalist theory. This is why I choose to limit my discussions here to Mohism and Daoism.

3. See Benjamin I. Schwartz, *The World of Thought in Ancient China* (Cambridge, MA: Harvard University Press, 1985), 146.

4. See Mei Ji and Lin Jinbao ed., *Vernacular Translation of Mozi* (Changsha: Yuelu Books, 1991), 1–7.

5. Although, as Graham points out, the end of *jianai* has more to do with the mutual provision of benefits than personal affection of love, there is nothing that prevents Mozi from using the term as a motivational requirement for one to inculcate the proper disposition that habitually leads to benevolent acts. Compare A.C. Graham, *Disputers of the Tao: Philosophical Argument in Ancient China* (La Salle, IL: Open Court, 1989), 41–42, and Schwartz, *The World of Thought in Ancient China*, 146–149. Thus, I follow the common translation of "universal love."

6. "Among ten thousand things, none is more noble than *Yi*." *Mozi*, "Ennoblement of *Yi*", 47: 1.

7. Of course, a Confucian gentleman also cares about benefits, if not so much to oneself as to others and to society in general. But he would not reduce a human being to primarily a profit-seeking creature, as a Mohist tends to do. See Wing-tsit Chan, Source Book in Chinese Philosophy (Princeton University Press, 1963), 215.

8. Thus, "*Ren* is to love closely"; "*Yi* is to benefit." *Mozi*, "Canon I", 40: 7, 8; see also "Exposition of Canon II", 43: 177.

9. *Hanfeizi*, "Prominent Schools", 50: 1.

10. Kongzi once says: "The institution of the Zhou dynasty borrowed in part from the two previous dynasties (Xia and Shang). How rich and civilized it is! I am for the Zhou institution." *Analects*, 3: 14.

11. See Fung Yu-lan, "An Outline of the Historical Development of Chinese Philosophy," in *A Collection of Papers on the History of Chinese Philosophy* (Macao: Xinfeng Books, 1962), 70–83.

12. Thus, "although the mourning should be carried out according to *Li*, its foundation is grief." *Mozi*, "Self-Cultivation", 2: 1. To be fair, I should point out that Kongzi himself also advocates for simple rituals: "in general the rituals should be made thrifty rather than extravagant; for the mourning ritual, sadness is more important than procedural completeness." *Analects*, 3: 4. The vulgar Confucians apparently ignored his advice.

13. So, "if a gentleman wishes to be a generous ruler, a loyal subject, a kind father, a filial son, a friendly older brother, and a respectful younger brother, then he must put into practice this principle of universality." *Mozi*, "Universal Love III", 16: 9.

14. "The principle of universality is the way of the sage kings, the means of bringing safety to the rulers and officials and of assuring ample food and clothing to the people." *Mozi*, "Universal Love III", 16: 9.

15. Mozi does mention "the constitution (*xian*) of the ancient kings" several times (see, e.g., "Against Fatalism I", 35: 3, 5; "Against Fatalism II", 36: 2), in which his utilitarianism serves as the universal and constant organizing principle.

16. *Mozi*, "Canon I", 40: 13.

17. *Mozi*, "Major Illustrations", 44: 4.

18. *Mozi*, "Universal Love II", 16: 2; see Burton Watson, *Basic Writings of Mo Tzu, Hsun Tzu, and Han Fei Tzu* (New York: Columbia University Press, 1967), 39.

19. On identifying Mohism as a strain of utilitarianism, see Fung Yu-lan, *History of Chinese Philosophy* (New Edition, vol. 1) (Beijing: Zhonghua Books, 1961), 115. Compare with Frederick W. Mote, *Intellectual Foundations of China* (New York: Alfred A. Knopf, 1971), 88.

20. See Philip L. Ralph, "Mo Ti and the English Utilitarians," *The Far Eastern Quarterly* 9 (1949): 42–52.

21. It is generally accepted that Mozi is the most religious among all traditional Chinese thinkers, see Chan, *Source Book in Chinese Philosophy*, 220–221.

22. Compare Hao Changxi, "Is Mozi a Utilitarian? On the Modern Significance of Mohist Ethics," *History of Chinese Philosophy* 2005 (1): 70–78, which denies Mozi as a utilitarian, but the author apparently has confused the Benthamite utilitarianism with self-centered hedonism.

23. See Hyung I. Kim, *Fundamental Legal Concepts of China and the West*, trans. Chen Guo-Ping et al. (Shenyang: Liaoning Renmin Press, 1989), 55–63.

24. See Mote, *Intellectual Foundations of China*, p. 88.

25. Here, I take the "intent" of Heaven (天意 *tianyi*) to mean the same as the "will" of Heaven (*tianzhi*).

26. *Mozi*, "The Will of Heaven II", 27: 8; trans. Watson, *Basic Writings of Mo Tzu*, 90, 92. "How do we know that Heaven loves all the people in the world? Because it enlightens them all. How do we know that it enlightens them all? Because it possesses them all. How do we know that it possesses them all? Because it feeds them all." *Mozi*, "The Will of Heaven I", 26: 5; trans. Chan, *Source Book in Chinese Philosophy*, 220; see also "The Will of Heaven III", 28: 4.

27. *Mozi*, "The Will of Heaven II", 27: 8; trans. Watson, *Basic Writings of Mo Tzu*, 92.

28. While "Kongzi valued benevolence, Mo Ti valued being for everyone, ...Yang Chu valued self". *Lü's Spring and Autumn Annals*, 17: 7; trans. Graham, *Disputers of the Tao*, 54.

29. In fact, Mozi apparently divides benefits in three levels: benefits to Heaven, benefits to the ghosts, and benefits to human beings, but in his theory these three kinds of benefits always coincide with one another. See, for example, *Mozi*, "The Will of Heaven II", 27: 7. For our purpose the first two kinds are irrelevant.

30. See Donald J. Munro, *The Concept of Man in Early China* (Stanford: Stanford University Press, 1969), 49–83.

31. In fact such arguments still support, among other things, the contemporary electoral system that heavily discriminated against the rural majority. Only in 2010 was the so-called one-quarter clause against the peasants in the election law eliminated. For an analysis concluding that the ability to stand for an election or select among candidates actually have little to do with one's level of education and theoretical knowledge, see Cai Dingjian ed., *An Election Report of China* (Beijing: Law Press, 2002).

32. *Mozi*, "The Instrument of Standards", 4: 3.

33. *Mozi*, "Minor Illustrations", 45: 4.

34. *Mozi*, "The Instrument of Standards", 4: 2.

35. *Mozi*, "Universal Love I", 14: 2.

36. Some argue that the Mohist equality is limited in that, although Mozi appeals to universal love, he merely suggests to treat other's father,

property, or state just as one's own father, property or state, respectively, never denying the differences in social obligations assigned to different social roles. See Sun Shiming, "On the Mohist Ethics: Comparing Confucian and Mohist Ethical Thoughts," *Qiushi Journal* 1994 (5): 19–24. While this can be true (even though Mozi says no more than "to love others' relatives just like one's own relatives", immediately follow by "to universally love everyone alike", "Major Illustrations", 44: 6), it is not inconsistent with the arguments made here, and Mozi never demands unequal love for parents and children or for king and subordinate officials.

37. *Mozi*, "Elevation of the Worthy II", 9: 4.

38. "If the Son of the Heaven does the good, the Heaven will reward him; if the Son of the Heaven does the evil, the Heaven can punish him." *Mozi*, "The Will of Heaven II", 27: 2.

39. As explained in more details below, Mozi's ideal social and political system is hierarchical rather than equalitarian, and assumes differences in rank, social prestige and remuneration, though advancement is to be open to all and depends on talent and virtue. So he is advocating, wisely, equal opportunity rather than equal results. See Ralph, "Mo Ti and the English Utilitarians," 45–46.

40. *Mozi*, "Will of Heaven III", 28: 4.

41. If one takes into account of the length of the works, then *min* appears in *Mengzi* even more frequently than *Mozi*. Unlike Mengzi, in which substantial arguments spread throughout the whole book, however, the major arguments in Mozi are concentrated in the first half of the book. Consider that large portions of *Mozi* in later chapters deals with matters irrelevant ethics and politics, one may come up with a different statistics: if one counts the first 28 chapters (ending with "The Will of Heaven") which include almost all major arguments in roughly 38,470 characters, then the words *min* and *baixing* appear 219 and 60 times, respectively.

42. *Mengzi*, 4B19.

43. "While rules of propriety (*Li*) should not be extended to the common people (*shuren*), penal punishments should not be applied to high officials (大夫*dafu*)." *Book of Propriety* (*Liji*), Ch. 1. Although it is doubtful that such a distinction was strictly carried out in practice, it remains a Confucian ideal and clearly reflects a class conscious mentality.

44. *Mozi*, "Against Music I", 32: 3; see Watson, *Basic Writings of Mo Tzu*, 111.

45. Since utilitarianism has this built-in property by counting everyone's pleasure and pain equally, it is not surprising that social and even moral status play very insignificant role in the Mohist value system.

46. Ralph, "Mo Ti and the English Utilitarians," 47–48.

47. There have been an enormous amount of news reports on the variety of social problems created by land expropriations associated with the widespread "demolition and relocation" (*chaiqian*) projects. Both peasants and city residents repeatedly complain that the amounts of compensations are two low, and the governments at various levels are colluding with the developers to maximize their shares of profits at the expense of the residents. See, for example, "To Cure the Pain of Demolition and Relocation", *Southern Weekend*, December 31, 2003; Ren Bo and Hu Yifan, "Reforming the Takings Law, Whither Should the Balance Be Tipped?", *Finance Biweekly*, March 20, 2004.

48. *Mozi*, "Indulgence in Excess", 6: 1–3.

49. *Mengzi*, 7A15, trans. Chan, *Source Book in Chinese Philosophy*, 80.

50. *Mozi*, "Against War II", 18: 3.

51. See, for example, *Mozi*, "Seven Calamities", 5: 3, where the government is supposed to maintain normal harvest, and so on. More discussions below on the role of government in promoting uniformities.

52. *Mozi*, "Indulgence in Excess", 6: 4. The plebeian-oriented ethics of Mozi also makes him condemn the kings of his time, who took numerous concubines, depriving many men and women of the opportunity to form procreative families. See *Mozi*, "Indulgence in Excess", 6: 5. By way of comparison, few if any Confucians had touched on this aspect of the court life; many had even sought social justifications for royal debauchery (as illustrated, e.g. in the long standing concubine system).

53. Conceivably, Mozi can be interpreted to support a limited government and active popular participation in social affairs. It seems that Mozi would have the government do less rather than more, in order to promote the welfare of whole society.

54. For discussions about moral dilemmas faced by Benthamite utilitarianism, see Bruce Ackerman, *Social Justice in the Liberal State* (New Havens, CT: Yale University Press, 1980), 314–320.

55. *Mozi*, "Universal Love II", 15: 2.

56. Otherwise, Mohism would have suffered from the same difficulty arising out of utilitarian balance, that is, the extravagant enjoyment of the king and the upper class might compensate the suffering of the lower classes.

57. *Mozi*, "Major Illustrations", 44: 3.
58. Thus, "the love of others does not exclude self, as love admits of no distinction between more and less"; "Love the kin of others, just as you love your own kin.... Love [everyone] universally alike; love [everyone] uniformly alike." *Mozi*, "Major Illustrations", 44: 4, 6.
59. For interpreting "universal love" as "impartial rational concern for all men," see Schwartz, *The World of Thought in Ancient China*, 149.
60. *Mozi*, "Exposition of Canon I", 42: 7.
61. See *Mozi*, "Against Offensive Warfare", 19: 2; "Gongshu", 50: 2.
62. See Wu Jin-an, *A Comparative Study of Confucian Humanity and Mohist Universal Love* (Taipei: Wenshizhe Press, 1993), 155–165.
63. *Mozi*, "The Will of Heaven II", 27: 1; trans. Watson, *Basic Writings of Mo Tzu*, 84.
64. *Mozi*, "The Will of Heaven II", 27: 2; see Watson, *Basic Writings of Mo Tzu*, 84. For the preeminence of Heaven over the Son of Heaven, "I have never heard of Heaven praying for blessings from the Son of Heaven. So I know that Heaven is more eminent and wise than the Son of Heaven." *Mozi*, "The Will of Heaven II", 27: 2; trans. Watson, *Basic Writings of Mo Tzu*, 85.
65. *Mozi*, "The Will of Heaven I", 26: 6; trans. Chan, *Source Book in Chinese Philosophy*, 220.
66. *Mozi*, "The Will of Heaven I", 26: 3; trans. *Chan, Source Book in Chinese Philosophy*, 218.
67. *Mozi*, "The Will of Heaven II", 27: 1.
68. Thus, "What the superior considers right all shall consider right; what the superior considers wrong all shall consider wrong." *Mozi*, "Identifying with One's Superior I", 11: 3.
69. This is not surprising given his unique theory of the state of nature. Mozi, who otherwise speaks sparingly of the inherent human nature, was the first philosopher to provide a state of nature theory. For him, human beings are not born good or evil; nor are they preoccupied with mere survival or material benefits. Rather, it is their basic nature to argue among themselves and find out what is right and wrong. The differences as to what is right predisposed them to struggle against each other, creating mutual harms and hatred. To end such a deplorable condition, there must be some uniformity in the conception of the right, enforced by a common power, which assumes the name and authority of the state. See *Mozi*, "Identifying with One's Superior I", Ch. 11.

70. *Mozi*, "Identifying with One's Superior I", 11: 3.
71. *Mozi*, "Identifying with One's Superior III", 13: 3, see Chan, *Source Book in Chinese Philosophy*, 230.
72. Fung Yu-lan, *History of Chinese Philosophy*, 141. Earlier Liang Qichao held the same view, see his *Case Study on Mozi* (Shanghai Books, 1992), 62–65.
73. See, for example, Fang Shouchu, *The Origin of Mohist Studies* (Shanghai: Zhonghua Books, 1989), 84–86; Liu Zehua ed., *The History of Chinese Political Thought* (Pre-Qin volume) (Hangzhou: Zhejiang People's Press, 1996), 447–453.
74. *Mozi*, "Elevation of the Worthy II," 9: 10.
75. See generally, Zhang Yongyi, *Mozi and the Chinese Culture* (Guiyang: Guizhou People's Press, 2001).
76. *Mengzi*, 5B9.
77. *Mengzi*, 1B8; trans. Chan, *Source Book in Chinese Philosophy*, 62.
78. It is interesting that Locke's famous notion "appeal to Heaven" corresponds quite closely to the Chinese "practicing the Way on behalf of Heaven" (替天行道*titian xingdao*), see his *Second Treatise*, Sec. 20, in *Two Treatises of Government*, ed. Peter Laslett (Cambridge: Cambridge University Press, 1988), 282.
79. *Mozi*, "Identifying with the Superior II", 12: 3.
80. See Xu Xiyan, "Studies on Mohist Political Thought," *Studies in Political Science* 2001 (4): 46–56.
81. *Mozi*, "Elevation of the Worthy I", 8: 10.
82. See his *Clarifications of Ancient History* (vol. 7b), 49, cited in Wang Keqi, "On the Relationship between Mozi and Kongzi, Laozi, and Han Fei," *Studies on Kongzi* 1997 (3): 92–99.
83. *Mozi*, "Identifying with One's Superior I", 11: 3.
84. *Mozi*, "Identifying with the Superior", 13: 1.
85. *Mozi*, "Universal Love III", 16: 5.
86. For an argument that Mozi can be interpreted to support a "theocratic democracy" under the will of Heaven, see Kim, *Fundamental Legal Concepts of China and the West*, 55–63.
87. *Mozi*, "Elevation of the Worthy I", 8: 4; trans. Watson, *Basic Writings of Mo Tzu*, 20–21.
88. See, for example, *Hanfeizi*, Chs. 12, 14, 18–19, 33–35.
89. On this point, see, for example, Zhang Qianfan, "The People's Court in Transition: The Prospects of the Chinese Judicial Reform", *Journal of Contemporary China* 12 (2003): 69–101; "How to Save the Cost

of Implementing the Edicts of Central Government", *Legal Daily*, August 12, 2004.

90. And the westerners also became interested in it because of its superficial similarity with Christianity. See Graham, *Disputers of the Tao, 7*; Mote, *Intellectual Foundations of China*, 90.

91. To be sure, Confucianism was not a closed system; over the time it did undergo self-transformation by absorbing the essence of many other schools of thought (e.g., Daoism and Legalism), and was divided into many sects. But the system of *Li* had preserved the central elements of traditional Confucianism. For the historical development of neo-Confucianism, see Chung-ying Cheng, *New Dimensions of Confucian and Neo-Confucian Philosophy* (Albany: State University of New York Press, 1991), 47–57.

92. A term used in Tu Wei-ming, "*Li* as a Process of Humanization," in *Humanity and Self-Cultivation: Essays in Confucian Thought* (Berkeley: Asian Humanities Press, 1979).

93. Cui Yongdong, "An Analysis of the Ideal Personality in Mohist Design," *Tsinghua University Journal* 1994 (2): 28–33.

94. Admittedly this could be quite a leap, since Mozi would have to substantially modify his doctrine about promoting uniformity, give up unrealistic hopes in mysterious intervention of Heaven in human affairs, and further develop confidence in the ability of the multitude to choose relatively worthy candidates for government posts. Yet, none of these should prove impossible for Mozi.

95. Of course, this idea is best expressed in James Madison's famous Federalist No. 51: "In framing a government which is to be administered by men over men, the real difficulty lies in this: you must first enable the government to control the governed; and in the next place oblige it to control itself." Alexander Hamilton, James Madison, and John Jay, *The Federalist Papers*, ed. Clinton Rossiter (New York: Penguin, 1961), 322. For Mozi, the first point is taken for granted, and the second point is yet to be comprehended, though this problem is not his alone, but shared by virtually all classical philosophers; even the Daoist is no exception.

96. In this aspect, Mozi does share with Bentham, who expressed in his will to donate his body for medical research after his death. See Laurence J. Lafleur, "Introduction," in Bentham, *The Principles of Morals and Legislation* (New York: Haffner Press, 1948), xii–xv.

CHAPTER 6

Primitive Freedom and Human Dignity in Daoism: A Comparison with Rousseau

INTRODUCTION

This chapter completes the previous discussions on the idea of human dignity in Confucianism and Mohism, and focuses on the original contributions made by the early Daoist philosophers in aspects that had been ignored by the Confucians and the Mohists. The most unique contribution of Daoism is that it brings the individual person—simple, uncultivated and, perhaps, selfish person—to the center of moral philosophy. Explicitly for the first time, active fulfillment of social duties ceases to be the unquestioned ground for moral encomium; a person is no longer viewed primarily in terms of relationships to others, but in his own right—more precisely, in his personal relation to the Way, that is, both his destiny and origin of birth. Rather than asking what a person ought to do for his family, the community, and the state—in a word, for others, the Daoist is daring enough to question the very legitimacy of human obligations, and asks instead, what a person should do for his own sake. More than the utilitarian Mohist, the Daoist brings into doubt not only a particular moral code enacted for a people at any particular time, but morality in general, which in one way or another restricts a person's primitive freedom to live as a natural animal. By criticizing the traditional morality and reviving the faith in a primitive, self-sufficient life, Laozi and Zhuangzi add an important dimension to the classical understanding of human dignity: individual

© The Author(s) 2016
Q. Zhang, *Human Dignity in Classical Chinese Philosophy*,
DOI 10.1057/978-1-349-70920-5_6

freedom, particularly the freedom of living under the minimum burden, direction, and oppression of the state.

The chapter is divided into three main parts. It first explores the Daoist moral philosophy centered on the Way and human freedom. Distinguishing itself from other schools of Chinese philosophy, the Daoist takes the self as the ultimate end of human pursuit, thereby recovering human dignity from excessive burdens of social or familial obligations that tend to crush individual personality. Second, it discusses the Daoist political program as a way to realize its moral ideals and examines the extent to which the early Daoists have succeeded in building a consistent theory to effectively pursue a free personal life. I argue that, although the Daoists express the romantic longing for personal freedom, their unnecessarily radical hostility against reason and institutional building has prevented them from formulating an effective mechanism to gain, protect, and maintain such freedom.

Finally, a comparison is made with Rousseau's account of the state of nature and the origin of civil society. Such comparison may be surprising to many since Rousseau is commonly viewed as a radical proponent of direct democracy, whose political position seems to be diametrically opposed to that of passively liberal Daoists. Yet, the Daoists share many views on human nature and ideal society with Rousseau, who also vehemently criticizes various aspects of modern civilization in his second *Discourse*.[1] Thus, a meaningful comparison can be made even though, in the end, Rousseau adopts a solution opposite to the Daoist one. Seeing clearly the impossibility of pulling back the clock, Rousseau would have the civilized society transcend its current condition to gain civilized freedom under the general will. The chapter ends with a brief critique of the inconsistencies shared by Rousseau's and the Daoist political theories.

THE WAY AND THE DAOIST FREEDOM

A Total Break with Traditional Morality

If Kongzi, followed by Mengzi and particularly Xunzi, seeks to preserve the traditional *Li* as a moral constitution for society, and Mozi seeks to reform the particular provisions of this constitution under the overarching utilitarian principle, then the Daoist proposes to abolish artificial rules and customs altogether. Like Mozi and his disciples, the Daoists as represented in the classic *Laozi* (道德经) and *Zhuangzi*,[2] criticize Confucianism for making social distinctions contrary to the Daoist understanding of the Way (道 *dao*) as the ultimate One. Thus, "[p]erfect humanity knows no kinship"; "Perfect humanity is unsurpassable; words like filial piety can never suffice to describe it."[3] But the Daoist has gone much further in that direction. While the writings of Mozi represent a limited attack on the obstinate insistence of the later Confucians upon the anachronistic and wasteful system of *Li* and *yue* (music), and a comparatively limited reform of such a tradition based on its utilitarian principle commanding universal love, Laozi and Zhuangzi propose nothing less than a total break with everything traditional and repudiation of all social distinctions in order for mankind to regain the true meaning of life. Thus, "from the view of the Way, things are neither noble nor ignoble.... Ten thousand things are equal as one. [How can we tell] which is shorter and which is longer?"[4]

Put together, the Daoist works constitute a grand indictment of human civilization. They seek to awaken the lethargic minds hitherto content with the accepted doctrines of morality based on social distinctions. In reality, what is branded as "moral" or "good" often amounts to no more than the adulation of the powerful, which renders a large part of moral teachings to mere hypocrisy. In the somewhat cynical view of Zhuangzi, "[he] who steals a buckle gets the death penalty; he who steals the state gets the lordship, and benevolence and righteousness are to be found at the lord's gates."[5] For Laozi and Zhuangzi, human problems, which they confronted over 2000 years ago, no less than we do today, are to be solved neither by moral indoctrination under the names of *Ren*, *Yi*, and universal love, nor by astute political schemes or severe legal punishments; all these artifices merely lead mankind further away from the natural Way that gives birth to everything existing—Heaven, the Earth, and mankind. Repudiate knowledge, sagely teachings, and clever reason, which have merely served to pollute the simple morals of the primitive people; discard every nicety that the civilization had manufactured to distract a person from living according to his own Nature; return to the primitive community where men and women, as simple and sincere as they were in their infancy, and live a natural life as destined by the great Way and where they regain the paradise of primitive freedom. The rulers, on the other hand, should do nothing (无为 *wuwei*) but maintain such a primitive state of affairs.

The Daoist rejects a tendency commonly present and seek something commonly absent in both Confucianism and Mohism. While Confucianism can be interpreted to support moral autonomy and personal independence, and even Mohism can be construed to require treating everyone as the end and not merely as means, in practice, they are all too easily disposed to immerse, and ultimately dissolve, an individual person in the relationship to others. Under the crushing burden of a myriad of social obligations and the stringent demand of universal love (which does *not* require anyone to sacrifice himself, but does require him to love everyone as he loves himself and his kin), a person can no longer live his own life; properly speaking, he is living primarily not for himself, but for others. He is no longer taken, by others or by himself, to be the person he is, but only a son of his father, a subject of his lord, or a universal servant whose worth lies solely in the benefits he confers to the world. He sees himself as the summation of the duties he owes to his kin and superior, and of the various sorts of comfort he may derive in turn from the duties others owe to him. In him as in everyone else, the very essence of personhood is lost. Such a person is necessarily deficient in dignity, just as dignity is lacking in a slave or an instrument used for purposes other than itself. The Daoist effort is precisely to rediscover and regain the essence of self that has been lost, perhaps in small steps, each imperceptible to human consciousness, along the path toward civilization.

The Self as the Ultimate End

Opposed to both Kongzi and Mozi, who lay heavy emphasis upon one's social duty and pay homage to those sage-kings who supposedly had saved society from dissolution, Laozi and Zhuangzi extol the virtue of private life and seek to convince men and women to return to their natural, easy, and simple way of living, by which they can live in touch with their true selves. This idea is pervasive in the work of Zhuangzi, who repeatedly preaches "the usefulness of being useless," as against turning oneself into a useful tool, thereby abandoning one's own nature. "The Truth of the Way is in looking out for oneself; its fringes and leftovers consist in managing the state; its offal and weeds consist in governing the empire."[6]

The Daoist principle is generally consistent with the teaching of Yangzi, who challenges his contemporary archrival, Mozi, by questioning *not* whether one ought to do useful and beneficial things, but what is truly useful and beneficial to life—one's own and everyone else's life.[7] While "Kongzi valued benevolence, Mozi valued being for everyone, ... Yangzi valued self"[8]; "Keeping one's nature intact, protecting one's genuineness, and not letting the body be tied by other things—these Yangzi advocated but Mengzi condemned."[9] The idea of Yangzi, it seems, is to leave everyone to benefit his own person and allow the others to do the same. Here, we have a flavor of the early Chinese individualism.[10] The way Yangzi views the self naturally leads him to value one's person as the ultimate end that is above everything else, whether wealth, high office or the honor it entails. Thus, "our life is our own possession, and its benefit to us is very great. Regarding its dignity, even the honor of being Emperor could not compare with it. Regarding its importance, even the wealth of possessing the world would not be exchanged for it."[11] As "regarding its safety, were we to lose it for one morning, we could never again bring it back,"[12] we ought to value ourselves and take things lightly.

The divergence in the view of human nature and society among Confucianism, Mohism and Daoism begins with the metaphysical meaning of the Way. Unlike "the Way of Heaven" (天道 *tiandao*) in Confucianism, the Way in Daoism, as the ultimate source of all things, is more fundamental than Heaven and the Earth. It is the eternal, spontaneous, nameless and indescribable One, the differentiation of which gives rise to Heaven, the Earth, humans, and other things.[13] While the Confucian and Mohist Heaven is the source of morality and universal love that governs the human world, such moral connotations are entirely absent in the Daoist Way. On the contrary, the Way, as a morally neutral principle that governs the whole universe, transcends the human concerns of good and evil. Everything in that universe has its own nature, and to change it is as futile as harmful. The duck's legs are short, just as the crane's legs are long; it would equally violate their nature to stretch the former and to shorten the latter in order to fit the aesthetic views held by parts of the human species.[14] No less than other animals in the universe, mankind too has its inalienable nature, and Zhuangzi wonders whether the man-made doctrines of *Ren* and *Yi*, imposed upon ordinary men and women by the force of social sanctions and legal punishments, are unlike the stretching and shortening of legs. Just like everything else, a human being has an innate Virtue (德 *de*) or natural character insofar as he spontaneously participates in the Way, free from the interference of human artifice.[15] Thus, "human beings model themselves after the Earth; the Earth models itself after Heaven; Heaven models itself after the Way; and the Way models itself after Nature (自然 *ziran*)."[16] As long as a person holds fast to his natural Virtue, he cannot be far from the Way and Nature. As Laozi reportedly says to Kongzi:

Heaven and the Earth hold fast to their constant ways, the sun and moon to their brightness, the stars and planets to their ranks, the birds and beasts to their flocks, the trees and shrubs to their stands. You have only to go along with Virtue in your actions, to follow the Way in your journey, and already will you be there.[17]

Thus, like Confucianism, the idea of treating oneself as the end and never as means is prominent in the Daoist thinking. But, unlike the Confucian who, seeing everyone as potentially a moral and rational being, requires a person to fulfill his social duties, the Daoist sees human beings as naturalistic, amoral animals who ought to shun all desires for honor, power, and socially imposed responsibilities in order to live with their true nature. It is the nature of every animal to remain free—humans no less than brutes, and freedom means more than any comfort of life. Mote is quite accurate when he points out that the Confucian value lies in humans, and the Daoist in nature.[18] It is too often forgotten that humans still belong to the animal kingdom and should not lose altogether the simple freedom common to the living species.

Human Dignity in the Daoist Universe

Like Confucianism, Daoism accords to human beings a high position in the universe, and the optimism about human nature has allowed the Daoist to develop a liberal view on government. According to Laozi, mankind is elevated to a status parallel to that of the Way, Heaven, and the Earth. "Thus, the Way is great; Heaven is great; the Earth is great; and humans are also great. There are four great things in the universe, and one of them is man."[19] Not surprisingly, however, the "great humans" here take a completely different meaning from the Confucian counterpart. He is not a moral and rational being in the conventional sense, as one may gather from the works of Mengzi and Xunzi; rather, he is free, natural, and spontaneous in the primitive sense, acting as he is destined by the amoral Nature. Thus, the perfect person is marked not by conventional moral virtues, which would only distract him from the Way, making him no different from those petty men who live in a way contrary to their true nature, but by free spontaneity achieved only through the intuitive (and somewhat mysterious) experience of the Way, when he is freed from desire and passions for external objects. Likewise, a perfect society is not one in which everyone is busy with such lofty principles as humanity, righteousness, or universal love, but a primitive community in which every member pursues his own life according to the inborn virtue. Such a society is not far from the state of nature described by Mozi, Mengzi, and Xunzi, except that it is characterized by a great deal more peace, joy and spontaneity, and much less violence, misery and incapacity so many thinkers have uncritically attributed to mankind in its natural state.

Thus, the Daoist account of state of nature differs completely from all other schools. To a Confucian and or a Mohist, the people in the state of nature were either incapable of providing for their own basic needs (Mengzi) or iniquitous to others' welfare, drawing themselves into a war of all against all (Mozi and Xunzi), the state of nature to Zhuangzi was a Garden of Eden, in which the primitive people enjoyed lives without the worries and desires multiplied in a modern society. Through the infamous Robber Zhi (盗跖), Zhuangzi provides a vivid picture of men and women living in a peaceful state of nature:

> In the age of Shen Nong, the people laid down peaceful and easy, woke up wide-eyed and blank. They knew their mothers but not their fathers, and lived side by side with the elk and the deer. They plowed for their food, wove for their clothing, and had no thought in their hearts of harming one another. This was Perfect Virtue at its height.[20]

Presupposed in these passages is the ability of ordinary human beings to provide for their own living. The primitive people are necessarily poor and perhaps ignorant, but they know enough to produce the basic means to sustain a peaceful, self-sufficient and, perhaps, reasonably comfortable life. They take no interest in sages, heroes, and statesmen because these are superfluities of a complex modern society. Nor are they interested in making themselves one of those types, for social honor to them is a burden, and luxury the very origin of debauchery and decay.[21] In a society with minimal needs and wants, the people can manage their own daily lives, and the government is necessarily relegated to a marginal role.

THE DAOIST GOVERNANCE

Toward a Minimal Government

Having identified the true good and the causes for true evil, the Daoist does not hesitate to propose radical measures in order to implement their primitive utopia.[22] They believe that the people can be restored to their natural conditions simply by abolishing all those nice artifices that come along with civilization. As Laozi puts it, "Abandon sageliness and discard wisdom; the people will benefit a hundred-fold. Abandon humanity and justice; the people will return to filial piety and deep love. Abandon skill and discard profit; there will be no thieves or robbers."[23] Following Laozi, Zhuangzi appeals to the complete abandonment of reason, knowledge and conventional morals.[24] A government does exist even in such a primitive society, but its function is neither to promote any positive good—because the people can supply enough of it with their own hands—nor to honor the worthy and virtuous—because the primitive people have no need for them—nor to punish and prevent crimes—because evils so prevailing in a civilized society are unknown to a people with so simple morals. Rather, its function is purely negative, that is, to guarantee that the people will continue to live in such a primitive and ignorant state, free from external disturbances—luxuries, wisdom, and, above all, those Confucian and Mohist sages, the culprits who have stirred up the human ambitions that break the serenity of a primitive mind. Once again, the dialectic teachings of Laozi reflect his deep insight into the evils inherent in a big "benevolent" government:

> The more taboos there are in the empire, the poorer the people. The more sharpened tools the people have, the more benighted the state. The more skill the people possess, the further novelties multiply. The more laws and orders are made prominent, the more thieves and robbers come into being. Therefore the sage says: I take no action, and the people of themselves are transformed. I prefer tranquility, and the people of themselves become correct. I engage in no activity, and the people of themselves become prosperous. I have no desires, and the people of themselves become simple.[25]

Thus, in contrast to all other classical doctrines, Daoism is in full support for a minimal state. Like the Confucians and Mohists, the Daoist condemns those tyrants who exploit their people for satisfaction of their sensuous desires, or muster troops and kill the people of the neighboring states merely for enlarging their own territories.[26] Joining their intellectual rivals, the Daoist insists that a government is to protect the people's lives, and avoid endangering their physical survival by all means.[27] While they all denounce political tyranny from which the people suffer materially, the Daoist sees further that the evil of a government lie precisely in its attempt or pretense of actively doing good for its people. In fact, the capacity of a government increases proportionally to the loss of the people's energy and purity. As Laozi puts it, "when the government is dull, the people are simple. When the government is searching, the people become cunning."[28] Once the government busies itself doing everything for the people, ordinary men and women would lay down in idleness and degenerate to the point where Mengzi finds them, capable of nothing but waiting for heroes and sage-kings to save them from chaos and calamities; a weak, domesticated civilization further necessitates a "benevolent government," keeping it permanently handicapped in serfdom. To the contrary, an ideal Daoist ruler always does the minimum, and leaves the people alone to provide for their own needs.[29]

The Daoist Inconsistencies

Laozi and Zhuangzi condemn every human artifice that was created under the name of humanity and righteousness, but more often than not turned out to be an instrument with which the stronger and the wicked can exploit the world more efficiently and legitimately. They propose a radical move back to a primitive society maintained by a minimal government acting in accordance with the Way. The Daoist rejection of reason, knowledge and civilized society is, however, at best a simplistic solution[30]; it is both unrealistic and self-defeating. First, although Laozi and Zhuangzi see the problems inherent in the existing morality, they have not shown the plausibility of returning to the primitive state without creating disastrous social consequences. In a way, the Daoist is even more conservative than the Confucian because, while the latter looks only to the immediate past (the Zhou Dynasty) to find the true principle of government, Laozi and Zhuangzi would require mankind to go all the way back to the beginning of human history. The Daoist fails to realize that their idealistic state of nature, if ever existed in human history, had irretrievably passed as soon as mankind entered the civilized condition; there is no way back, and nothing constructive is accomplished by simply demolishing the current morality.

Second, the Daoists contradict themselves by presupposing a supremely wise government that keeps everyone else in that society primitive and ignorant (in order to live according to the Daoist nature), while refraining from abusing its monopolized knowledge and power. This is no more than a wishful dream, to be realized only (if ever) in extremely rare cases of the true "sage-kings." In order to keep the people naive and ignorant, the Daoist opens the door to heavy manipulations of the ruling elites, the surest road toward tyranny. In seeking to implement an impractical mechanism to preserve primitive freedom, the Daoist is compelled—more than the Confucian and Mohist—to pin his hopes solely on the elite-monopolized powers, which are necessarily inimical to liberty itself. Thus, the Daoists are confronted by the same fundamental problem that confronts the Confucian and Mohist—how to design a rational government? And they have failed to provide a feasible solution.

The failure of Daoism is rooted in its radical attitude toward reason and in its implicit distrust of the rational capacity possessed by ordinary human beings.[31] Although the people are capable of providing for their own means of life, the Daoist writings have nothing to suggest that they are also capable of governing themselves in a relatively complex society. To the contrary, it seems that the people are bound to either remain ignorant or misuse their knowledge and wisdom—the very means that make a civilized society possible. As a result, the only solution feasible to a Daoist is the resurrection of primitive society, in which the government rules over a mass of people kept as ignorant infants. True self-government is as (if not more) illusory in Daoism as it is in Confucianism and Mohism. Having abandoned reason and wisdom in favor of primitive freedom, the Daoist ultimately fails to gain any freedom in the practical world. Freedom is cherished, but without the aid of reason, it remains an unfulfilled dream. In the end, Daoism is reduced to a passive ethic, merely providing a private sanctuary for those who were disheartened by the corrupt political and social realities.

Rousseau as a Western Daoist?

The Daoist is, of course, not alone in romanticizing primitive men and women in the state of nature. Many centuries later, a "citizen of Geneva" paints very much the same portrait of a robust and content savage. Jean-Jacques Rousseau, who is to be remembered not only for the first book bearing the title of "social contract," but also for providing Kant with the inspiration for his categorical imperative in shaping the theory of human dignity, distinguishes himself from his predecessors, Hobbes and Locke, and particularly the former by picturing the state of nature as an innocent paradise rather than a sinister jungle. Here, we find a pervasive Daoist shadow. Both the Daoist and Rousseau reject the unproved presuppositions, whether Hobbesian, Mengzian, or Mohist, on the deplorable miseries of primitive societies; both assume that the primitive person is simple, healthy, and self-sufficient, and both advocate for small states. Their similarities end here, however, for ultimately Rousseau disagrees with the Daoist that such state of being is a realistic option. Instead of indulging in the golden age of Eden permanently lost, Rousseau proposes a radical solution, in which man is to be "forced to be free" if his myopic selfishness makes it necessary; having departed from primitive natural liberty, according to Rousseau, the humans have no choice but acquire civil liberty through a social contract.

The State of Nature

To Rousseau as to the Daoist, the state of nature in which a savage lived was an innocent paradise—poor but sustainable and self-sufficient: "Being naked, homeless and deprived of all those useless things we believe so necessary is no great misfortune for these first men, and above all no great obstacle to their preservation."[32] And Rousseau's savage, like the primitive inhabitants in the Daoist writings, was simple and content precisely because he was poor and ignorant:

> *savage man, wandering in forests, without work, without speech, without home, without war, and without relationships, was equally without any need of his fellow men and without any desire to hurt them, perhaps not even recognizing any one of them individually. Being subject to so few passions, and sufficient unto himself, he had only such feelings and such knowledge as suited his condition; he felt only his true needs, saw only what he believed it was necessary to see, and his intelligence made no more progress than his vanity.*[33]

Thus, living under extremely simple conditions and without knowledge of progress, luxury, or envy, the savage desired few things beyond sheer physical needs, thereby preserving his psychological tranquility. Could such a condition be so miserable as supposed by Hobbes and others? Rousseau emphatically rejects such conventional wisdom, which wishfully pictured the lot of a savage not in his own condition, but in an already civilized state in which the modern men and women were living. It is often said that the state of nature is a jungle in which the strongest rules, but the savage for Rousseau has neither means nor intent for oppressing others:

> *What is intelligence to people who do not speak, or cunning to those who have no commerce with others? I hear it constantly repeated that the stronger will oppress the weak,...but how will he ever be able to exact obedience? And what sort of*

chains of dependence could exist among men who possess nothing? He is obliged to expose himself voluntarily to much worse trouble than the trouble he wishes to avoid, or gives to me.[34]

To the contrary, the moral world of a savage was just as simple as his physical world: "One could say that the savage are not wicked precisely because they do not know what it is to be good, for it is neither development of intelligence nor restrains of laws, but calm of passions and their ignorance of vice which prevents them from doing evil."[35] In fact the savage had a good deal more compassion than modern man, as "pity becomes all the more intense as perceiving animal identifies itself more intimately with suffering animal."[36] It is only when he was "dazzled by enlightenment, tormented by passions, and arguing about a state different from his own"—in a word, when he began to be civilized—that he became a miserable animal tormented by a variety of desires and iniquitous ideas. While "the savage man breathes only peace and freedom; he desires only to live and stay idle,"

Civil man, being always active, sweating and restless, torments himself endlessly in search of ever more laborious occupations; he works himself to death, he even runs towards grave to put himself into shape to live, or renounces life in order to acquire immortality.... The savage lives within himself; social man always lives outside himself; he knows how to live only in opinion of others, and it is, so to speak, from their judgment alone that he derives sense of his own exist.... We have only facades, deceptive and frivolous, honor without virtue, reason without wisdom, and pleasure without happiness.[37]

Corruption of the Enlightenment

Thus, Rousseau is almost repeating Mengzi when he writes: "Men are wicked, melancholy and constant experience removes any need for proof; yet man is naturally good."[38] When and how did this fatal transition take place? Once again Rousseau shares with the Daoist that the ultimate source of corruption is human reason and knowledge which, far from procuring what the conventional wisdom purported to be "progress," permanently destroyed the peace both within the soul and in the outer world.[39] In his inclination against reason, knowledge, and progress, Rousseau seems to be another romantic Daoist.

For Rousseau as for the Daoist, the sin began with knowledge. "It is reason which breeds pride and reflection which fortifies it; reason which turns man inward into himself; reason which separates him from everything which troubles or affects him."[40] From knowledge and introspection arose comparison, valuation, and perception of inequality—the seed of evil and violence: "He who sang or danced the best, he who was most handsome, the strongest, the most adroit or the most eloquent became the most highly regarded; and this was first step towards inequality and, at same time, toward vice."[41] The initial inequality was further engrossed by education, which not only "establish differences between cultivated minds and those which are not, but it increases the difference among cultivated minds in proportion to their culture; for when a giant and a dwarf walk the same road, every step each takes gives extra advantage to giant."[42] As a result, the modest distinctions of the natural qualities developed into fully blown social inequality, hypocrisy, and other modern vices:

> *Behold, then, all our faculties developed, memory and imagination brought into play, pride stimulated, reason made active and mind almost at point of perfection of which is capable. Behold all natural qualities called into action, rank and destiny of each established, not only as to the quantity of his possessions and his power to serve or to injure, but as to the intelligence, beauty, strength, skill, merit or talents; and since these qualities were only ones that could attract consideration it soon became necessary either to have them or to feign them. It was necessary in one's own interest to seem to be other than one was in reality. Being and appearance became two entirely different things, and from this distinction arose insolent ostentation, deceitful cunning and all vices that follow in their train.*[43]

Characteristic of a modern society is its distinction, mutual cooperation, and interdependence, all of which are needed for producing a variety of goods perceived to be necessary for maintaining a civilized life. To Rousseau, however, this was precisely where the first slavery and servitude took place: "since bonds of servitude are formed only through mutual dependence of men and reciprocal needs that unite them, it is impossible to enslave a man without first putting him in situation where he cannot do without another man, and since such situation does not exist in the state of nature, each man there is free of yoke, and the law of the strongest is rendered vain."[44] However, "from the moment that one man needed help of another, and it was realized that it would be useful for one man to have provisions enough for two, equality disappeared; property was introduced, work became necessary and vast forests were transformed into peasant fields which had to be watered by the sweat of men, and in which slavery and misery were soon seen to germinate and flourish with crops."[45]

From economic cooperation, many goods and progresses are achieved, the material and social lives of the civilized world are greatly enriched, and from Adam Smith onward, liberal economists have always preached that such a mutually dependable and cooperative state is not only best for procuring human prosperity, but also the very condition for sustaining peace and order. To Rousseau, however, such state of things is not only less charitable in reality than it is in scholarly imagination because it is invariably accompanied with grave inequality, which produces both poverty and indolence, but also susceptible to crimes and treacheries:

> *Admire human society as you will, it is nonetheless true that it necessarily leads men to hate each other in proportion to the extent that their interests conflict, and to pretend to render each other services while actually doing each other every imaginary harm…. We each find our profit at the expense of our fellows, and one man's loss is nearly always good fortune of another…. If I am answered by the assertion that society is so constituted that each man gains by serving others, I shall reply that that would be all very well but for the fact that he would gain even more by harming them. There is no profit so legitimate that it cannot be exceeded by what can be made illegitimately and the injury done to neighbor is always more lucrative than any service. The only problem that remains is that of finding ways of assuring one's impunity, and this is the end for which the powerful use all their strength and the weak use all their cunning.*[46]

In fact, crimes and violence were natural incidents to the civilized society, in which valuation, comparison, vanity, and anger were pervasive. The primitive savage was permanently transformed to civilized man, whose passion for revenge replaced tranquility of mind, and even the harshest criminal law was insufficient in keeping violence in check. Here Rousseau joins the Daoist again in observing that, in the civilized state, greater punishments simply beget more crimes.

Toward Civil Liberty

Ultimately, however, Rousseau is no Daoist. Unlike the Daoist, who seem to be unconditionally opposed to reason, Rousseau claims only that human reason was put to wrong use in the unwitting process toward civilization and that, far from indiscriminately abandoning science and knowledge, mankind is obliged to acquire real science, that is, the science about human being itself, in order that knowledge is put to the proper use that truly benefits human lives.[47] Nor is Rousseau unswervingly clung to the golden past, as is the Daoist, since it is practically impossible to return to the past and recover the innocent freedom of the savages. To him, the rise of civilization had its own cause that need be explored precisely with human reason so as to learn the lesson of its faltering; it is much more constructive to devise institutional mechanisms through which mankind can cure the vices of the civilized life and regain freedom, albeit in a new dimension.

Rousseau does not explain the exact events that drove human race toward the first enlightenment, but he makes a plausible argument that the early civilization confronted certain urgent need for survival.[48] From the scarcity that made the primitive living unsustainable were derived agriculture, metallurgy, and property rights. Thus, "for philosopher it is iron and wheat which first civilized men and ruined the human race."[49]

How do we escape the predicament imposed by the enlightenment? Rousseau's solution is no less than a radical transformation of the natural state, which could no longer remain natural as a consequence of the civilized perversions, through a social contract made with unanimous consent:

> *Each of us places his person and all his power in common under the supreme direction of the general will; and as one we receive each member as indivisible part of the whole. At once, in place of individual person of each contracting party, this act of association produces a moral and collective body composed of as many members as there are voices in the assembly, which receives from this same act its unity, its common self, its life and its will. This public person ... at present takes the name republic or body politic.[50]*

This process is a voluntary act of one's free choice, since "in giving himself to all, each person gives himself to no one. And since there is no associate over whom he does not acquire the same right that he would grant others over himself, he gains the equivalent of everything he loses, along with the greater amount of force to preserve what he has."[51] This dramatic act produces, of course, significant changes to mankind, since it imposes a variety of civil obligations over the hitherto physically free individuals, who were no longer free in a perverse civilization:

> *This passage from state of nature to civil state produces quite a remarkable change in man, for it substitutes justice for instinct in his behavior and gives his actions moral quality they previously lacked. Only then, when the voice of duty replaces physical impulse and right replaces appetite, does man, who had hitherto taken only himself into account, find himself forced to act upon other*

*principles and to consult his reason before listening to his inclinations. Although
in this state he deprives himself of several of advantages belonging to him in
the state of nature, he regains such great ones. His faculties are exercised and
developed, his ideas are broadened, his feelings are ennobled, his entire soul is
elevated to such height.*[52]

To Rousseau, this fundamental choice is free precisely because it is
good for everyone. Of course, an average person may nevertheless fail to
see its good due to his myopic selfishness, and thus may have to be "forced
to be free."[53] On the whole, Rousseau believes that the "balance sheet" is
so clear enough and everyone would agree that the gains to be achieved
by entering a true civil society outweigh the losses:

*What man loses through the social contract is his natural liberty and the unlim-
ited right to everything that tempts him and that he can acquire. What he gains
is civil liberty and proprietary ownership of all he possesses. So as not to be in
error in these compensations, it is necessary to draw careful distinction between
natural liberty (which is limited solely by the force of individuals involved)
and civil liberty (which is limited by the general will), and between possession
(which is merely the effect of force or right of the first occupant) and proprietary
ownership (which is based solely on positive title). To the preceding acquisitions
could be added acquisition in the civil state of moral liberty, which alone makes
man truly master of himself. For to be driven by appetite alone is slavery, and
obedience to the law one has prescribed for oneself is liberty.*[54]

Thus, liberty remains the focus of Rousseau's social contract, which
merely substitutes the unsustainable natural liberty with reliable civil
liberty. To Rousseau, "[the greatest good] boils down to two principal
objects, liberty and equality. Liberty, because all particular dependence is
that much force taken from the body of state; equality, because liberty cannot subsist without it."[55] It seems that equality, thought by many to be the
ultimate motive behind Rousseau's theory, is only secondary to liberty—
only as a necessary condition for its subsistence. And at least certain passages from the *Social Contract* suggest that Rousseau's equality is far from
an absolute end,[56] but only equal right before the law. Such equality is to
be forcefully maintained, merely because it is too easily destroyed by the
free play of forces, but is never meant by Rousseau to outweigh liberty.
In fact equality can even be viewed as a key element in the mutuality of
the voluntary act from which the social contract derives its binding force:
"Since citizens are all equal by social contract, what everyone should do

can be prescribed by everyone. On the other hand, no one has right to demand that someone else do what he does not do for himself."[57]

Since the social contract is a purely voluntary act, individual consent is absolutely necessary. It seems to Rousseau that human freedom, unlike mere physical freedom of other animals, is above all freedom of will, which makes mankind both wicked and hopeful: "while nature alone activates everything in operations of a beast, man participates in his own actions in his capacity as free agent. The beast chooses or rejects by instinct, man by act of freewill, which means that beast cannot deviate from laws which are prescribed to it, even when it might be advantageous for it to do so, whereas man often deviates from such rules to his own prejudice."[58] And this is precisely why slavery is absolutely unacceptable since it alienates the basic personality of the slaves. This dehumanizing coercion of slavery, which destroyed the very essence of a free person, cannot coexist with Rousseau's ideal civil society, in which human freedom is recovered through the exercise of free will and everyone is to be ruled by laws expressing the general will of which he is a part.

Rousseau's free will is far from an unrestrained display of one's own passion, much less a lawless anarchy. To the contrary, not only that everyone is to be ruled under law, but the laws are to be made in accord with the "general will," which is the soul of the sovereign established by the social contract and is to be formed in the process of collective deliberations in a general assembly attended by every citizen. To Rousseau, laws made in such process are regarded as an act of free will exercised by all citizens: "when the entire populace enacts statue concerning the entire populace, it considers only itself."[59] Such laws are not only general, "like the will that enacts it," but also just "since no one is unjust to himself."[60] In this way, Rousseau thinks, the conundrum of maintaining freedom while subject to laws is resolved, "since they are merely record of our own wills."[61] Bound by the social contract, a citizen is obliged to render services "as soon as the sovereign demands them," but such services cannot be onerous, since "for its part, the sovereign cannot impose on subjects any fetters that are of no use to community. It cannot even will to do so, for under the law of reason nothing takes place without cause, any more than under the law of nature."[62]

Rousseau is not altogether optimistic about the wisdom of ordinary citizens in discovering suitable laws through which the sovereign acts. In fact, like the Daoist, he at times feels necessary to have a ruler of supreme wisdom, even fictions of divine power, to impose wise rules for the ignorant, myopic and easily confused mass: "Discovering rules of society best suited to the nations would require superior intelligence that beheld all passions of men without feeling any of them; who had no affinity with our nature, yet knew it through and through; whose happiness was independent of us, yet who nevertheless was willing to concern itself with ours; …Gods would be needed to give men laws."[63] On the whole, however, Rousseau trusts the democratic process through which common people reach the general will and suitable laws that will bring felicity to the community.

Rousseau's Inconsistencies

Rousseau did not, of course, write his *Social Contract* on a plain slate. Like the Daoist, he also takes the prototype of his ideal society from the past; unlike the Daoist, however, his ideal is not the original state of nature, but the classical polity exemplified in the Athenian democracy. In this sense, *Social Contract* is not so much an intellectual revolution as a restatement of classical democratic tradition, which serves as the intellectual and political foundation for Rousseau, a foundation obviously unknown to the Daoist. In fact, the very concept of "republic," alien to the Daoist, is central to Rousseau: "I therefore call every state ruled by laws republic, regardless of the form its administration may take. For only then does the public interest govern…. Every legitimate government is a republic."[64] And Rousseau's ideal type of republic is the Athenian city-state, in which citizens directly participated in making every public decision.

Like the Daoist but for different reasons, Rousseau prefers small states to large empires. To Rousseau, small size is decisive for a direct participatory democracy. Rousseau's preference for small states derives partly from his insistence on the unity of the sovereign, which will be destroyed in a federation of states, and partly from his somewhat peculiar objection to representative democracy, the institutional precondition for building a large federal state that the American Founders held to be more advantageous for protecting individual liberty.[65] Laws for Rousseau are identified with the direct expression of the general will, which must be decided by the people directly rather than through their representatives, because he somehow insists that the elected representatives cannot be made responsive to their constituencies beyond the election day: "The moment a people gives itself to the representatives, it is no longer free; it no longer exists,"[66] so does the general will.

More fundamentally, Rousseau shares with the Daoist in presupposing that an ideal community is necessarily small and simple. Small community is crucial for maintaining a tight social bond among the members of community, which a large state cannot secure. Increasing the size of the state, you will not only multiply the difficulties in communicating among the citizens given the technological conditions at Rousseau's time, but also tend to dissolve the bonds among citizens by bringing in more diverse interests, mores and customs, which cannot fail to obscure and destroy the general will:

> When the social bond begins to relax and the state to grow weak, when private interests begin to make themselves felt and small societies begin to influence the large one, the common interest changes and finds opponents. Unanimity no longer reigns in votes; the general will is no longer the will of all. Contradictions and debates arise, and the best advice does not pass without disputes.[67]

Thus, "it is always evil to unite several towns in single city, and ... anyone wanting to bring about this union should not expect to avoid its natural disadvantage."[68] It is much better to have a small state, in which the general will can be easily ascertained from a simple and cohesive set of preferences of similar citizens: "the manner in which general business is taken care of can provide rather accurate indication of the present state of mores and of the health of the body politic. The more harmony reigns in the assemblies, that is to say, the closer opinions come to unanimity, the more dominant too is the general will. But long debates, dissensions, and tumult betoken the ascendance of private interest and the decline of the state. Since citizens have but one interest, the people had but one will."[69] For these reasons, Rousseau summarizes several conditions to be fulfilled before his social contract can be put to practice:

> First, very small state where it is easy for the people to gather together and where each citizen can easily know all others. Second, great simplicity of mores, which prevents multitude of public business and thorny discussions. Next, high degree of equality in ranks and fortunes, without which equality in rights and authority cannot subsist for long. Finally, little or no luxury, for luxury either is effect of wealth or it makes wealth necessary.[70]

Even for a simple and small state, however, these conditions are not necessarily fulfilled. Deliberate and heavy-handed measures would have to be taken, presumably by the government, to equalize the "rank and fortunes," to suppress wealth and luxury, and, above all, to censor opinions. But who will be the censor? How to keep his power from turning into an arbitrary exercise of personal whim rather than the rational command of the general will? To these questions Rousseau has offered no answer, just as the Daoist cannot answer the question of finding a virtuous and supremely wise king, who is trusted to forcibly maintain the community in its ignorant primitive state without exploiting such formidable power for his private gain. Eventually we are led to question the consistency in Rousseau's arguments, which purports to preserve civil liberty through a social contract, in the same way we question the consistency in the Daoist arguments, which purports to preserve primitive liberty by returning to the primitive community: how much liberty is ultimately preserved in such a unitary and simple state maintained under force and manipulation of opinions?

This is not a place to provide a systematic critique of the inconsistencies in Rousseau's pitting the "general will" against private wills, or of the rationale in maintaining small democracies as opposed to federal republics.[71] To be sure, it is methodologically fatal to presuppose that the independent wills of individual persons can be united to form a fictitious "general will," in which the unanimity of interests, opinions and votes are magically reached. Rousseau writes that "so long as several men together consider themselves to be one single body, they have but single will, which is concerned with their common preservation and general well-being."[72] Such a condition is impossible to attain even in such a small unit as an average Chinese village. It suffices to point out here that the root problems in Rousseau's theory lie in the obstinate insistence on direct participatory democracy by which absolute liberty can be preserved in a civilized state and the unrealistic presumption that individual wills can be united in a general will as long as the community is kept sufficiently small to make the interests simple and identical. He is quite accurate to foresee the vices in modern large democracies, where the interests have multiplied to an extent where the "general will" is beyond the possibility of identification and the bewildered voters are often fooled by the unaccountable politicians. But his simplistic solution of ironing out individual differences, far from curing these problems, implies the dangerous tendency of eliminating the very liberty it strives to preserve; the "terror of Robespierre" near the end of the French Revolution tragically illustrated the unintended consequences of ruthlessly suppressing the social differences under the name of the "general will."

ROUSSEAU, DAOISM, AND BEYOND

Rousseau has taken a giant step beyond the Daoist nostalgia with the primitive community and arrived at almost its direct opposite by inventing the notion of "general will," which would suppress all dissents and differences in order to maintain a simple community life. But here they share many points in common. They both continue to indulge in the idyllic versions of a primitive community, except that Rousseau's society has undertaken a fundamental civil transformation; both are unaware of the dangers inherent in such primitive state and, particularly, in employing whatever means necessary to maintain such state; both are loath to large complex societies ridden with crimes and treacheries, and pessimistic on the feasibility of building more complex institutions to check against the abuses of powers. Ultimately, Rousseau seems to lack confidence in the capacity of the common people to settle their differences through direct dialogues and parliamentary deliberations, and to shelve their differences by mutual respect and tolerance. As envisioned by the Framers of the US Constitution, the multiplicity of interests and individual differences in a large republic is precisely the social condition that both inculcates social toleration and calls for a confederate constitution, which limits the public power in order to preserve individual liberty. The end of imposing a uniform, supreme and unlimited "general will" is not liberty, but tyranny.

The Daoist is wise to stay with the original notion of individual liberty rather than invent such a fictitious one as "general will," by which different preferences among free individuals somehow dissolve and disappear in the collective. But the Daoist solution is even less tenable and needs be fundamentally reformed. It seems that, to maintain human freedom— if no more than primitive physical freedom, a consistent Daoist should not object to building a realistic theory of constitutional government that can protect at least the most vital individual liberties, even if the social conditions may oblige mankind to relinquish certain natural liberties. He should not merely retrieve into a passive, private life, but actively pursue human and social science to gain genuine knowledge about the Way in order to live with his nature. It is true that human reason creates its own dialectics; we do not know whether we can ever use reason properly as a means to advance a worthy goal, or we will be merely bequeathed by its inevitable misuse at the end. Yet, the problem of reason is not resolved in any sense by simply renouncing it. The only alternative available to mankind lies in nowhere other than the reason itself; it encumbers on human reason alone to experiment within the bounds of human capacities in order to find effective protection for every free human being. A healthy society can neither do away with wise laws and social rules that help an individual to inculcate innate virtues and constrain or redirect inordinate passions and desires, nor fail to lay down those checks and balances to prevent egregious abuses of the political powers.

In short, to maintain a minimal government and a self-sufficient life consistent with the Way, the Daoist should support the effort to design a constitution that is acceptable to every reasonable mind and consistent with the most advanced state of knowledge about human nature, and to maintain and renovate such a basic law over time in order to effectively pursue worthy ends in a changing society. Like Confucianism and Mohism, Daoism has an end worth pursuing; by bringing the individual person to the fore, it presents itself as the antidote to Confucianism and Mohism that tend to mistake the conventional morality for unerring truth, thereby supplying the very foundation for human dignity—individual liberty. Like its intellectual rivals, however, it is yet to find—through human reason—a consistent means toward that end.

NOTES

1. See Jean-Jacques Rousseau, *Discourse on Origin and Foundations of Inequality among Men*, trans. Maurice Cranston (New York: Penguin Books, 1984), 24.

2. The existence of Laozi and the authenticity of his work have been extensively debated and remain inconclusive, but this issue is quite irrelevant here. See Benjamin I. Schwartz, *The World of Thought in Ancient China* (Cambridge, MA: Harvard University Press, 1985), 187, and Hu Shih, *The Outline of Chinese Philosophy* (vol. 1) (Taipei: Commerce Press, 1969), 32; cf. A.C. Graham, *Disputers of the Tao: Philosophical Argument in Ancient China* (La Salle, IL: Open Court, 1989), 216–217, and Fung Yu-lan, *A Short History of Chinese Philosophy*, ed. Derk Bodde (New York: The Free Press, 1948), 30–37. I refer "Laozi" (sometimes translated as "Lao Tzu") to the author(s) of the work under that name. The same is meant for "Zhuangzi" (sometimes translated as "Chuang Tzu"), whose work is commonly thought to be the product of many hands. See Zhang Yi ed., *Modern Translation of Laozi* (Beijing: China Books, 1992), 1–10; Zhang Geng Guang ed., *Complete Translation of Zhuangzi* (Guiyang: Guizhou People Press, 1991), 1–14.

3. *Zhuangzi*, "The Evolution of Heaven," Ch. 14.
4. *Zhuangzi*, "Autumn Flood," Ch. 17.
5. *Zhuangzi*, "Rifling Trunks," Ch. 10; see Burton Watson, *The Complete Works of Chuang Tzu* (New York: Columbia University Press, 1968), 110.
6. *Zhuangzi*, "Yielding the Throne," Ch. 28; see Watson, *Complete Works of Chuang Tzu*, 312–313.
7. The rivalry of two schools is represented in *Mengzi* (7A26) and other works. While Mozi travels all over China seeking to help out every single human being that needs help, the negative teaching of Yangzi is reduced to the extreme of selfish hedonism and total withdrawal from social life—a position which Laozi and Zhuangzi have never explicitly endorsed: "Men of antiquity did not prefer to sacrifice one single hair to benefit the world. Nor did they choose to have the world support them. If everyone refrains from sacrificing even a single hair and if everyone refrains from benefiting the world, the world will be in order." *Liezi*, "Yangzi Chapter," trans. Chan, *Source Book in Chinese Philosophy*, 311. For a rebuttal by Mozi, who argues that pure selfishness is self-contradictory, see *Mozi*, 46: 18; see Graham, *Disputers of the Tao*, 60–64.
8. *Lü's Spring and Autumn Annals*, 17: 7; trans. Graham, *Disputers of the Tao*, 54.
9. *Huainanzi*, 13: 10B; trans. Graham, *Disputers of the Tao*, 54.
10. See LüZhenyu, *The History of Chinese Political Thought* (Beijing: Renmin Press, 1980), 138.
11. *Lü's Spring and Autumn Annals*, "Importance of Self," 1: 3; trans. Fung Yu-lan, *A Short History of Chinese Philosophy*, trans. Derk Bodde (New York: The Free Press, 1948), 63.
12. *Ibid.*
13. See *Laozi*, Ch. 1.
14. *Zhuangzi*, "Webbed Toes," Ch. 8.
15. *De* is sometimes translated as "potency" (Graham, *Disputers of the Tao*, 186–189) or "latent power" deriving from the virtue inherent in a thing, but virtue, defined in the Aristotelian sense to be the excellence of a thing in performing certain functions, seems at least equally adequate. See Chan, *Source Book in Chinese Philosophy*, 136–8, 788–790.
16. *Laozi*, Ch. 25; see Chan, *Source Book in Chinese Philosophy*, 153.
17. *Zhuangzi*, "The Way of Heaven," Ch. 13; trans. Watson, *Complete Works of Chuang Tzu*, 150.

18. See Frederick W. Mote, *Intellectual Foundations of China* (New York: Alfred A. Knopf, 1971), 71.
19. *Laozi*, Ch. 25; see Chan, *Source Book in Chinese Philosophy*, 152.
20. *Zhuangzi*, "Robber Zhi," Ch. 29; see Watson, *Complete Works of Chuang Tzu*, 326.
21. Thus, when Shun tried to cede the kingship to a hermit farmer (善卷 Shan Juan), the latter declined in the passage at the beginning of this chapter. *Zhuangzi*, "Yielding the Throne," Ch. 28; see Watson, *Complete Works of Chuang Tzu*, 309–310.
22. The Daoist utopia is simple and unambiguous, as expressed by Laozi. *Laozi*, Ch. 80; see D.C. Lau, *Tao Te Ching* (Hong Kong: The Chinese University Press), 1982, 115–116; cf. Chan, *Source Book in Chinese Philosophy*, 175. See Watson, *Complete Works of Chuang Tzu*, 112.
23. *Laozi*, Ch. 19; see Chan, *Source Book in Chinese Philosophy*, 149.
24. *Zhuangzi*, "Rifling Trunks," Ch. 10; see Watson, *Complete Works of Chuang Tzu*, 111.
25. *Laozi*, Ch. 57; see Chan, *Source Book in Chinese Philosophy*, 166–167; Lau, *Tao Te Ching*, 84–85.
26. See *Zhuangzi*, "XuWugui," Ch. 24.
27. Thus, Confucians and Daoists share the favorite story about the Great King Dan-Fu, the grandfather of King Wen of Zhou, who was willing to give up his throne in order to divert a potential bloodshed due to the invasion of the neighboring herdsmen:

> *To live among the older brothers and send the younger brothers to their death; to live among the fathers and send the sons to their death—this I cannot bear. My people, be diligent and remain where you are! What difference does it make whether you are subjects of mine or of the men of Di (a northern minority race)? And I have heard that one must not injure that which he is nourishing for the sake of that by which he nourishes it.*

Zhuangzi, "Yielding the Throne," Ch. 28; see Watson, *Complete Works of Chuang Tzu*, 310. In other words, the lives of his people are (or ought to be) far more precious to the ruler than the possession of his territory and property.
28. *Laozi*, Ch. 58; see Lau, *Tao Te Ching*, 85.
29. See Chan, *Source Book in Chinese Philosophy*, 148.
30. For a critique of Daoist counter-intellectualism, see Yu Ying-Shih, "Counter-Intellectualism and the Chinese Political Tradition," in *The*

Modern Interpretation of Traditional Chinese Thought (Nanjing: Jiangsu People Press, 1989), 72–81.

31. See Yu Ying-shih, "Couner-Intellectualism and the Chinese Political Tradition," 72–81.

32. Rousseau, *Discourse on Inequality*, 86.

33. Rousseau, *Discourse on Inequality*, 104.

34. Rousseau, *Discourse on Inequality*, 105.

35. Rousseau, *Discourse on Inequality*, 35.

36. Rousseau, *Discourse on Inequality*, 36.

37. Rousseau, *Discourse on Inequality*, 135.

38. Rousseau, *Discourse on Inequality*, 44.

39. Rousseau, *Discourse on Inequality*, 44.

40. Rousseau, *Discourse on Inequality*, 101.

41. Rousseau, *Discourse on Inequality*, 39.

42. Rousseau, *Discourse on Inequality*, 105.

43. Rousseau, *Discourse on Inequality*, 118.

44. Rousseau, *Discourse on Inequality*, 106.

45. Rousseau, *Discourse on Inequality*, 40.

46. Rousseau, *Discourse on Inequality*, 147, note I.

47. "The most useful and least developed of all sciences seems to me to be that of man.... What is more cruel is that the whole progress of human species removes man constantly farther and farther from his primitive state; the more we acquire new knowledge, the more we deprive ourselves of the means of acquiring the most important knowledge of all; and in a sense, it is through studying man that we have rendered ourselves incapable of knowing him." Rousseau, *Discourse on Inequality*, 67.

48. Rousseau, *Discourse on Inequality*, 89.

49. Rousseau, *Discourse on Inequality*, 116.

50. Rousseau, *On the Social Contract*, 24.

51. *Ibid.*

52. Rousseau, *On the Social Contract*, 26.

53. *Ibid.*

54. Rousseau, *On the Social Contract*, 27.

55. Rousseau, *On the Social Contract*, 46.

56. *Ibid.*

57. Rousseau, *On the Social Contract*, 76.

58. Rousseau, *On the Social Contract*, 87.

59. Rousseau, *On the Social Contract*, 37.

60. *Ibid.*
61. *Ibid.*
62. Rousseau, *On the Social Contract*, 33.
63. Rousseau, *On the Social Contract*, 38.
64. *Ibid.*
65. Alexander Hamilton, James Madison and John Jay, *The Federalist Papers*, ed. Clinton Rossiter (New York: Penguin, 1961), 77–84.
66. Rousseau, *On the Social Contract*, 75.
67. Rousseau, *On the Social Contract*, 80.
68. Rousseau, *On the Social Contract*, 72.
69. Rousseau, *On the Social Contract*, 81. And it is even worse to maintain the general will out of a diverse community since that means much force has to be used to hammer out dissenting interests, and such force grows in proportion to the size of the state: "since the subject always remains one, the ratio of the sovereign to the subject increases in proportion to the number of citizens. Whence it follows that the larger state becomes, the less liberty there is. Now the less relation there is between private wills and the general will, that is, between the mores and the laws, the more repressive force ought to increase. Therefore, in order to be good, the government must be relatively stronger in proportion as the populace is more numerous." Rousseau, *On the Social Contract*, 50.
70. Rousseau, *On the Social Contract*, 56.
71. Hamilton et al., *The Federalist Papers*, 77–84.
72. Rousseau, *On the Social Contract*, 79.

CHAPTER 7

Conclusions: Human Dignity Revisited

This book has compared the Confucian conception of human dignity with those of the Mohist and Daoist, and demonstrated that all three classical schools, if rationally construed, should support the view that the establishment of a liberal constitutional scheme is necessary to preserve dignity for every human being who lives in a modern society. In conclusion, I will recapitulate the common merits and limitations in all three schools of classical Chinese philosophy. Although the traditional Chinese thinkers, limited by the context of political and social practices at the time, had never discovered the modern notions of liberal democracy and human rights, and this conclusion stands firm even if most sympathetic interpretations are lent to liberal Daoism and egalitarian Mohism, the classical schools are not inherently repugnant to these notions. Indeed, as I have argued throughout this book, the classical ideas about human dignity require the establishment of a constitution, which will limit the power of the government, protect and help to inculcate the innate virtues, maintain moral independence as against the potential infringements by social and political powers, and provide for a minimum welfare to every human being.

© The Author(s) 2016
Q. Zhang, *Human Dignity in Classical Chinese Philosophy*,
DOI 10.1057/978-1-349-70920-5_7

HUMAN DIGNITY: A COMMON THREAD OF CLASSICAL CHINESE PHILOSOPHY

The previous discussions have illustrated many differences among Confucianism, Daoism, and Mohism. While Confucianism takes gentleman as the ideal personality and humanity and righteousness as the central principles of the Way of Heaven, Mohism is based on mutual benefits and universal love under the will of Heaven, and Daoism endorses the amoral Way and Nature, which destine mankind to live a free and primitive life. Taken together, however, the three schools of thought do converge on a common moral precept: to treat every human being as the end in itself and not merely as means to other things. All three classical schools, I argue, imply in essence the notion of human dignity, even though they do differ as to what dignity consists of. For Confucianism, human dignity is fully illustrated in the ideal personality of a gentleman, who has cultivated innate virtue through learning and the practice of *Li*; he takes humanity and righteousness as the highest principles, and follows the Principle of the Mean by which he gains moral independence. For Mohism, everyone ought to love everyone else alike, and everyone equally deserves at least a minimum concern for well-being.[1] Daoism rejects conventional morality as hypocritical and worthless practice, and seeks human dignity in a free, self-sufficient, and spontaneous life; like Confucianism, it also values an independent moral character, but insists that personal independence and freedom can be maintained only in a simple and primitive lifestyle. All three schools, particularly Daoism and Confucianism (possibly except Xunzi), take an optimistic view of human nature, and recognize the intrinsic worth in every human being. While the Confucian emphasizes the duty of self-cultivation and practice in developing the virtues, the Daoist objects to external interferences that distract men and women from their true nature; in comparison the Daoist pins more hopes on the people's own initiatives, and the people themselves should not be active in pursuing profits (like Mohists) or reputation (like Confucians). Yet, all schools at least imply that the intrinsic worth of every human being should be respected and protected. Thus, human dignity, though understood in different (but mutually complementary) ways, seems to be a common element that can be extracted from all three schools of thought.

Yet, the classical moral ideas (re)interpreted above remained unfulfilled in the traditional practice in China. Among the three schools of thought in classical China, the Confucian system of *Li* had no doubt dominated the social practice. As we have seen, although Daoism made strong appeal to personal freedom, it lacked a realistic scheme to implement freedom on the social and political scale. Mohism suffered from a great decline during the violent unification of Qin (229–221 B.C.) and became extinct in the seventh century, and was not revived until it was rediscovered nearly a millennium later.[2] The Confucian *Li* had served as a moral constitution, as it were, of the traditional Chinese society, maintaining a degree of order and harmony. From different perspectives, both the Mohist and Daoist critiques can be constructive in correcting the defects in Confucian *Li*. While the Mohist advocates the universal utilitarian principle that governs everyone equally, thus alleviating the subordination of children, women, and subjects of the rulers, the Daoist brings forward the concern for personal freedom, without which a person is but a selfless slave.

Even when different schools join together, however, the classical Chinese philosophy on human dignity has still been made defective by the traditional practice. After all, it is practice that both gives life to and defines the content of a moral concept. The visions and imaginations of the traditional Chinese philosophers were severely limited by the political realities of their times. Unlike ancient Greece, where polities of different nature interacted and competed for prominence, China had been settled in one monolithic authoritarian government since the earliest historical record; the seven warring states were offspring of the same parent, the Zhou regime, which in turn derived its form from the earlier regimes with dubious historical records. If there was a stage when the primitive people wandered freely in woods and managed their own lives with a minimal government, such a history would remain an unverifiable Daoist fiction, and was in anyway irrelevant to the civilized communities. The Daoists themselves, who longed to return to primitive lives, could only wish a wise and benevolent king to reign someday, and the way of governance, simplistic, and impractical as it was, still appeared identical to a typical Chinese monarchy. Here, Daoism was no less inconsistent than Confucianism: while the Confucians believed that the vast majority of ordinary people are morally inferior "petty men," they nevertheless hoped that the government would be run by the virtuous gentlemen; the Daoist hoped that everyone must live in ignorance in order to be happy, but the king must be supremely wise to maintain an ignorant state. In order to make moral theories relevant to practical life, the classical theories need be reconstructed. If freedom is anything more than romantic imagination and matters in practical life, it must come to terms with the needs and necessities of real social life. In a civilized society, it means that freedom is to be maintained by a reasonably capable government, and to coexist with its competence and possible abuses. This requires a science that the traditional Chinese thinkers were never given the opportunity to explore—the science of making a liberal constitution, by which the power of the government is confined to certain limits.

TOWARD A CONSTITUTIONAL PRINCIPLE

If it is correct to argue Daoism, Mohism, and Confucianism all have a vision for human dignity, then it seems to be only consistent to require that such moral visions be adequately carried into practice, primarily through social and political institutions. Respect for human dignity commands that a legitimate public power must treat everyone always as the end and never merely as means—neither to others (e.g. for the sake of social order or political control) nor to one's own desires and impulses. To express in the Confucian terms (which do not necessarily conflict with the Mohist or Daoist teachings), everyone is born with the innate moral and intellectual virtues, capable of being developed fully in a mature person. To respect human dignity, then, the state and society must take such a moral belief seriously and refrain from any positive acts that would impede personal development of virtues; human dignity is violated whenever a person is deprived of the opportunity to fully develop his innate virtues, and any deprivation under the name of public authority must be seen as illegitimate exercise of power. Further, the state and society may be required to create such positive conditions as to provide everyone with the opportunity of moral and intellectual development. Rather than preoccupied with the provision of material goods, the public power ought to be primarily concerned with the provisions of developmental and educational opportunities, and perhaps establish and maintain a system of social rules and norms in its curriculum, which helps to "make" the gentlemen who respect others in the same way they respect themselves. Heaven has endowed human beings with innate virtues; it is their task to develop them through their own efforts—through the establishments of a civil society, the state, and a constitution that lays down the fundamental principles under which the state and society shall operate.

Such a constitution is indeed very much consistent with the spirit of classical Confucianism, which is deeply concerned with the actualization of potential virtues through moral education and practice. The traditional

Confucians used to support rule of virtue by the few because it was only feasible for the few to succeed in acquiring the virtues; but nothing prevents the modern civilization from helping everyone to develop the innate human virtues, by which a value-based democratic society is made possible.[3] Such a development should be welcomed by the Mohist, since human experiences have taught that the best way to promote universal love and social welfare is not by producing equal result for everyone through political coercion, but by guaranteeing equal opportunity with which everyone can freely pursue one's own interest and aspirations. It should equally be welcomed by the Daoist since the government can now become truly restrained (if not minimal) and the people retain their freedom—not because they remain ignorant, but precisely because they are wise, mature, and competent in governing themselves in a complex modern society.

Traditionally, Daoism is opposed to Confucianism in theory, but complements it in practice; while Confucianism governs one's public life, Daoism takes over once one has retired to private life. The split in the personal philosophy of the same personality was largely attributed to the sharp division between the public and private spheres in the Chinese society—between the ruling class of active elites and the vast majority of the ruled who remained politically passive. As I have argued in Chap. 2, however, a gentleman shall transcend such a division and acquire a mature, self-governing and dignified personality in all spheres. Whether staying alone, in family, or before the sovereign state, he will act in such ways as to preserve and improve his dignity; he respects the dignity of others, and requires a reciprocal respect for his own dignity. To be consistent with such a moral aspiration, he should seek to implement and maintain—with the consent shared by all members of society—a constitution by which his dignity and that of others are equally protected. And the fundamental principle of this constitution, commonly acceptable to the classical Chinese schools, is the respect and protection of human dignity, against which the legitimacy of every social action and political regime is to be measured.

NOTES

1. Although it is more difficult to derive the notion of human dignity directly from Mohism, it at least implies the idea of treating everyone as ends and not merely as tools. As discussed in Chap. 5, it is perhaps easiest to derive from Mohism, among the three schools, the moral support for a democratic and constitutional regime.

2. Compare A.C. Graham, *Disputers of the Tao: Philosophical Argument in Ancient China* (La Salle, IL: Open Court, 1989), 7; Frederick W. Mote, *Intellectual Foundations of China* (New York: Alfred A. Knopf, 1971), 90.

3. Even with the basic principle settled, practical questions are bound to arise in circumstances where individuals may fail to act in accord with the dignity principle. For example, should a citizen be required that the vote he casts has gone through a serious evaluation? Should the voters be required to pass a literacy test so as to prove that he is equipped with the ability of casting an intelligent (at least informed) vote? Is human dignity violated if the unemployed are required to participate in compulsory training programs rather than passively waiting for the delivery of social welfare? These and other issues are still debatable in the contemporary world and may continue to be debated in future.

BIBLIOGRAPHY

Gabriel A. Almond, *A Discipline Divided: Schools and Sects in Political Science* (Newbury Park, CA: SAGE, 1990).

Kenneth J. Arrow, *Social Choice and Individual Values* (2nd Ed.) (New Haven: Yale University Press, 1963).

Robert Axelrod, "The Emergence of Cooperation among Egoists," *American Political Science Review* 75 (1981): 306–317.

Robert Axelrod, *The Evolution of Cooperation* (New York: Basic Books, 1984).

Robert N. Bellah et al., *Habits of the Heart: Individualism and Commitment in American Life* (Berkeley: University of California Press, 1985).

Peter L. Berger, *The Sacred Canopy: Elements of a Sociological Theory of Religion* (Garden City, NY: Doubleday, 1969).

Peter L. Berger and Thomas Luckmann, *The Social Construction of Reality: A Treatise in the Sociology of Knowledge* (Gardon City, NY: Doubleday, 1966).

James M. Buchanan and Gordon Tullock, *The Calculus of Consent: Logical Foundation of Constitutional Democracy* (Ann Arbor: University of Michigan Press, 1962).

Cai Dingjian ed., *A Survey Report of the Chinese Elections* (Beijing: Law Press, 2002).

Chan Wing-tsit, *A Source Book in Chinese Philosophy* (Princeton: Princeton University Press, 1963).

Chen Da-qi, *The Theory of Xunzi* (Taipei: Huagang Press, 1971).

Chen Fei-long, *Studies on Xunzi's Theory of Li* (Taipei: Literature, History and Philosophy Press, 1979).

Chen Guidi and Chun Tao, *The Chinese Peasant Investigations* (Beijing: People's Literature Press, 2004).

© The Author(s) 2016
Q. Zhang, *Human Dignity in Classical Chinese Philosophy*,
DOI 10.1057/978-1-349-70920-5

205

Chen Song ed., *Selected Papers on the East-West Cultural Debates Around the May-Fourth Movement* (Beijing: China Social Science Press, 1983).

Chen Zheng-xiong, *A Study on the Political Thought of Xunzi* (Taipei: Wenjin Press, 1973).

Chung-ying Cheng, *New Dimensions of Confucian and Neo-Confucian Philosophy* (Albany: State University of New York Press, 1991).

A.S. Cua, "Dimensions of Li (propriety): Reflections on an Aspect of Hsun Tzu's Ethics," *Philosophy East and West* 29 (1979) 373–382.

A.S. Cua, "Li and Moral Justification: A Study in the Li Chi," *Philosophy East and West* 33 (1983) 1–17.

Homer H. Dubs, *The Works of Hsuntze* (Taipei: Cheng-wen Publishing Co., 1966).

J.J.L. Duyvendak, *The Book of Lord Shang* (Chicago: University of Chicago Press, 1963).

Jon Elster, *The Cement of Society: Study of Social Order* (Cambridge: Cambridge University Press, 1989).

John King Fairbank, *China: A New History* (Cambridge, MA: Harvard University Press, 1992).

Lon L. Fuller, *The Morality of Law* (New Haven, CO: Yale University Press, 1969).

Francis Fukuyama, *The End of History and the Last Man* (New York: Avon Books, 1992).

Francis Fukuyama, *Trust: The Social Virtues and the Creation of Prosperity* (New York: Free Press, 1995).

Esson M. Gale trans., *Discourses on Salt and Iron: A Debate on State Control of Commerce and Industry in Ancient China* (Taipei: Chengwen Press, 1967).

Clifford Geertz, *The Interpretation of Cultures* (New York: Basic Books, 1973).

Guo Jian, "Ren in Confucianism and the Chinese Legal Culture," in *Confucianism and Legal Culture*, ed. Research Committee on Chinese Confucianism and Legal Culture (Shanghai: Fudan University Press, 1992).

David L. Hall and Roger T. Ames, "Getting It Right: On Saving Confucius from Confucians," *Philosophy East and West* 34 (1984) 3–24.

Garret Hardin, "The Tragedy of the Commons," *Science* 162 (1968) 1243–1248.

Russell Hardin, *Collective Action* (Baltimore: Johns Hopkins University, 1982).

David Hume, *A Treatise of Human Nature*, Ernest C. Mossner ed. (London: Penguin Books, 1969).

Thomas Hobbes, *Leviathan* (New York: Penguin, 1985).

Eric Hutton, "Does Xunzi Have a Consistent Theory of Human Nature?", in *Virtue, Nature, and Moral Agency in the Xunzi*, ed. T.C. Kline III and Philip J. Ivanhoe (Indianapolis: Hackett, 2000), 220–236.

Hu Shih, "The Question of Constitutionalism," *Independence Review* 1 (1932) 1.

Hu Shih, "The Natural Law in the Chinese Tradition," in E.F. Barrett ed., *Natural Law Institute Proceeding* 5 (1953) 119–153.

Philip J. Ivanhoe, *Confucian Moral Self Cultivation* (New York: Peter Lang, 1993).

Philip J. Ivanhoe, "Human Nature and Moral Understanding in the Xunzi," in *Virtue, Nature, and Moral Agency in the Xunzi*, ed. T.C. Kline III and Philip J. Ivanhoe (Indianapolis: Hackett, 2000), 237–249.

Jiang Qing, "From Heart-Nature Confucianism to Political Confucianism," in Liu Shu-xian et al., *Collection of Papers on Contemporary Neo-Confucianism* (Taipei: Wenjing Press, 1991), 153–178.

Jin Bingcai, "The Modern Meaning of Xunzi Philosophy," in *The Modern Interpretation of Traditional Confucianism*, ed. Zhou Boyu (Taipei: Wenjin Press, 1994), 167–174.

Jin Chun-feng, *New Examination of the Time of Zhouguan's Writing and the Culture and the Epoch It Reflected* (Taipei: Dongda Book Press, 1993)

Li Ri-gang et al. ed., *A Collection of Studies on the Three Li* (Taipei: Cultural Enterprise Press, 1981)

Jin Guantao and Liu Qingfeng, *Prosperity and Crisis: On the Super-Stable Structure of Chinese Society* (Hong Kong: Chinese University Press, 1992), 158–180.

Immanuel Kant, *Critique of Practical Reason*, trans. Lewis White Beck (Indianapolis: Bobbs-Merrill, 1956).

Immanuel Kant, *Grounding for the Metaphysics of Morals* (3rd Ed.), trans. J.W. Ellington (Indianapolis/Cambridge: Hackett, 1993).

Immanuel Kant, *The Metaphysics of Morals*, trans. Mary Gregor (Cambridge: Cambridge University Press, 1996).

James Legge, *The Four Books* (Hong Kong: Wei Tung Books, 1971).

James Legge, *The Sacred Books of China* (vols. 27 & 28.) (Oxford: Clarendon Press, 1885).

Lin Yu-sheng, *Thoughts and Characters* (Taipei: Lianjing Press, 1983)

Lin Yu-sheng, "Dilemmas Confronting neo-Confucians in Pushing for Theories of Democracy and Science in China," *China Times*, September 7–8, 1988.

Lin Yu-sheng et al., *The May-Fourth Movement: A Pluralistic Reflection* (Hong Kong: Sanlian Books Press, 1989)

John Locke, *Two Treatises of Government*, ed. Peter Laslett (Cambridge: Cambridge University Press, 1988).

John Knoblock, *Xunzi: A Translation and Study of the Complete Works* (3 vols.) (Stanford: Stanford University Press, 1988/1990/1994).

Richard Madsen, Morality and Power in a Chinese Village, Berkeley: University of California Press (1984).

Avishai Margalit, *The Decent Society*, trans. Naomi Goldblum (Cambridge, MA: Harvard University Press, 1996).

Montesquieu, The Spirit of the Laws, Anne Cohler et al. (trans. & ed.), Cambridge: Cambridge University Press (1989).

Mou Zongsan, Xu Fuguan, Zhang Junmai, and Tang Junyi, "Declaration of Chinese Culture to the World: Our Consensus on Chinese Scholarly Research and on the Future of Chinese Culture and World Culture," in *Tang Junyi's Collection*, ed. Huang Kejian et al. (Beijing: Qunyan Press, 1993), 475–525.

Donald J. Munro, *A Chinese Ethics for the New Century* (Hong Kong: The Chinese University Press, 2005).

Douglas C. North, *Structure and Change in Economic History*, trans. Chen Yu and Luo Huaping (Shanghai: Sanlian Books Press, 1981).

Mancur Olson, *The Logic of Collective Action: Public Goods and the Theory of Groups* (Cambridge, MA: Harvard University Press, 1971).

Elinor Ostrom, "A Behavioral Approach to the Rational Choice Theory of Collective Action," *American Political Science Review* 92 (1998) 1–18.

Talcott Parsons, *The Social System* (New York: The Free Press, 1951).

Talcott Parsons and Edward A. Shils ed., *Toward a General Theory of Action* (Cambridge, MA: Harvard University Press, 1954).

Samuel L. Popkin, *The Rational Peasant* (Berkeley: University of California Press, 1979).

Qu Tongzu, *Chinese Society and Chinese Law* (Beijing: Chung Hwa Book Co., 1981)

William H. Riker, Liberalism Against Popularism: A Confrontation between the Theory of Democracy and the Theory of Social Choice, San Francisco: Freeman (1982).

Heiner Roetz, *Confucian Ethics of the Axial Age* (Albany: State University of New York Press, 1993).

Henry Rosemont, Jr., "State and Society in the Xunzi: A Philosophical commentary," in *Virtue, Nature, and Moral Agency in the Xunzi*, ed. T.C. Kline III and Philip J. Ivanhoe, Indianapolis: Hackett (2000), 1–38.

Jean-Jacques Rousseau, *A Discourse on Inequality*, Maurice Cranston trans. (New York: Penguin Books, 1984).

Jean-Jacques Rousseau, *On the Social Contract*, Donald A. Cress trans. (Indianapolis: Hackett, 1987).

Benjamin I. Schwartz, *The World of Thought in Ancient China* (Cambridge, MA: Harvard University Press, 1985).

J.B. Schneewind, *The Invention of Autonomy: A History of Modern Moral Philosophy* (Cambridge: Cambridge University Press, 1998).

James C. Scott, *The Moral Economy of the Peasant* (New Haven: Yale University Press, 1976).

Leo Strauss, *Natural Law and History* (Chicago: University of Chicago Press, 1953).

Julia Po-Wah Tao, "Two Perspectives of Care: Confucian Ren and Feminist Care," *Journal of Chinese Philosophy* 27 (2000): 215–240.

Michael Taylor, *The Possibility of Cooperation* (Cambridge: Cambridge University Press, 1987).

Tu Wei-ming, "The Creative Tension between Jen and Li," *Philosophy East and West* 18 (1968) 29–38.

Tu Wei-ming, "Li as a Process of Humanization," in *Humanity and Self-Cultivation: Essays in Confucian Thought* (Berkeley: Asian Humanities Press, 1979).

Tu Wei-ming: *The Challenge of Singapore* (Beijing: Sanlian Books, 1992).

Edna Ullmann-Margalit, *The Emergence of Norms* (Oxford: Clarendon Press, 1977).

Qingjie James Wang, "The Golden Rule and Impersonal Care: From a Confucian Perspective," *Philosophy East and West* 49 (1999): 419–438.

Burton Watson, *Hsün Tzu: Basic Writings* (New York: Columbia University Press, 1963).

Burton Watson, *Han Fei Tzu: Basic Writings* (New York: Columbia University Press, 1964).

Burton Watson, *Basic Writings of Mo Tzu, Hsun Tzu, and Han Fei Tzu* (New York: Columbia University Press, 1967).

Sandra A. Wawrytko, "Confucius and Kant: The Ethics of Respect," *Philosophy East and West* 32 (1982): 237–257.

Max Weber, *The Protestant Ethic and the Spirit of Capitalism*, Talcott Parsons trans. (New York: Charles Scribner's Sons, 1958).

Barry R. Weingast, "The Political Foundation of Democracy and the Rule of Law," *American Political Science Review* 91 (1997) 245–263.

Paul Weiss, "The Golden Rule," *Journal of Philosophy* 38 (1941): 421–430.

Weng Hui-mei, *Xunzi on Studies of Man* (Taipei: Zhengzhong Books, 1988).

Dennis H. Wrong, *The Problem of Order: What Unites and Divides Society* (New York: Free Press, 1994).

Xu Fu-guan, *The Time of the Writing of Zhouguan and Its Intellectual Characters* (Taipai: Student Books, 1980).

Yu Ying-Shih, *The Modern Interpretation of Traditional Chinese Thought* (Nanjing: Jiangsu People's Press, 1989).

Yu Ying-shih, "Modern Confucians and Democracy," Speech on Cultural China Conference, August 30, 2004, http://www.gongfa.com/rujia.htm.

Zhang Qianfan, "Rule of Virtue, Rule of Law, and Constitutionalism," *Studies in Law and Business* 2 (2002) 34–39.

Zhu Xi, *Collective Annotations of the Four Books* (Ji'nan: Qilu Books, 1992).

INDEX

A

altruistic, 8, 120, 137n35, 138n39
Analects, 39n17, 39n21, 40n33,
  41n44, 46, 47, 49, 52,
  88n11, 89n18, 89n21,
  89n23, 94n87, 98n148,
  165n10, 166n12
a priori, 6, 31, 56
Aristotle, 4, 41n45
Augustine, 4
authenticity, 35n21, 194n2
autonomy, 11n2, 22, 36, 82, 84,
  88n7, 129, 131, 163, 175

B

baby, 24, 55, 63, 64, 92n54
benevolence, 35, 45–87, 139n51, 157,
  167n28, 175, 176
benevolent politics, 51, 58, 60, 68

B (right column)

Bentham, Jeremy, 147, 148, 154–6,
  166n22, 169n54, 172n96
Book of Rites, 105, 127, 133n12

C

categorical imperative, 5, 9, 47, 50,
  88n7, 145, 182
Cheng. *See* authenticity
chi. *See* shame
Christian, 4–6, 15n52, 15n53, 37,
  90n29, 95n105, 148, 172n90
Civil Rights Movement, 2
classical, 2, 3, 7, 10, 17, 18, 24, 30,
  33, 38n3, 42n61, 58, 66–8, 72,
  75, 80, 101, 107–11, 144, 148,
  149, 151, 152, 172n95, 173,
  180, 190, 199–203
Clinton, William, 30, 32
Confucian. *See* Confucianism

© The Author(s) 2016
Q. Zhang, *Human Dignity in Classical Chinese Philosophy*,
DOI 10.1057/978-1-349-70920-5